# IDEOLOGIES

# IN THE

# NEAR EAST

1946-1972

# Ideologies

# in the

# Near East

1946-1972

MOSHE ZELTZER

**VANTAGE PRESS**

New York    Washington    Atlanta    Hollywood

FIRST EDITION

Copyright© 1975 by Moshe Zeltzer,

Published by Vantage Press, Inc.
516 West 34th Street, New York, New York 10001

Manufactured in the United States of America

Standard Book No. 533-01100-0

# CONTENTS

# IDEOLOGIES

# IN THE

# NEAR EAST

# 1946-1972

# INTRODUCTION

A book, unusually structured, in part anthologized, invites criticism. It was not my intention to add to the vast volume of writings on the Near East a new piece of what could arguably pass for science, political or social, or combined.

A proper contribution seemed to me to let actors and observers, mainly from within, speak their mind, thereby conveying the mood of the times and the atmosphere of the struggle, that is, the hotbed of facts.* A people's mind stands guard, conditioning the birth or adoption of ideas, their evolution, their presentation and application. Of course, pitfalls are unavoidable.

There are levels of self-revelation: official communications and interpretations, spontaneous utterances, theoretical expositions, intra-party or inter-party exchanges of views, controlled or explosive. There are publications varying with the addressee. There is a question of choice and preference, even stress, through size and sequence, finally of dispassionateness and its motivations.

Added to this, the countries concerned are afflicted with various degrees of lack of freedom of expression. And last but not least, one has to contend with three kinds of inflation: inflated language, be it native or ideological

---

* Admittedly, any attempt to apply oneself to a people's mind is of experimental validity, intellectual and moral.

1

rhetoric; overheated millennial ideology, national or social; inflation of struggle.

The best of intents to let actors and orators speak their mind through their idiom faces another pitfall, too. Common usage speaks of letter and spirit of a statement as if separable; simplifyingly we urge joining the spirit, by implication, at the expense of the letter. Justice is to be done to two languages, to the author and the reader. Should translation be literal and, as far as bearable, preserve even the original turn of a phrase and the structure of the sentence? Even literal translation is only approximating the original. It seems preferable, since it is the only way to capture the uncontrolled flow or burst of words — what is termed the stream of consciousness. Of course, it could be argued that the source material presented here — word, phrase and sentence — had come about, to a large degree, by way of translation of ideas, terms, phrases, line of argument into Arabic. Hence the original is far from being original. True, it is a predominantly borrowed world, only the process of arabization, absorption or part-assimilation, is Arabic. As against this, joining the spirit means one's mind attempts rationally to filter into an alien mind and interpret content and meaning. In a way, it is the translator's rationalization. Running the risk of being unreadable, I prefer to keep close to the original.

Reliance on verbal evidence may seem clay-footed. It is not suggested to take the word for the deed. But in our context the word is more than itself; drawing strength from the realm of fantasies, it may precipitate and condition action. By being carried away by rhetoric one also betrays intimate longings, variously stimulated. In authoritarian states the autocrat, seemingly fearless, is also prisoner of his sense of destiny as well as of the expectations excited in the masses.

To Adonis, the Lebanese poet, "A European language rests on causal liaison; it is a language of logic, convention and custom." As for Arabic it is a "language of effusion,

2

radiation, of vision, flash and inspiration." "Our Arabic language is poetic in the first degree, hence personal to a wide limit, shuns terms and logical definitions, gushes out and explodes in a motion from depth."[*]

Since the late 'fifties, Arabic is intensely made to serve Marxist analysis and scientifism. Here a distinction is to be made between the impact of affluent Arabic and that of linguistic poverty, as is often the case with a writer who has no intimate knowledge of literary sources. In both cases the author is pressured by overheated ideologies, the result being inadequate or negligent use of their idioms of argument. Cadence of demagoguery may collide or merge with cadence of genuine Arabic style. Sometimes, thorough assimilation of an idea or a line of argument makes the author argue lucidly without damaging the identity of Arabic.

This study attempts to trace the convulsive evolution of national and social thought, epitomized in what is termed "Arab socialism," since about 1946. Except for a few groups upholding views of social reformism, probably then conceived as revolutionism, the preceding period stood, in the main, on a ground of unqualified nationalism. In the 'twenties the mainstream of Arab nationalism still sustained the traditional values of Arab society while trying to emulate political, cultural and to a negligible extent social values of Western parliamentarianism and democracy. The interplay of attraction to and rejection of the mandatory powers or their metropoles is well worth considering.

The 'thirties offered to a militant nationalism, notably to the youth, a new alternative to endorse: the militancy of Fascism with its strong appeal to emotions of aggression and revenge, its call for might and glory, its "anti-imperialism," including Zionism and Judaism. The beauty snags of Italian Fascism such as the events in Ethiopia

---

*Tajribati al-shi'riyya (My Poetic Experience), al-Ādab, March 1969. By this the identity of classical Arabic is hardly exhausted.

and Libya didn't deter from adulation. German national socialism had no chance to effect all its real ambitions. (Similarly, the events in Hungary and Czechoslovakia obviously didn't affect the attitude of this area to the Soviet Union.)

At the end of the Second World War socialism became a near-universal *cri du coeur* and a battle cry even of some traditional—lay and Islam-bound—parties vying for prevalence. The growing awareness of social ills, the pressure of the new generation imbued with a stronger sense of social justice, emergence of new parties—all combined to make socialism, once variously confused with communism, an epitome of social justice corroborative to nationalism. The outcome of the 1948 war was to quicken the pace. Within one generation socialism evolved to a many-faceted ideology said to be variously implemented in at least seven Arab countries, in all combining, by way of military coups and violence, word and sword. Furthermore, to segments of the new generation, yesterday's revolutionary regimes have become, at best, exponents of a socialism conserving and promoting the interests of the small bourgeoisie and the new bureaucracy issued from her. To them, exponents of social and political feudalism are eliminated, but a feudalism of a New Class, led by a secretive tiny elite, more exclusive and more authoritarian, is to be contended with.

In spite of sharp divergencies one characteristic is common to all, *i.e.;* militancy against a three-headed enemy— "imperialism, Zionism and native reaction"—and ardent espousal of revolutionary romanticism as embodied in national liberation fronts and guerrilla movements. Of course, it remains to detect the real motives, even the various degrees of opportunism behind a predilection for these new ways and means of activity.

Common to all, though to a varying degree, is Marxization of socialism in the direction of Leninism and rejection of Western socialist legacy, notably since the arms

4

deal with the Soviet Union in 1955. Ba'th, initially utopian and messianic, assumed more and more "scientific" coloring. The younger generation, no less imagination-drawn than the older one, turned away from "socialist subjectivism." In Syria Ba'th split by a violent coup into "Right" and "Left" (1966); the former entrenched itself by a coup in 'Iraq (1968) and the latter was again reinterpreted by a coup in Syria (1970), it seems up to ideological diminution. Egypt's ideology moved from avowedly "pragmatic" to "scientific" socialism grafted on a metaphysical outlook, which necessitated quasi-Marxist reinterpretation of Islam as well as Islamic vindication of "scientific" socialism. Both offshoots of the Arab Nationalists Movement espoused Leninist Marxism strongly leaning toward Maoism. A common dimension of revolution in permanence and guerrillism, as recently applied by Palestinians, ensures an air of romanticism somehow rooted in traditional warfare.

This study has not done full justice to the title. It dwelt cursorily on earlier strains in Arab ideology that don't lack some originality in fusing concepts drawn from foreign sources. Jumblat's philosophical musings, combining East and West, violence and nonviolence, and his dissimulative behavior in politics as embodied in the Progressive Socialist Party, are well worth pursuing. It is a local Lebanese apparition. Likewise the Syrian Popular Social Party in its metamorphoses, at whose inception rising Fascism stood pat, had some unusual ideas to propound: ideas of a "Syrian nation" and of the Fertile Crescent having a distinct geographical and ethnic identity, thus excluding Egypt, and with some reserve substituting Syrianism for or aligning it with Arabdom. It explicitly stood for separation of religion and state and "removal of the sectarian barriers between the communities through restriction of communalism to merely religious matters."

The completion of this study coincides with events that couldn't but signify a watershed in Arab politics, hence also in the realm of ideology. This may help towards the summing up of an era. Without the privilege of hindsight it could unfailingly be forecast that what was possible under 'Abd al-Nasir, who was believed to commune with his people's destiny, would no longer work under his successor. For some sixteen years 'Abd al-Nasir succeeded in keeping the "power centers" of the regime from falling apart. After him it proved a mirage of monolithism.

Sadat's coup — depending on one's view, a pre-emptive strike — has shown how ephemeral and vioceless was the Arab Socialist Union with its nominally millions-strong membership, how powerless was its casual leadership in the face of those who, backed by the military, proved more adept. Succession in a dictatorship excludes a majority decision even within its limited confines. Sadat's struggle for power could, from some angle, pass for manipulation of "rightist" with "leftist" tactics. An experiment of markedly enlarging the base of actual power to the "right" without excluding the "left" could not but be an interim measure.

The al-Asad coup in Syria is unique in that it is a coup within a coup within a coup, all in the name of Ba'th. It resulted in a "national front" government ensuring the leading role of the author of the coup, subsequently elected president of Syria. It remains to be seen how a no-choice-regime will find its way to a regime of some choice conceded to semi-legal factions by the "leading party," itself curtailed in its choice by the strong man of the coup.

Having no military backing and no strong social base, the Moscow-centered Communist parties are engaged, for reasons of self-preservation, in a kind of political mimicry. Since the Soviet Union is heavily involved in this area — in the long run the benefactor may be more dependent on his beneficiaries than vice versa — the local communists pursue tactics of supporting the Soviet stand, sometimes by taking a negligible, grudgingly conceded, part in the government. They don't shun "partnership" with the rightist Ba'th in 'Iraq, nor with the leftist Ba'th, now Ba'th of Asad's coinage in Syria. Their past stand notwithstanding, they have called to vote for a federation of Egypt, Syria and Libya.

Palestinian *fida'ism* had a short heyday to its credit. The ominous conflict within the Communist orbit, the quasi-accommodating policy of the Soviet Union versus the U.S.A., the brand-new *realpolitik* of People's China, the decline of revolutionary guerrillism in the world, finally the lot of *fida'ism* in Jordan — all this has dampened its ideological fervor and reduced to its real substance.

Its rise and decline recalls the 'thirties in Palestine, when the Nashashibis (National Defence Party), a more accommodating party sharing the views of the then Amir 'Abdullah of Transjordan, were assassinated by the hundreds by the uncompromising Husaynis (Arab Palestine Party), inspired and encouraged as they were by the then current fascism and National Socialism. Carried away by lofty ideas of liberation, the *fida'iyyun* claimed to act not only on behalf of Palestine; they variously deemed themselves liberating, by word and sword, Jordan, Lebanon and other Arab states, even taking part in the world movement of national liberation.

It was a shortlived apparition. Praised as "the conscience of the Arab nation," they were said to usher in a new era in the "Arab revolution." A variety of factions outbid each other in revolutionism, in devising methods of violence. Overawed screen commentators, journalists and theorizing intellectuals in the West, reared on contemporary sophistry on violence, seemed fascinated with the bursting flames of a Palestinian revolution. Recalling the near past, is it heresy to maintain that constructive work done by Arab pioneering youth for the rehabilitation of the Palestinian refugees would have furthered the cause of "Arab revolution" an incomparably longer stretch?

In this context, the events in Pakistan seem to have

some relevance. They have shown what was to be expected: the inadequacy of Islam for forging a nation and the actual meaning of Islamic solidarity. The controversy between Afghanistan and Pakistan over the land of the Pathans is also a case in point. They have also incontrovertibly proved the ephemeral worth of the concept of Islamic socialism, not only the versions propounded in both parts of former Pakistan. Still more, no authoritative Muslim voice was raised against the massacres of multitudes of Muslims by Muslims in Yemen and East Pakistan.

In Bangladesh, Islam as ideology of greater Pakistan is replaced by nationalism; in Pakistan, in view of a varied Muslim opposition and ethnic divergencies, there is no reason to invoke Islam as a religious or ideological bond.

The era in question, utterly ideology-bound, seems fading away. Egypt's ideology has been molded and remolded by men in power. Initially Ba'th and ANM concepts have grown out of discussion, and only upon accession to power their variations are being imposed on the people. To suit their purposes, men in power may modify an ideology, or simply reinterpret it without modification, put it aside or let it languish to be invoked in case of need. The newly proclaimed "Federation of Arab Republics" and the merger of Egypt and Libya are a case in point. Men in power undertake to federate or merge their countries thereby manipulating, adjusting or equalizing their ideologies.

As long as the "army," concretely the man who wins the allegiance of some commanding officers, more precisely, of the commander of the air force and of the tank units guarding the approaches to the airfields, can impose its own version of ideology, with its ensuing torrential verbalism, it will never take root in the people's mind. On the morrow of a new upheaval it is bound to wane. An awakened sense of justice sharpened both by these

8

ideologies in word and by their abuse in action, and the un-extinguishable quest for the dignity of man are again and again to press their claim.

In his *The Game of Nations*, Miles Copeland has not applied himself to the part of ideology in the "amorality of power politics." Still, it has a great part in the "game." The impact of ideology on man's mind, its originator, is an issue to be argued about. At least initially man attempts to live by it, even to die for it. The role of ideology and its variants in the struggle for power, often as a means of delusion or self-delusion, is undeniable. Multitudes formulate and interpret it, popularize it, arouse masses, rationalize their actions by it and stage coups for its sake.

In *The End of Ideology*, Daniel Bell speaks of "an exhaustion (in the 'fifties) of the Nineteenth-Century ideologies, particularly Marxism, as intellectual systems that could claim *truth* for their views in the world" ("ideology, which once was a road to action, has come to be a dead end").

And yet the succeeding decade saw a burst of ideological revivalism, to those exegetes who touched it off—unavowedly repentant Communists or neo-Marxists of refined sophistication—ideological creativity. Instead of the proletariat—once hailed as an inevitable messenger of liberation—a new trinity was seen to carry the message: the Third World with its national liberation movements, student power to champion guerrilla activities, underprivileged workers and other oppressed minorities. To underpin the ideology of the "new," in fact to aid faltering Marxism, even Marxism-Leninism, anarchism and other carriers of dissidence (Bakunin, Trotsky, Rosa Luxemburg) had been summoned. In the Near East we witnessed what, in another context, Abdallah Laroui termed arabization of the newly discovered ideological values.

Ideology being, as axiomatically argued, a kind of super-structure, it was to expect—on account of the lessons from Bolivia, Uruguay and Jordan, of the confrontation between People's China and the Soviet Union, finally of the reversal in their non-ideological relations with the U.S.A.—that the star of ideology, except for professional pursuits of intellectual sophistication, should be dimming. The Near East followed suit Except for Lebanon, in all the Arab states, "conservative" and "progressive" alike, Islam is made state religion.* In Egypt, denasserization is making great strides; Asad's Ba'th and Bakr's Ba'th appear to have changed roles as to "left" and "right." 'Iraq harbors a Baluchi-Liberation Front and Syria's theorist of guerrilla warfare (in the vein of Guevara) pays homage to King Faysal; Libya and Sa'udi Arabia, both fundamentalist and betraying affinity with Muslim Brotherhood, promote Islam in General Amin's Uganda and battle communism in 'Uman.

Egypt's ideology, born of desolation and protest and enhanced by an urge for sole power and its concomitants, ventured to blend two visions—past in its purity and socialist future. Libya's new "ideology," born of wealth of oil and conscious of its power, hatches a socialism bent to a primitive, ferocious concept of Islam and molds a socialism in its image.

Whatever the untold attitude, the actual attitude of Asad's Syria and Bakr's Iraq is conditioned on regional and confessional stresses. The ways and byways of ideology and its motivations are hardly fathomable. Men in power bend and twist it, in word and deed, even without mastering it.

Ideology-bound violence once fervently extolled, has failed. Is violence, stripped of social ideology and reduced to traditional dimensions of bare opportunism, to succeed?

*In Syria, Islam is being made the religion of the head of state.

Chapter I

# MYTHOLOGY OF THE THIRD WORLD

Up to the early 'thirties contemporary Middle East was hardly seen worthy of scholars' research. It was Hans Kohn who in the late 'twenties launched pioneering work in this field. His main concerns were political evolution and what was then termed spiritual trends underlying the nascent or militant nationalism. In point of belief in progress—technology, and education—the "twenties seem a promontory of the Nineteenth Century in an onrushing sea of horror and violence.

Toynbee supervised, in the Chatham House publications on the Middle East, the recording, at first glance painstaking and dispassionate, of events and their immediate background of struggle and negotiations, unfortunately without giving due attention to the larger scene of power politics enmeshed in Nineteenth-Century notions of domination and prestige and affected by salvation-minded Soviet politics; still less, to the economic and social forces conditioning native politics. British scholarship had dealt, in the main, with the political destinies of the dependencies and with problems of administration. Steeped as it was in an imperial world and adverse to theory, it was not eager to explore various facets of human cohabitation, still less to envisage problems which would arise after decolonization. Events and structural statics, not root causes and dynamics were the focus of interest.

Still, even official reports contain priceless material. In justice, owing to the background of the authors, social and economic problems of the Middle East could not have been of acute concern; furthermore, the tools of research had then been near-primitive. British officials on the spot-political agents or soldiers-were cautiously, some exaltedly, treading in descriptive works and yet their records of tribal life, of somehow romanticized desert travels, of local politics, add up to a unique legacy. They also attest to a world of yesterday. Freya Stark added an artistic, hence humanist dimension to a genre of travelogue combining archeological, historical and present-day interests.

The French humanist, all-inclusive approach stands supreme. It resulted in an edifice of *géographie humaine*, a lasting monument to devoted scholarship *de long haleine* and to deep insights into North African humanity. The twenty years of the mandate regime in Syria and Lebanon had yielded enlightening — some near-classical — monographs, notably on minorities and places. Soviet scholarship, from its own viewpoint ideal serving, is, on the whole, time-serving even in regard to the past. And yet, some aspects of topics may have been, if overstressedly, elucidated by it. The U.S.A. part in this field was rather negligible.

After the Second World War Middle East studies have become a discipline no longer disputed. Bent on quick-results research, many of the new generation of impatient scholars seemed to drag their feet behind foreign policy pathfinders. Added to this, specialization blurred the over-all scenery. In fairness, communist championship of anticolonialism, an exciting song of the day, has led to outbidding. The U.S.A., reminiscent of the golden age of anticolonialism, had indulged her past glory by projecting

12

it into Africa and Asia. Scholars, elated over the surge of a new nationalism with lofty notions of freedom, of independence and self-determination, joined the chorus.

These new scholars, many insufficiently steeped in the past, still less in the culture of the emerging states, seem to have had no intimate acquaintance with the evolution of the national idea and movement in Central and Eastern Europe. Between the 'nineties and the First World War social reformers, scholars and publicists there had intensely probed into problems of nation and minorities. Deep human concern informed their deliberations, out of which a body of theory had grown.

The multi-national empires of Austria-Hungary and Russia headed what may be called a scholarly movement in this field. Definitions of nation and minority vied with each other and solutions were devised —federation, confederation, autonomy (regional for territorial, national-cultural or personal for non-territorial minorities). After 1918 some of their solutions had been applied —daringly but not unfailingly —in some nation, or nation states of Europe (by way of granting independence, unification or cession of territories, or some kind of autonomy). On the other side, new wrongs resulted from the peace settlement or, later, from *faits accomplis*.

The new scholars of the 'Forties were hardly capable of guiding, still less warning of gathering storms. Swayed by the tide of enthusiasm for freedom, this instant scholarship has not sufficiently concerned itself with the implications of the fact that neither linguistically and ethnically nor by reason of common historical past, time-honored community of destiny, were there everywhere prerequisites for nation states. Concepts of nationalism have been applied to tribal agglomerations, once arbitrarily joined and held together by sheer force, at best by the authority of a foreign administration. Their real sense of identity often derived from tribal loyalties, supplemented or blurred by aversion to foreign rule and temporary cohesion of a fissiparous elite. Once the heyday of anticolonialism was over and the surge for independence subsided, the centrifugal forces came to the fore.

It is not claimed here that Western scholarship should or could have devised patterns of government as a panacea for countries of a variety of ethnic backgrounds and stages of social and economic life. But it definitely defeats itself by neglect, by resorting to short-term exercises instead of thorough investigation of the widest range of aspects of societies in which the menace of explosions is ever present. Search for answers lies within the scope of scholarship, too. Even bold problem setting prompts answers. By incessantly ramifying problems, social or human sciences claim more and more analytical prowess, implicitly responsibility.

In fairness, there have been voices crying in the wilderness, some still, some outspoken. Independent-minded journalists defied the temptations of conformity and in fearless judgment involved themselves in the destinies of a rediscovered world.

World War Two has set off demographic upheavals such as flight or transfer of populations and resettlement of areas. Ideologies of solidarity notwithstanding, a sharp trend of fragmentation gains momentum. Nationalism or regionalism suck in social ideologies, diluted as they are by a universal trend of so-called *embourgeoisement*, in the wake of implementation. Theories once considered "monolithic" fall to pieces, and older ones, thought doomed to oblivion, raise their heads. Human realities such as tribal or regional identity, historic reminiscences, spoken idioms, folklore, even geographic distinctness feed this trend of self-assertion. It seems a cyclic reversal of the mental tide of integration once aiming at cosmopolitanism, later at internationalism. Discontent feeds also on the practice of salvation-minded theories or on the excessive drive of capitalism.

14

It is an era of re-evaluation of values, in some respects of a future-minded neo-romanticism looking backward for "authenticity." This new soul-searching proves no less fissiparous than the older global theories. Curiously, this trend yielded also a modest contribution — the national liberation ideology — of the Third World to the West.

The native leadership of the colonies claimed the integrity of the colonial legacy with its borders once arbitrarily drawn or redrawn. Under pressure of Communist and "non-aligned," also from contending Western powers, some colonial powers felt impelled to throw considerations of good sense overboard. Congo and West Irian are cases in point; Biafra, preceded by Zanzibar, and the mass slaughter of the Tutsis in Rwanda (1959-1963) and, in 1972, followed by Uganda and the mass slaughter of Hutis by Tutsis and vice versa in Burundi are the horrid result. By slowing the pace or by effecting territorial adjustments in a democratic spirit eruptions of violence and new iniquities could have been averted, at least reduced. Eloquence of "charismatic" leaders carried on the crest of excited masses had won the day.

In fairness, the native leaders reasoned that disruption of territorial entities would cause chaos and bloodshed. But disregard of the ethnic, tribal and linguistic heterogeneity of the colonies does not prevent bloodshed either, and the inherent contradictions are not to be resolved by force, nor by social reforms of Third World no-choice socialisms. It is all-inclusive cultural and economic dynamism, enhanced by a democratic process of governing, that helped make the U.S.A. a " melting pot. " The formal unanimity of the Organization of African Unity with regard to the integrity of the former colonies, numerously violated, is dictated by a convention of solidarity or by common fear of loss or endless disruption.[1] This new nationalism, based on a status quo and on coercion to preserve it, seems an inexhaustible source of dissension.

15

Once the concept of self-determination by, humanly speaking, genuine criteria, and of rule by consent, is thrown overboard, the sole saviors seem indispensable. It is a mere deception to claim that some of these large territories could be kept intact by an iron fist, if socially promising or claiming socialism. They carry with them the seeds of disintegration and no semblance of pan-African or Afro-Asian unity can avert it.

The avowed sense of human solidarity of peoples for whom justice won the day does not apply to issues of internal argument. The magic of national liberation front that has inspired much sympathy in the Third World, India included, does not extend to all the rebellions of oppressed or of those claiming to be oppressed in the Third World. It is power politics overlaid with ideology that decides the legitimacy of a national liberation front. It may be supported beyond one's own borders and suppressed at home.

Member states of AOU may foster rebellions in one or some states and reject them in others. The Southern Front in the Sudan was rejected, and the National Liberation Front in Eritrea is thought progressive and is supported by Syria. Marxist-Leninists differed in their attitude to Pakistan and India. The National Liberation Front under the auspices of U Nu in Burma is set to remove a military regime pursuing the "Burmese road to socialism." The incorporation of Tibet was to People's China an act of "revolutionary legitimacy." The Naga and Mizo movements in India, once supported from China, are seccessionist. Ironically, the rebellion of the Mizo hillmen is being subdued by "regrouping thousands of villagers in security camps bordering main communication routes," an experiment "based on the American regrouping system used in Vietnam."[2]

From its inception the concept of Third World could not but be self-defeating, at best illusory. It sprang from a common revolt against colonialism, a kind of moral solidarity of two continents. (Later on Latin America was thought fit to join in, although here the predominant white race had a different part to play.) In the euphoria of anti-colonialism nearly all the Asian and African states and colonies, some representing old regimes of native coercion, hastened to attend the Bandung conference in 1955. The myth of intrinsic solidarity soon exploded within and between states. The India-China war proved it convincingly. A confrontation within a non-white race or between non-white races could be as fierce as between whites and non-whites. Given the ethnic, linguistic and political background of the African peoples south of the Sahara, *négritude*, a "watchword of African cultural nationalism," could not but be a passing state of mind.[3] And how different are the problems of the potentially eight-peoples state of Burma, of Pakistan comprising the distinct Pathans and Baluchis in the north, of Thailand and Laos.

One day a contemporary history of the newborn Third World will have to be candidly written, just as the dominance of the white race has been presented. Light will have to be shed on the sordid story of Zanzibar, in 1963; Egypt's vision of foster parentage there waned due to a coup sustained by agents of popular democracies. There followed massacres of Arabs in the two islands Zanzibar and Pemba, burning of children and deportation.[4]

As a result of a rebellion in West Irian, hastily handed over, under pressure of the United Nations and others, to the then "progressive" Indonesian "liberators," multitudes of tribesmen have been killed or made refugees seeking sanctuaries in the interior or in Australian territory. In an agreement with the Dutch, in 1962, Indonesia pledged to the people of West Irian, while planning annexation, freedom of speech, movement, and assembly and the right to self-determination "before the end of 1969."

"Colonialist" Australia treats the population of Papua

17

New Guinea in a democratic and generous spirit and guides the country toward independence.[5] Strangely, unlike the activities of the National Liberation Front in 'Uman, those of the Papuan Liberation Front under the former regime of "guided democracy," didn't warrant coverage in the Third World.

What Paul Theroux terms the "Third World's War" feeds, basically, on one issue: the refusal to concede within and between the infant states what was asked of the colonialist, namely the right to make a choice and dissent.[6] Parodixically, India initiated the new era in Asia by foisting "freedom" on Goya. Not that leaders of human entities are always capable of making the best choice or that self-determination could or should always mean secession. Not all the knots of human cohabitation can be unravelled by it. Contrary to a truism, experience was also to prove that at an age of ideologies converging on new states fascinated by newly won freedoms, sweeping social reforms do not eliminate traditional manifestations of kinship making for stronger cohesion. As in the West, authoritarian and centralist approach is to aggravate the problems.

Socialism and revolutionism are watchwords in the Third World, but, as within the communist orbit, in point of territorial status quo, utter conservatism is the rule. With the emergence of Pakistan and India, a status quo, in more than one way beneficial to the subcontinent, was upset, assumedly to do justice to two segments of a community whose only link is religion that should have ensured political coalescence in common statehood. Probably a component of enmity against India reinforced it. A genuine essay in democracy — economic and political — would have helped cement this unusual formation. It is the much scorned Western democratic processes that helped India to ride storms.

In an incisive study, *New Nations*, Dr. Mair speaks of a micro-nationalism of territorially based ethnic "groups with common language, culture and tradition... which cannot meaningfully be called tribes" ("it is no use deploring small-scale patriotism and thinking people can be lectured out of it"[7]). Strictly, they are not what is termed "historical" nations but in some respects they fit in with the definitions of a nation variously given in Europe.*

One does not dare to envisage Indonesia with her multitudes of peoples and languages applying the extremely considerate methods of Switzerland, but one day, one should hope after Biafra and East Pakistan, the key problem of human cohabitation will be seized upon. It is extremely multifaceted: we witness monotribal regionalism, multilingual tribalism within one region, essays in multiparty system intended to do away with tribal divisions and merge various tribal elements within parties, ultimately to end in a one-party system, sometime with one tribe dominant and others bent into it. In Africa, a continent of some 3000 ethnic groupings and 500-600 languages, only a few states have boundaries co-extensive with one tribe; the rest are made up of small or two or three powerful tribes.[8]

To the many reasons put forward for "erosion of democracy" should be added the moral vindication provided by the "popular democracies." In Chad, a group Florina, styled revolutionary and Arab socialist, draws its vocabulary from the Red Book, but in fact its motive power is "tribal-religious," hatred from members of Arab and Muslim groups.[9] Libya fomented it and it may make it subside. To speak with Gilbert Compte, "the reality of 1969 (in Africa) is fundamentally different from the situation that existed in 1960." To him, it is by force of habit that we maintain the myth of two Africas—so-

---

*It is utter simplification to see them as "simply by-products of social change," or even focus the analysis on "linguistic, economic and religious differences." Here too "community of destiny" could be applied, a term coined by Otto Bauer with regard to a nation.

called "reformist" or "moderate" (in the idiom of "revolutionaries" — "reactionary") and "progressive" Africa experimenting with the backing of USSR and People's China.[10]

For all the basic differences, the root problems are common to the Third World countries regardless of system.

One of the priorities for consideration seems to be the language problem. Moving up from a stage of "underdeveloped" country involves education. The assimilationist belief in adopted or native mono-lingualism, urged from a centralist or simplist, i.e., progress-oriented approach, is more than open to question. A fifty-year effort of francisation in Alsace has not resulted in displacing the German dialect, still spoken by eighty per cent of the population. Literary German is insufficiently taught and French is still an acquired language, so that the threat of alingualism is not to be shrugged off. The values of genuine bilingualism are far from being made true.[11]

Even Switzerland, perhaps unique in her subtle handling of problems of human cohabitation, has to face, despite active promotion of the native languages, various complexities: stirrings of regional nationalism somehow mollified by religious versus national affiliations; changes within linguistic frontiers (immigration and migration in the wake of industrialization and urbanization disturbing the linguistic equilibrium); technology and communication overcoming the seclusion of some linguistic areas, even weakening topography-based political entities. Added to this, the relationships between multilingualism and multiculturalism are far from being identifiable.

In India, where eighty-seven per cent of the 1652 dialects are covered by the fourteen languages recognized by the constitution, the decision to make Hindi the sole official language by January 1965 has come to nothing. The Hindi states are changing to Hindi, spoken by a third of the population, "with aggressive speed" and "the non-Hindi states are becoming fanatically monolingual."[12]

Ideally, demographic planning, consequently delimiting areas of homogeneous or least heterogeneous entities and redrawing of borders, by consent or arbitration, could be suggested. Since parts of some tribal entities live within contiguous borders of several states, methods of political or cultural federalism, nowadays anathema, could be considered. There will hover the question of a language of culture: should or could a spoken tongue be fostered to become a written language, or should, by consent, a majority language become the state language. Consent may not be achieved forever. The experience of India, where some areas had to be redrawn on linguistic lines, points to the reverse. Some argue for a foreign language spoken by the native élite and somehow rooted in the country to become a unifying bond. A guiding line can be only utmost concern for human identity.

Rule by force, be it in guise of a Third World socialism, may seem an expedient solution; by no means can a no-choice socialism check an irrepressible urge of self-preservation through self-expression. On the contrary, it exacerbates this urge, even fans the potential elements of aggression in it. At the back of some minds there may lurk a possible solution by reducing human entities as in the case of East Bengal. Otherwise human entities can be moved toward dignified cohabitation only by strong cultural and social incentives and economic dynamism, by substituting higher values for the existing ones. Inalienable rights, once claimed from foreign rulers, have validity in de-colonized countries, too. Unless peaceful means are devised (political, constitutional, cultural) for the adjustment of rights and claims, Africa and Asia are heading for grave convulsions.

Fanon has not lived to witness the lot of Africans in the Sudan, of Biafra, of the Kurds in 'Iraq and Syria, of the West Irians in Indonesia and other calamities in the Third World. "Racial hatreds, slavery, exploitation," deplored by Fanon, had existed before the rise of the white man, and, it seems, will not cease with his decline.[13] Colonialism and imperialism had been practiced by non-whites since time immemorial. We now witness anticolonial ideologies practicing colonialism on native ground. Undeniably, the West reimbursed Africa and Asia with values and concepts — moral, cultural, social — by which the Third World will have to live.

The new battlecry against neo-colonialism does not blind one to the aggressive behavior toward the weak between and within the decolonized areas. In fact, with the decolonization native colonialism or imperialism have stepped in. India seems to have drawn a lesson from the practice of Afro-Asian solidarity after her clash with People's China. Who would deny the background of non-Western imperialism of the India-Pakistan war? The target of anti-colonialism is not pre-destined always to be Western. It is a case in argument within the Communist orbit, too.

To sum up: by throwing overboard basic problems of society's existence, the Afro-Asian world — in its structure an upshot of imperialism, old and new — is bound to unleash forces of destruction to such a degree that the volume of violence involved in white domination would pale into insignificance. In the first decade of independence Africa had some thirty coups, no doubt a corrupted version of change of guards — "ins" and "outs" — in a democratic multi-party system. Due to the new ideology, the Third World may become an arena even of tribal "national liberation fronts." By subduing Biafra and disclaiming East Pakistan the basic problems of Northern Nigeria and West Pakistan remain acute as ever. Social reforms and experiments are bound to come to grief with the issue of minority and majority at any level—ethnic, tribal, political—and be cancelled out.

The recurrent upheavals, culminating in apocalyptic killings, make remedies of subtler nature seem utopian. Doubters shelter behind problems said to be more pressing: "underdevelopment," want or hunger. But the minority versus majority condition affects the pace of development too. In this sense, too, African and Asian countries have much to profit from the workings of federalism at various levels in Switzerland. The position of the Swedes in Finland (7 per cent of the population) and the linguistic stress and strain of the two constituent peoples in Belgium could also shed light on possible ways and means.

The problem of tribe and national minority *vis-à-vis* the state in the Third World makes other adversities such as alienation, rejection of the West coupled with neo-assimilation recede behind. It cannot be tackled under secretive, totalitarian régimes, at the mercy of military parvenus and "ruling cliques, decked out . . . in ideological verbiage and modern weaponry, but otherwise exhibiting all the vices, and few of the virtues, of the tribal monarchies which imperialism dethroned."[14]

### Footnotes

1. The pledge of OAU, whose aims were to be "freedom, equality and dignity" of all African peoples and elimination of colonialism "in all its forms," to abstain from interference in the affairs of the member states was never honored. There has been interference in the affairs of Congo, Kenya, Ethiopia, Nigeria, Uganda, Chad, and other states.
   On the inside of OAU see Charles Mohr, **Herald Tribune**, June 22, 1971.
   On India's supreme efforts to subdue the Naga movement see **Observer**, October 1, 1972.
2. Peter Hazelhurst, **Times**, May 28, 1969.
3. Eric Pace, **New York Times**, July 30, 1969.
4. Martin W. Duyzings, **Weltwoche**, May 1, 1964; Keith Kyle, **Spectator**, January 24, 1964.
5. Michael Donald, **Observer**, June 1, 1969.
6. **Christian Science Monitor**, October 19-21, 1968.

7. London, 1963, p. 118.
8. See Roy Lewis, "African Style Political Game of Ins and Outs," **Times**, September 3, 1969; also "Problems of Nomads at Core of Conflicts," **ibid.**, March 31, 1967; also: "A Pride of Tribes — Africa's Big Headache," **ibid.**, September 18, 1972.

   In his essay "Africa in the 1970's" (**Survey**, Spring 1972), Ali A. Mazrui sees what he terms "pendular model of change" conditioned by the suddenness of political change, cultural ambivalence and dualism of political behavior, i.e., indigenous and acquired ways of politcal response. For a while African nationalism, precisely racial nationalism in Africa, glossed over the artificiality of the colonial framework left intact. Manifold forces — tribalism, ethnocentrism, territorial nationalism and racialism — are inter- or counteracting, to be confounded by the problem of parties versus soldiers. Hence what A. Mazroui calls "retribalization."

   In his stimulating but somewhat apologetic essay "Tribalism through corrective Lenses" (**Foreign Affairs**, July 1973), A. R. Zollberg seems to have been inhibited by a pervasive sense of guilt ("To say that the boundaries of contemporary African countries are 'artificial' tells us less about Africa than about our own historical myths concerning the emergence of nation-states"). Having easily dismissed the contemporary problems of "boundaries," he calls "to tackle the problems of 'tribalism' at their source by moving toward greater equity of political and economic life." We are also being told that "the potential consequences of the introduction of representative democracy amounts to nothing more or less than a social revolution."
9. Jean Pouget, "**Le Tchad contre la partition**," **Le Figaro**, August 20, 1970; also **Le Monde**, September 23, 1969.
10. "**Les deux Afrique**," **Le Monde**, November 12, 1969.
11. G. Wyott, "Pour un vrai bilinguisme en Alsace," **ibid.**, February 4, 1970; also Henri Deligny, **ibid.**, August 3, 1971; Michel Legris, **ibid.**, October 1-7, 8-14, 1964.

    There are cases apart.

    The Bahutu, Batutsi and Batwa, distinct ethnic entities, are to be found in all regions of Burundi; they speak one language and have lived together for centuries. To Romain Forscher, "**Ce n'est pas une lutte tribale qui a déchiré ce pays, c'est le déchainemént et le triomphe du tribalisme érigé en politique (Esprit**, 7-8, 1972).
12. Sandar Rajan, **Reporter**, May 6, 1965. Another version mentions 170 languages and 544 dialects. The fourteen languages are spoken by 90 per cent of the population.

    The 2.5 million natives of Papua New Guinea speak about 700 languages and dialects. See **Neue Zürcher Zeitung**, August 1, 1970.

    Chad comprises ethnic entities speaking 169 dialects.
13. By strange logic Latin America is included in it, although it, too, is "built up with the sweat and dead bodies."
14. Paul Johnson, **New Statesman**, January 12, 1973.

## Chapter II

## THE RISE OF NASSERISM (NASIRIYYA)

Egypt's new ideology has been expounded in various terms: political, economic, less so social, but least of all in view of a people's or man's mind. Hence the recurrent disillusionment with Egypt, resulting in modification of attitude, to some social-minded observers even in a love-hate attitude.

It is a truism that, moral or intellectual stimuli apart, political exigencies, motives of tactics, of party or personal power, make men in power generate, adopt or affect ideas, even modify the interpretation of codified sets of ideas; ideas of religious concern are no exception. The more so, under an authoritarian régime that has no open critique to contend with. It is a long way from the reform-minded Liberation Rally of 1952-1956 to the National Union holding to "pragmatic, cooperative democratic socialism" (1956-1961) to "scientifically" oriented socialism (since 1961), an Egyptianized version of Marxism unobtrusively studded with Leninist ingredients. Only the attachment to Islam has remained intact and has been made to vindicate the ideological evolution all along.

One is tempted to adopt a one-man centered view of an authoritarian régime. Within political and ideological, hence, in point of an obligate creed, also philosophical confines, the written and publicly spoken word in Egypt

25

has been monopolized or, at least, strictly supervised. But the media of information and the strata of addressees to be enlightened are numerous; no wonder that conflicting or diversified statements are frequent. Besides, the ideological itinerary of a writer may account for some deviant backsliding. Since unequivocal criticism is eliminated, strong inhibitions deriving from self-criticism dwindle too. Conformity is an overwhelming element in man's behavior even in a, humanly speaking, free society. When imposed with an iron fist, it inevitably weighs man's mind down. How tormenting must it be for a trainee of Western culture, when he is made to adopt and to plead for what amounts to a creed. What is more, even the ideological debate, stimulated or condoned by the régime in times of crisis, notably after 1967, be it as a safety valve or as a result of self-examination, often sounds, in its evasive sophistication, self-streamlined.

A scrutiny of the vast volume of authorized, inspired or tolerated ideological literature shows a variety of levels of approach. The emotionally charged and slogan-studded *National Charter* dominates the whole of it. On it draw the Islamic preacher, the pious popularizer, the one-voice radio commentator, and both the reasoning social essayist and theorist. This unquestioned source of inspiration feeds all these channels of enlightenment. Actually, it seems to rank third to the Koran and *hadith*.[1]

At the turn of the century Islamic reformers in Egypt employed much ingenuity of reasoning, supported by the Koran and *hadith*, to prove that Islam is compatible with modern science. The cherished notion that all the knowledge, even the knowledge to come, is indicated or alluded to in the Koran, has helped sustain the reformers' zeal. Throughout the centuries the Koran was exposed to Islamic interpretation on various levels—literal, early rationalistic, allegorical-mystical, positivist, recently Gandhi-centered. The Nineteenth

Century reformers had much to endure at the hands of the conservatives then supported by the régime. Now conservatives are on the defensive, if not silenced, and reformers, allied with the régime, are conformists: they labor, willingly or unwillingly, to prove that Islam is the fountainhead of socialism. In this way intellectual thought becomes a derivative of religious thought or vice versa. Even externally: books and pamphlets that deal with secular problems often invoke religious sanction by being introduced or closed by a religious formula. One may argue that all problems could or should be of religious concern, but here the association of religion and socialism is dictated and not to be questioned, inevitably in many a matter of convention or expediency. Exposition of problems in the light of socialism, that is to say in the light of Islam, necessitates knowledge of religious literature, first and foremost Koran and *hadith*. But in the course of time unchallenged exegesis has become patterned in style and content. Sayings, again and again repeated, may make up for dearth of knowledge.

Egypt's constitution of 1924 declared Islam — a majority religion — the country's religion. But now the regime has incorporated a religion into a manmade ideology. In a sense Egypt's socialist creed is super-totalitarian. Being Islam-based, it also implies a metaphysical outlook. In this respect an alien creed is imposed, not without some resistance, on members of the Christian Coptic minority numbering some six millions, about a sixth of the population.[2]

Moreover, by joining the Arab Socialist Union, the only political formation in Egypt, the considerable, perhaps overwhelming, agnostic segment of the intelligentsia is made to be professing Muslims.

The notion of Islamic socialism is not the régime's innovation. In the 'thirties Young Egypt and the Muslim Brethren viewed sympathetically German national socialism. Islamic socialism gained currency in their idiom toward the end of the Second World War, and more so in the late 'forties. At that time, socialism became a battlecry of nearly all the Egyptian parties. No doubt, by retaining the attachment to Islam, even monopolizing its interpretation, Egypt's new ideology is also given some historic, hence conservative background. Is Islamic socialism to help secure the attachment of the rural masses to the régime or stem the tide of secularization caused by urbanization and industrialization? To placate Muslim theologians, or to take the wind out of the Muslim Brethren's sails? It is also argued that "Nasser may indirectly accelerate the secular process by making political use of a religious instrument."[3]

The noted dictum of Ahmad ibn Hanbal, the great Ninth Century theologian: "The *jihad* (holy war) should be pursued alongside all *imams* (leaders of the nation), whether good or evil-doers; the injustice of the tyrant or the justice of the just matters little," is called to mind.[4]

In line with this, Rashid 'Ali's revolt against the government of Nuri Sa'id and the "infidel British" in 1941 was endorsed by the religious authorities of 'Iraq as a "holy war"; even the Sunni Mufti of Lebanon followed suit. In 1962, the new Mufti of Egypt announced that the Prophet was the first socialist. But the cliché of the church being blended with the state in Islam does not blot out the fact that throughout the centuries Muslim theologians and scholars, including ibn Hanbal, resisted the pressure of the authorities to conform and often paid for it with their life. The struggle between "old" and "new" in Islam never ceased, but the terms "old" and "new" have now become confounded. Nowadays institutional Islam has to argue out differences with or conform to exclusive salvation-minded teachings.

Let us present Egypt's Muslim scholars in their own idiom, with no attempt to tell possible convention from circumvention. Ahmad Hamad, preacher general in Cairo:

Islam is a religion of true socialism: in worship, when the leader (*imam*) and the led stand before God, in fasting and pilgrimage, in consulting the Muslims (*shura*), in collective responsibility in Islamic society, both the humble and the powerful (said the Prophet: Everyone of you is a shepherd, and everyone is responsible for his flock). Basic rights can be insured only in socialism: the right to life, the right of freedom and knowledge, the right to dignity, political freedom (said the Prophet: Every person has the right to stand up before his *amir* (prince) and speak his opinion).

"Economic freedom is a means not a goal." Socialism of Islam derives from human nature and dispositions. Islam respects private property as long as it promotes the well-being of society. It is to be taken away only when it harms man. "The basis of socialism is mutual help and solidarity between classes, not a war of one segment against the other."

Communism rejects the right of private property, kills personal initiative, does not value mind or ability. "Competition between men creates classes, and the existence of classes in Communist society means war between men." The basis of relations between the in-fighting classes in communism is atheism, negation of personal feelings and moral values. "Possibly, communism derives its principles from Satan (*iblis*)." Communism does not trust men.[5]

Said Ahmad Hasan al-Zayyat, an al-Azhar University teacher and editor of *Majallat al-Azhar*:

"Allah's religion is socialist by its very nature and message.... His is the property, His is the capital, and the poor are His wards, the rich are His servants."

The fast of Ramadan is "spiritual socialism," manifestation of "spiritual association among Muslims all over the world." Without a solid base of spiritual socialism, material socialism will neither come into being nor last.

> "This spirit is Allah's secret in every living being, and in society. .... It unites the hearts of fellow citizens to worship one God, to love the common homeland ...to obey the leader-commander."

When this spirit weakens in the souls of men they do not help each other in distress, and socialist laws and cooperative statutes become words without meaning.[6]

Socialism in Islam stands, among other things, for rights to human freedom (man is not owned); religious freedom (socialism of Islam aims at freeing man's mind from superstitions and chimeras, so that it could be employed to observe the creation of heaven and earth); "scientific freedom" (division of the Koran, hadith, law, kalam (dogmatics), history, philosophy, mysticism, medicine); political freedom: to choose the head of the state, to criticize the ruler. It is a "human service" and a "compelling national necessity" to call for socialism of Islam.

> "Socialism of Islam is godly in its sanctity, Muhammadan in its guidance, Arab in its characteristics and human in its world trend and message."[7]

To Mahmud al-Sharqawi, Islam is "liberation of conscience" and social solidarity; complete human equality (in another place, as far as possible) between rich and poor, man and woman; social justice; participation of the nation in the affairs of government (in "constitutional width,"

Islam is ahead of the most modern parliamentary order); nationalization (said the Prophet: "Men are partners in three things: water, bread and fire"). In some versions salt is added, hence every necessity could be included.[8]

Abu Dharr, the Prophet's Companion and "the first revolutionary socialist in the world," is said to epitomize Egypt's official concept of Islamic socialism that "has widely surpassed the French Revolution."[9]

Islam has also put socialist practice to use. "All the precepts of Islam aim at the realization of public utilities." "Hence every means that is in line with the Islamic law, also by way of analogy, is legitimate."[10]

*Ta'mim* (nationalization) is not synonymous with corresponding terms in Arabic (*waqf*, charitable endowment, and so on), but they meet in the meaning of common ownership.[11]

The value of handiwork is highly stressed (said the Prophet: "The best livelihood is man's work with his hands"). A true believer does not shun any work whatsoever as long as he pursues a public interest or a private interest that does not harm public interest. (The Prophet pastured sheep, travelled for business, dug trenches, split rocks, carried earth; the prophet Noah built ships.) All works of civilization and culture and science attest to Allah's wisdom in man. Belief is a "basic pillar" of work, so that a nonbeliever, whatever his standing, carries no weight with Allah, and his work, whatever it is, is valueless. Work is measured by its motive and incentive; it is a "natural fruit" and "final result" of belief. The word *'amil*, in other languages meaning *worker*, was given in Islamic society to governors and rulers. There is no difference between the work of workers, merchants, heads of departments and companies. "Religion is neither passivity nor negation."[12]

Shaykh al-Baquri, rector of al-Azhar university, adduces proper reasons for exercising birth control, including one by al-Ghazali, an Eleventh Century Muslim thinker, and alludes to a method thereof as indicated by some Companions of Muhammad and in Islamic jurisprudence *(fiqh)* that takes into consideration "freedom of the woman."[13]

The new interpretation of the Koran launched by the High Committee on Islamic Affairs at the Ministry of Waqf" contains judicious observations of biologists, physicians, psychologists, sociologists, and other scientists, explaining some allusions to these sciences in the Koran that were not known at the time of its revelation and are proofs of its miraculousness." Likewise there are in the Koran "stipulations about honoring freedom, human dignity, justice and equilibrium between rights and duties. These notions became known in later centuries."[14]

Islamic or Islam-minded writers make excessive use of the term "revolution" *(thawra)* and its derivations, which is not particular to Egypt. *Thawra* gained currency with the rebellions against the British and the French after the First World War, and ever since came to denote any military *coup d'etat* in 'Iraq and Syria. With the emergence of the Ba'th party, *thawra* (also *inqilab*) assumed, beside the nationalist, also a socialistic coloring. It seems to provide some sense of grand doing and an illusion of accomplishment. It perfectly fits into a process of speech, in which reason dissolves in Egypt *thawra (thawri)* is also used to stress precedence over reformism, or Western style socialism.[15]

A large volume, dedicated to "the commander of the Arabs... and leader of free men! To the people's hope and expectation of the hearts! To the guardian of freedom... to President 'Abd al-Nasir," and studded with sayings from the Koran and *hadith*, is a kind of pan-revolutionary presentation of history, which is "a set of revolutions of liberation."

   Revolution is a genuine expression of society's spirit and of people's emotions; it is the successivs breaths on volcanos' mouths and in heroes' breasts. . . .

Revolution of the United Arab Republic for the sake of the liberation of the world and benefit of life . . . and welfare of humanity. Revolution of innovators in religion! Revolution of scientists, inventors, and discoverers! Revolution of giants among the people's leaders! Revolution of heroes among the war commanders! Revolution of reform leaders! Revolution of philosophers and rulers! Revolution of toiling and struggling peoples in Africa and Asia, revolution of free revolutionaries of 23 July (1952).[16]

A cornerstone of Egypt's new ideology is execration of Jews. In the past official Egypt was least affected by it. Now it is state-authorized and it is being injected, in the main, into popular and Islam-centered ideological writings. The spoken word has its target in Israel and Jews and the written also in Judaism.

A thorough scrutiny shows the parentage of this literature, namely the *Protocols of the Elders of Zion*. The *Protocols* became a book of guidance.[17] In the 'Fifties they had fed a booklet—*Haqiqat al-shuyu'iyya (The Nature of Communism)*—prefaced by 'Abd al-Nasir. In it communism and Judaism jointly strive for domination of the world. It is a horrible concoction of falsehoods and ignorance.[18]

A few representative pieces of argument from other sources:

This is the history of the Jews with Muhammad, full of their treachery and betrayal and violation of pledges and treaties . . . They disbelieved Moses and Jesus nor had they held to religion, moral or virtues . . . Throughout the centuries theirs was ingratitude to those who favored them, cowardice in battlefield and seeking protection with the allies of Satan . . .

... After all this do they deserve that a hand be stretched to them? ... Do they deserve a free and honest life in the shadow of the Arab countries? History is full of their misdeeds and lowliness. Humiliation has been granted as their lot (Sura 3:112) at all times and places .... * Hated by all peoples and all hearts. They kill prophets unjustly.[19]

Karl Marx, the "Rabbi of Israel," and "messenger of communism" was one of the masters of this heavy conspiracy. He knew that the Jews "embody the nature of hate and human squalor," strive to dominate the world and destroy religion and nationalism. The Jews are standard bearers of these two destructive creeds (communism and capitalism). Max Nordau devised a plan for this destructive work. He asked to rear a new generation on lies, falsehoods and gainseeking. Jews said that the Russian revolution was of their planning, due to their mentality.

Zionists admit that they were the first to call for communism. Often have the Jews stated that they made communism a means to exploit world resources. It is agreed that Lenin was a Jew.[20]

Within a few years, communism has been divorced from Zionism. The editor of *Majallat al-Azhar* pins hopes on the Three Continents Conference in Havana "to look into the problems of imperialism and the way of its elimination." Conferences of prominent people from Asia and Africa are to "cooperate for good and against evil" and "help spread world peace."[21]

A composite apologia of Islamic socialism, presented as popular maxims and corroborated from a multitude of sources of human thought, is to be found in another of al-Sharqawi's works. Ancient naïveté as well as modern con-

---

* Another translation: "They are debased .... " In 1972, Anwar al-Sadat presented these views in public.

cepts of social justice, scholarly research into Islam and new psychology, all combine to prove the author's suppositions.

The Charter's premise that political democracy cannot be divorced from social democracy is supported by Nehru's view on economic democracy, from Laski's, Cole's and Erich Fromm's works, from the Prophet's and his Companions sayings such as:

A leader who shuts his door to the needy, miserable and poor will find that Allah shuts the doors of heaven to his misery and need.

The best of your leaders are those whom you love and who love you, who pray for you and for whom you pray.... The worst leaders are those whom you hate and who hate you, whom you curse and who curse you.

'Umar was running behind a straying camel from the treasury. When asked: O, prince of the believers, should not we pursue it so that you would rest? He answered: Why, then, am I a governor and a prince to man? By Allah, should a cord of camels get lost in 'Iraq, I would be afraid that Allah might ask me about it saying: Oh 'Umar! We have entrusted you with the people's property and you sleep? If responsibility for the people's title to a cord is rated so high, how does he rate the people's title to freedom?

To al-Sharqawi, Christ's message had a great impact in "freeing the world from Jewish materialism," and Islam called for socialism from its inception. Islam limited property and freed slaves. Levi-Provençal and Dozy showed how Islam rescued the low classes from feudalism.

Islamic socialism rests on a regime of limited property, of socialist production and distribution, of urge to work and of wiping out materialist tyranny.[22]

It is a long distance from liberal and humanist thinkers such as the late 'Ali 'Abd al-Raziq who discarded the caliphate, for him an institution born of violence and greed, from intrinsic Islam, to the new Egyptian one-voice interpretation of Islam.

A religion that even in our days was made to bear the sublimest interpretation (from Iqbal to Azad in India) is being made to display affinity with the Protocols of the Elders of Zion. The ideological streak of Jewphobia is clearly Nazi-patterned. A dictated Egyptianization of Islam is meant to be valid for all Muslim and Arab lands.

There seems to have come about a division of labor between Islam-centered and more culture-minded intellectuals. Of course, a measure of protective coloring on the part of Marxist or Muslim converts to Nasserism is not to be excluded. To both segments ideological creativity is bounded by the National Charter, the fountainhead of argumentative and interpretative thought. One is tempted to a crude discrimination: to the second segment, the ideology of the Charter flows from Islam; to the first, vice versa.[23]

The more culture-bound stress, varyingly, Arabdom in socialism, and often gloss over the religious element in it; others such as the writers of *al-Tali'a*, barely address themselves to it. Ideologically Egypt had to monopolize the grasp of Arabdom, too. A messianic, salvation-minded creed couldn't but discard other variations of Arab socialism. True, hard lessons of latter days mitigated this attitude. Since 1967, with the slow sunset of Nasserism, Egypt's exclusivity is toned down. Implicitly, the legitimacy of other patterns of Arab socialism is conceded.

At times and in some respects, the two sets of standards of theorizing and appeal seemed to draw nearer; in others, with the wave of Marxist radicalization, farther apart. One was geared to the masses, *i.e.*, harping on emotions of hate or affectionate self-indulgence and sustaining them from religious sources. Here Freud was presented as a destroyer of spiritual values and Marx as an author of Jewish world conspiracy. Of course, some allowance could be made for insufficient knowledge or ignorance. And one allowed the educated a semblance of deliberation in a few periodicals: here Marxist reasoning enjoys leeway of exercise; theorizing may be seen as a substitute for practice. Here, too, deficient study or undisciplined presentation call for some consideration. In *al-Katib*, an ideological "journal for educated Arabs," started in 1961, Freud and his disciples (Erich Fromm and Ferenczi) are intently discussed, and Marx's *Jugendschriften* quoted. Harold Laski's works are respectfully expounded.[24] No doubt, the authors of the Chart had drawn, though inconsistently, on his *Grammar of Politics* and *Liberty in the Modern State*. Since about 1966, relics of democratic socialism have been eliminated, consequently intellectual tolerance vanished; "Third World" and Communist features and exploits dominate the scene.

It is much more difficult to pursue the evolution of ideological thought in the periodicals with no religious accent. The term secular would be misplaced; here too secular thought — unmentionable heresy — is nonexistent. Distinction is to be made between dailies, popular weeklies and journals of intellectual sophistication. The daily *al-Ahram* is an institution in itself; its editor, extremely pragmatic and pliable, has contrived to ride the crest of many an upheaval. It seems appropriate to start with *al-Katib*. At its inception in local terms broadminded and less given to sloganeering, it joined in the 'sixties the streamline of revolutionism.

What is specifically Arab in Egypt's socialism? Socialism is a European concept, and European reasoning feeds Egypt's socialism even in terminology. No doubt, closer ties with U.S.S.R. have later induced theorists to argue out ideological differences with Marxism instead of communism. Anyhow, economic and social commonplace reasoning sounds much on the line of Marxism.

37

This is the presentation of Kamal Rif'at, ideologist of a Marxist past and one-time member of the Presidency Council.

The 1918 revolution in Egypt "erupted from the base of fellahin and workers." The revolution was put down not by imperialism but by the bourgeois classes themselves. It was complementary to the "1881 revolution" as was the "1952 revolution" to the "1918 revolution '

No revolution is devoid of social content. The collision between capital and the "nature of production" in a capitalist society leads to an "absolute solution" of harmonizing the "collectivist nature of production" and the ownership of the means of production. Naturally, the means of production become collective property.

Egypt's national capital could not stand up to world capital and monopolies. There were two ways: to raise the capital by heavy dues, to curb imports and speed up local production, or to "socialize national capital."

Arab socialism differs from "other socialisms" in that it attaches to consciousness a "great and central importance." Other socialisms hold that consciousness is a "reaction to development" and that "existence determines consciousness."[25]

We are presented with a blend of economic Marxism tempered with some non-Marxism. Being much given to simplifying and generalizing, Egyptian theorists do not apply themselves to the evolution of Marxist thought and its derivations. But the differences between Marxism and Arab socialism are carried further.

"Arab socialism believes in Allah, His books, His messenger, His heavenly messages sent to man any time and any place, and in religious and moral values." Arab socialism establishes "an equilibrium between the claims of the individual and the society," as stated in the Charter: a free person is the basis of a free society. The basic rights of the individual are: freedom to shape his future of "positive participation in directing the evolution with all his thoughts, experience and hope."

Arab socialism believes in a "healthy democratic life," not in the rule of a certain class, not in party democracy, but in "democracy of the people as a whole, after having purged it from agents of imperialism, reactionaries and exploiting capitalists." This belief in the myth of a purge — once and for all—runs through all the trends of Arab socialism. In fact, this means had been applied, with no lesser severity, to defeated factions within formations of Arab socialism and, of course, between the formations themselves.

Along with this purge, Arab socialism believes in "melting the differences" between classes and in peaceful solution of conflicts, through a new pattern of distribution of riches and income, "insofar as work is their basic source."

Private capital and inheritance rights are lawful, but a distinction is made between "exploitative capital," a "tool to corrupt society," and property that fulfills a social function. National capital is a basic element of "the elements of people's forces," which implies cooperation between the public and private sectors. "People's rule over all the means of production does not necessitate the nationalization of all means of production."[26]

Arab socialism is revolutionary; right-wing and British socialism is evolutionary. Supplanting capitalism by socialism is unavoidable, they are "two opposites that cannot meet." The mentality of man should be transformed "from that of the capitalist exploiter's to a socialist just" one.

"Arab socialism is national socialism, not party socialism," not a target for party maneuvers or "a place for counter-reformist forces to attack." A coalition of "people's forces" within the framework of the Arab Socialist Union is "the best safeguard against deviation from goals."

Arab socialism sees in the sanctity of religions a basic factor of spiritual forces and of life of love, charity and solidarity, which gives it a distinct characteristic and makes a realistic socialism, far from the utopian socialisms of the Nineteenth Century.

Religion is a basic axis to solve the social problem, and the main ideological factor in Arab socialism.

Religion means justice, means freedom, means humanity in its sublime forms.[27]

Arab socialism strives to "establish a classless society of legal equality in which opportunity for decent living will be provided for all." Right wing socialism "does not wish to realize this goal"; it rests upon classes and tries to compose conflicts and implement social justice within the framework of the present social order.

To face the "inevitable natural struggle" between the classes, Arab socialism does not resort to violence. Class conflicts will be resolved "within the organized national entity."[28]

Marxist socialism stands for a one-party regime, even non-classbased, is a kind of tyranny, dictatorship. The people's demands reach the rulers only through this party.

Against this, the Arab Socialist Union is an "accomplished people's organization." It comprises, after removing the reactionary and opportunist elements, all the individuals of the working people. It does not approve of class rule, even of the fellahin and workers class.

This accords with the principles of Islam that does not approve of partisanship nor of a multi-party system, but calls for solidarity, mutual help and compassion.[29]

The discerning reader, familiar with Marxist thought, cannot but find this argument over socialism, proceeding from tacit identification of Marxism and communism, superficial and inaccurate. The ideological edifice is pieced together from titbits of socialist thought with, depending on one's viewpoint, Islamic thought grafted onto or underpinning it. The reader will have to contrast this edifice with the background of an authoritarian régime and an extreme cult of personality. And yet it is asserted that Egypt's socialism, being "experimental, applied Arab socialism .... has not borrowed its principles from abroad," "it assumed its character according to the people's nature, the political climate and the regional framework."[30]

"Scientifism" and "scientific socialism" appear as strong pillars of this edifice. To 'Abd al-Nasir, a revolution deserves its name only if it adopts a scientific method, in theory and practice. Revolution is the "science of comprehensive and deep social change, intended to create new life that meets the demands and hopes of the revolutionaries."[31]

The premises of Egypt's kind of scientific socialism are distinct, too.

The Arab theory of scientific socialism rejects the dialectical materialist view on religion, but at the same time holds to the scientific method in the study of problems of nature and society. Likewise it rejects, in response to the conditions of the new historic era and of the Egyptian patriotic revolution and Arab nationalism, the proletarian way of implementation of socialism, *i.e.*, dictatorship of the proletariat and leadership of the Communist party.

Since the Nasserite patriotic way of socialism is... not merely a response to specific Egyptian conditions, it offers a theory of revolution that will have to be repeated under similar conditions. Possibly world guidance is assigned to the socialist revolution of liberation in Egypt—the vanguard of socialist revolutions of liberation in Asia and Africa.

The bases of scientific socialism are:

Scientific method of history.
Scientific theory of history.
Scientific analysis of economics.
Indispensability of class strife and revolution.
_ Nationalization of the means of production.
Democracy of the whole working people (as against dictatorship of the proletariat).
Leadership of the socialist vanguard (as against Marxist-Leninist leadership).
Non-aligned internationalism (as against aligned internationalism).

In branding reformist socialism as false and opportunistic, Lenin's attack on Ed. Bernstein is cited.[32]
There remains to harmonize "class strife" with peaceful "melting of differences."
From the alleged collusion of Zionism and communism, induced by "Rabbi Karl Marx," a point stressed by Islam-centered writers and in the 'Fifties implicitly approved by 'Abd al-Nasir, Egypt's ideologists moved to Marxist vindication of Jewphobia, thus making it palatable to world-minded readers. Marx's *Zur Judenfrage*, translated into Arabic, is drawn upon. We are told that Bergson called upon the Jews to assimilate with non-Jews. "But the problem is not so simple."

Shakespeare's Jew Shylock is an inevitable phenomenon, not a personal accident. The Jew's separatism is but an expression of his feeling of being rejected for his financial operations. They turned to these very operations for two reasons: first, the spread of Christian feudalism in Europe induced the church to ban the régime of interest, so that the Jews alone seized this lowly opportunity to exercise this occupation; second, the Jews were small minorities in Europe's countries, and the only way for minorities striving to dominate society is the way of capital.

"In other words, a Jew is a despicable capitalist."[33]

After the massacres in Rhineland, France and England, the Jews took up the same occupation. Upon their return the crusaders found that a class of "big Jewish capitalists" took possession of a great part of the economic resources. This recalls "what Freud terms death wish."[34]

The class attitude to Zionism is to be elaborated as follows:

> Uncovering the class basis of Zionism as a movement that serves the interests of world capitalism and colonialism.
>
> Uncovering the historical basis of the Jewish problem that has no relation to an Arab homeland.
>
> Uncovering the aggressive and colonialist nature of Israel's policy in matters of liberation, socialism and peace.
>
> Pointing out the racialist and aggressive colonialist existence of the State of Israel.
>
> Elucidation of the nature of the battle waged by the U.A.R. against Israel as a battle for socialism, liberation and peace.
>
> Presentation of the democratic patterns of our new political life that hold their own in any formal comparison between Israel's trumpeted bourgeois democracy and the socialist democracy in our country.
>
> Shedding light, by means of intellect and art, and an objective method corroborated by proofs on the misdeeds of Zionist massacres in Palestine in the 'forties and condemning the savagery of Israelis who trade in Europe in the massacres of the anti-semites.[35]

Against this, Zionism is credited with having "set off the explosion of the strongest forces of the socialist revolution of liberation in the Arab countries." Were it not for the Zionist seizure of Palestine the Arab revolution would have possibly come years later. There is no Arab national or progressive movement that does not understand this, though they differ in the degree of understanding.[36]

Contradictions in this ideology vary also with the levels of exegesis. A rude awakening through a shakeup of the régime may reduce the whole edifice to a shambles.

In the strife with the Muslim Brethren, means were employed peculiar to the Muslim Brethren themselves, even the same ornate, cadenced style. The Muslim Brethren are "Satan's party," a "group of traitors" and dissidents (khawarij) "whose ends justify means," "in quest of spoils or power or splendor . . . They marched under the wing of colonialism, helped the usurping occupant . . . In their eagerness they allied themselves with communism, Zionism, Satan and enemies of Allah, fatherland, Arabdom and Islam." They carried the injunctions of religion in directions "willed by Malenkov, John Bull, Uncle Sam and Cohn." Their "criminal ways" contradict the principles of the Islamic mission ("call to Allah's path with wisdom and fine admonition").[37]

The Koran and hadith might supply sayings in support of both camps. Moreover, Egypt's Arab Socialist Union and the Muslim Brethren fight each other over some semantically identical ends of "Islamic democracy," Islamic socialism, both thereby manipulating notions borrowed from the West: freedoms, equality of ruler and ruled, social justice, solidarity (said 'Umar: all men are like the teeth of a comb). To both Islam is the "apogee of lawgiving." Both condemn multi-party rule. In essence, even the notion of "explosion of populist atom" is not alien to the Muslim Brethren.

Indiscriminate use of hadith seems to depreciate the much extolled aspect of "scientifism" of the régime. It also implies discarding free research into hadith. All kinds of ideologies could be borne out by it.[38] But most striking is the notion that "scientifism" is compatible with taboo as regards religion. Not unlike divines and former Islamic modernists, present scientific socialists are supposed to keep transmitted beliefs unquestioned. In this respect it is a new link in the chain of apologetics.

We witness reinterpretation of *hadith* in the light of socialism. The creative imagination that generated *hadith* is so to speak resuscitated and applied to socialism, thus picking up the lost thread of *hadith* creativity. In this case the notion that the Koran contains even all knowledge to be is extended to *hadith*. Furthermore, we could assume some identification with the creativity of the Prophet and his Companions on the part of present interpreters. In a preface to *Ishtirakiyyat Muhammad (Muhammad's Socialism)*, Mahmud Shalabi illuminates the immense potentialities of this identification.

> Every edition needs additions or improvements!! It is because Muhammad, God bless him and grant him salvation, is above the level of our minds.
>
> His word will be ever new.
>
> Whenever you ascend to it you see from it horizons not seen before!!
>
> Even if this book will be printed again and again until the Day of Resurrection.
>
> The word of Muhammad is not a thing of his own. It is a revelation revealed. ...
>
> It is summit of summits of light. The more you ascend ... the more you understand.[39]

From within, only Khalid Muhyi al-din's discernment of the relationship between Islam and socialism, that is, his interpretation of the Charter is subtler and could even be seen more than slightly sophisticated, even deviant. Islam is not presented as mainspring of socialism nor identified with it. "To us, Islamic values of justice and

45

ideals brought forth by the first Islamic revolution through the Messenger... represent, in their overall and general features, a method that steers us, when asking for their guidance under conditions of our age and our society... , to one road, that is, the road of socialism as a natural extension of the first revolutionary experiment in Islam."

We are told that "from the first moment" Islam met with ferocious resistance of big merchants and the propertied in Mecca and "religious reaction" there. Abu Dharr, with the poor Muslim masses behind him, declared goods and wealth property of Allah, hence property of Allah's servants as a whole, administered by the state, whereas the caliph 'Uthman considered wealth as a property of Allah and the ruler in lieu of Him. Islamic religion is also said to have originated a "legal way" to harmonize constantly with science and scientific discoveries. Hence the institution of renovators (*mujaddidun*) in Islam.

Furthermore, Muhyi al-din applies Marxist, hence relativist reasoning to the evolution of Islam. "There is no one way of understanding the teachings of Islam. Naturally, with the change of societies, classes and social forces, varying concepts wrestled in line with the struggle of the interests that produced them."

"This controversy is natural and logical. Being religion, world and ideology, Islam suits any time and any place. Naturally, it limits its appeal to overall ideals and principles, so that the door is open to *ijtihad* (individual judgment)."[40]

Thus a large latitude of sophistry makes one oscillate between the concept of the Muslim Brethren and *ijtihad* with its immense potentialities of interpretation and vindication.

A Marxist interpretation of Islam that gives free rein to imagination makes one wonder if it is innocent piety or analogous sophistication. Islam is presented in the vein of the verdict that history of society is a history of class struggle. The key tune is: "idealism of the Left and opportunism of the Right."

Left is the socialist trend. It rejects in principle the idea that the end justifies the means. However complex things are, however pressing the necessity, it will never reach its just goal with unjust means.

The socialist trend in Islam didn't die with 'Ali's death. The revolutions of the Left didn't cease after his murder; they expanded throughout Islamic history, at every age assuming a new form, befitting this age.

The bonfire started in Islam by its Prophet and the first Companions, thereafter kept alive by the caliph 'Ali, never went out . . . through all the ages, this trend never ceased to appear in this or that form as a social revolution demanding justice for the weak from the powerful and wealthy, from exploiters and autocrats.

In the ranks of the Right, crime is a weapon always resorted to. 'Umar was assassinated, then al-Ashtar, one of 'Ali's strong aides, was treacherously poisoned. Abu Hanifa's son was killed, likewise Muhammad, son of Abu Bakr, then Hasan, son of 'Ali, was poisoned in his home.

This method of getting rid of foes is not new with the leaders of the Right, not only at this time but at all times.[41]

Another landmark of Islam, again contrary to total idealization:

The history of Islam shows the struggle between two basic ideas—the idea of social solidarity and the idea of personal rule. When we speak of the receptiveness of the Arab peoples to the socialist idea, we actually mean this heavy legacy of heroic struggles—sacrifices and martyrs—that started with Islam; and when the features of Arab socialist implementation are drawn on the basis of this legacy, it means natural continuance of the early socialist ideas based on long-range and deep-rooted historical reality. The modern Arab socialist idea is not drawn from other sources, not derived from mere local reality, it is a revolutionary extension of the spirit of Islamic revolution, it is deep rooted and un-fathomable, goes back to the glorious struggle of the Islamic Left.

We could objectively say that the 23 July revolution, its revolutionary success and socialist application through revolutionary action crystallized in the Na-tional Charter, is a decisive success of the leftist trend that goes back farther than many imagine.

In Husayn, the Left found a hardy leader and a firm commander, but the Islamic Left was not one homogeneous block; it was full of rifts, and from these rifts the arrows of Mu'awiya pierced the Left's camp.[42] (The reader's attention is called to Egypt's leader).

Once this line of exegesis is taken up, Arab régimes, bent on self-assertion or vying for prevalence, had to follow suit. Egypt's attitude is challenged not only from orthodox quarters, themselves prompted to react through reforms. Tunisia's Destourian socialism, evolutionary and West-incliined, pursues reformist policies also designed to "restore Islam to its purity... rehabilitating it for its role as a factor of progress."[43]

Under Ladgham (1969-1970) an attempt was made, pro-bably by reason of closer realignment with Arab politics, towards conservative presentation of Islam. In this spirit Bourguiba's dicta had been interpreted.

In its ideological evolution the régime of Algeria has moved oscillatingly, then near abruptly, from "modernism" towards Islamism. Here too contradictory interpretation is unavoidable. It is argued that the Prophet rejected class war and violence. On the other hand, Abu Dharr is supposed to have said, "It would be strange if a man whose stomach is empty doesn't take up his sword to fight the rich. The Prophet himself made raids against his opponents who were slave owners. Is this not justification of class war?" He even said, "My God, let me live poor, make me die poor and place me in the ranks of the poor on the Day of Judgment."[44]

We are confronted with various and varying concepts of "purity of Islam," at best all intended to further progress with the least harmful results.[45]

In the 'twenties, 'Ali 'Abd al-Raziq attempted to strip the concept of Islam of temporality. To him, "the caliphate never ceased to be distressing to Islam and Muslims, a source of evil and corruption. ... It is not easy to doubt that from 'Ali and Mu'awiya to the last caliph all reached their position in the shadow of a sword and on tips of lances. ... The Prophet's authority was spiritual; actions in the Prophet's life that seem authoritarian were only means to strengthen and spread Islam." Politics and religion are far apart.

> "There is nothing in religion that prevents Muslims from competing with other nations in all the sciences of society and politics... to destroy the antiquated system they submitted to and to build the bases of sovereignty and a system of government in accord with the most modern achievements of the human mind."[46]

In 1933, 'Abd al Raziq went even further. "A government that leans both on the force of religion and on the force of politics is absolutist."

It took Europe a revolution to separate religion from politics and lessen the authority of both. Europe's new culture implanted principles of human freedom, freedom of thought and democracy. Egypt followed suit and moved from glorification of the caliphate to its negation.

The authority of the 'ulama of al-Azhar diminishes more

and more. "The Egyptians cut, or almost cut, the knot of religious rule, and perhaps are going to cut the knot of political rule and the despotism of political rulers."[47]

With the new and officially sponsored interpretation Islam is to respond to all human problems, what is more, to approve the doings of a regime. Of course, against the decreed islamization of man's thought militates preoccupation with Western and Communist civilizations, in essence the phenomena of secularization.

The socialist argument presents stages of metamorphosis. At the start, communism, associated with Zionism, was battled head on. Since 1955-56, probably for reasons of political realignment, Marxism replaced communism as a focus of argument. By this, the argument was doomed to be sterile. Non-Marxist socialism is not the invention of Arab socialism nor is Marxism identifiable with communism. As to political and social democracy, Egypt's theorists may not have applied themselves to the deliberations of Max Adler, a Marxist thinker of Austria, but they surely have been more than impressed, in the early days of Nasserism, with Harold Laski's writings. However, Adler and Laski, each in his own way, never questioned the inalienable right to free exchange of ideas — the mainspring of intellectual life. They never resorted to a myth that once the "remnants of exploiters and reactionaries" are eliminated, a one-voice national unity is to emerge and ensure social harmony.

Finally, dissociation from Marxism has given way to tacit assimilation of Marxism, even up to courting its recent offshoots and deviations. In writings designed for the educated, Marxism, *i.e.*, Leninist argument and policies, became presentable for deliberations of equals. Communist practice such as invasion of Czechoslovakia is given approval.

Strangely, in spite of vociferous semantics of Arabization and Afro-Asiatization, Westernization of Arabic

50

grows faster and faster. An Egyptian daily reads like a foreign daily; it is the elements of vernacular and relics of classical Arabic that slow its being alienated. The modern novel Europeanized the language in sentence, imagery, idioms. No wonder that Arab scholars complain of indiscriminate borrowing from foreign languages even when excellent native equivalents are at hand. On the other hand, European modernist poetry helped make Arabic poetry leap a century's distance forward. At long last Arabic poetry, direct and immediate, will be read without dictionaries. The late Salama Musa, a Coptic writer who helped promote a style straining after art and economy, unequivocally endorsed Europeanization of literature. Now it is brought about under blazons of Arabization and regimentation.

In a wide range of humanities the West has the upper hand. Western works are translated, adapted, expounded—in political and social science, economics, linguistics, psychology, philosophy. American patterns of analysis are emulated—in problem setting, in techniques, in terminology, and in extremely jargonized deliberations. Western art of governing is rejected, and yet it is Western arts and science that mainly excite and engage. Of course, by a stretch of imagination some equivalents, at least allusions, may be found in Islamic literature.

What are the mental repercussions of Westernization in a charged atmosphere of Easternization? In plain terms, how do the thousands of West-trained young Egyptians fare when, upon return, they have to close their minds, discard or shelve assimilated infectious ideas and unquestioningly respond to the exhortation of the régime? How is the regime accepted by the multitudes of intellectuals, increasingly doubters, who have to deliberate within the injunctions of the National Charter? Either way theirs is a road of self-denial.

What is the impact of the many translated, albeit hastily, standard works of Western philosophy, sociology and historiography? Suffice it to mention J. S. Mill, Bertrand Russell, Cole, Laski. They come to know that, beside capitalism, the ills of past imperialism and "neo-colonialism," the West has been a treasure-house of values, moral and social, ultimately, after convulsive experimentation, to be resorted to.

It is the West that stimulates inquiry and holds up the right to doubt that endangers all kinds of conformism, old and new. It is the West that incessantly sounds the warning that the inalienable right to differ and respect for human dignity are indivisible and universally-valid.

Egypt's intellectual links to the West are of longer duration; it is the West that induced her literary awakening. In the 'twenties we witnessed voluntary fascination of her intelligentsia with Western patterns of democracy. There were then many lights of attraction—Gandhi's non-violent struggle, the Pharaonic and Arab pages in Egypt's history, the nascent Arab movement, the stirrings of pan-Africanism, but the West outshone them, at least deep down in man's mind. Now a kind of socialism blended with Islam is enforced by an autocracy and all the vehicles of propaganda and exegesis are placed at its service. The "age of authoritarianism" is ever present.

The concept of religion, as applied within the confines of an exclusive ideology, is not to be questioned here; no deviation can be voiced within or without the Arab Socialist Union. As to political and social views, they revolve round premises of the National Charter and the statutes of the Arab Socialist Union, with varying accents or shadings of interpretation. As said, Western notions of social democracy are rejected, but the attitude to various trains of communism and guerrilism is of strong sympathy, the stress being on national liberation front ideology as represented by Hanoi, Cuba and China.

The conglomerate of notions christened New Left, Marcuse being its focal point, is much deliberated on, but the infinitely praised heroes are the men of action: Castro,

Che Guevara, Debray, Ho Chi Min, and Giap. As to the Soviet orbit, only Lenin is presented as a mainspring of inspiration. No total commitment is discernible; Garaudy is discreetly held in esteem. Yugoslavia, once in the ascendant in the minds, because her defection loosened "monolithic," hence no-choice communism, has nearly faded as ideological factor. In the fields of artistic pursuits, cultural eclecticism prevails. The interest in the West is not diminishing, but, in comparison with the early 'Sixties, the East and the Third World are given more and more attention, which may also be politically motivated.

In an exhaustive attempt to delineate the main trends in the debate after the 1967 war, *Middle East Record* 1967 (pp. 563-570) follows a "tripartite schema offered by Egyptian sources — 'rightist,' 'leftist' and 'status quo' (an equivalent to conservative)." The debate is made to revolve around national unity, democracy, the Arab Socialist Union and foreign policy. Bearing in mind, alongside of the independent-minded Zakariya Muhyi al-din, that "right and left are relative terms," one could speak of pragmatic, doctrinaire and power-based trends. Unfortunately, 'Abd al-Nasir's stand or tactics in this debate remains obscure.

After the June 1967 war *fida'ism* (Palestinian guerrillism) has held emotional sway in Arab letters; judging by the literary output and by the air of excitement it seemed to take an equal place with or precedence over Nasserism. Arab states failed, for the third time, to assert themselves in their contention with Israel. Egypt's Yemen adventure reached a dead end. In South Yemen, the National Liberation Front prevailed over the Egyptian-sponsored Front of Liberation of South Yemen (Flosy). The by-now aged ideologies — Nasserism, the two wings of Ba'th, ANM before its conversion to "Maoism" — had not asserted themselves in real trials. New ideological winds — a Third World concept embodied in national liberation fronts, the panacea of "power" culminating in rural and urban guerrillism, a seemingly revivified Marxism-Leninism — helped embolden the new critics.

Fida'ism became the magic formula — self-realization of the Palestinians through self-sacrifice. No more object of Arab politics, the Palestinians themselves are to forge their destinies. Defeat of Israel is to be the work of the victims of Israel. In the heat of excitement, fida'ism was even seen pioneering, ahead of all the ideas of Arab liberation. Arab states and parties paid homage or tribute to it. In a way it seemed to infuse strength into Nasserism, too.

Egypt's press abounded in variations on this theme as well as on all kinds of new power ideologies.

*al-Fikr al-Mu'asir* (1969) carried articles on: intellectual rebellion in France; the concept of cultural revolution; Unamuno and contemporary Christianity; unionism as norm of progressivism and revolutionism; Black Power and bankruptcy of the policy of nonviolence; freedom of intellect in our era.

*al-Katib* (1969) deals with the Palestinian revolution, its dimensions and problems; *fida'i* work and responsibilities of the Arab revolutionary; the Palestinian armed revolution as conscience of the Arab nation; the Jewish state and the Jewish problem in the light of scientific socialism.

*al-Tali'a* (1969): International dimensions of Israel's designs; democratic Korea and her experiment in world liberation struggle; new horizons for the Palestinian revolution; theoretical weapon in liberation battle, and so on.

Louis Awad speaks of "general shabbiness of Egyptian speculative, analytical and critical thought in the field of politics, economics, sociology, and moral philosophy." Beside "over-concentration upon the practical and immediately useful" and "adulteration of knowledge that always goes with democratic expansion," the third given reason should perhaps take precedence, namely, "the one-way traffic of ideas or the lack of sustained dialogue between Egyptian intellectuals and their compeers in more advanced countries."[48] The Egyptian periodicals seem alert to the newest trends of thought: to the revival of Hegel, to the "revolution of the angry men," to Garaudy, to Rosa Luxemburg and Neruda, to problems of alienation, to Ho Chi Min, Gorki and Gandhi, to Che Guevara and Stokely Carmichael, to the averted "counter-revolution" in Czechoslovakia. But behind these deliberations the tablets of the Charter and the ideological "big brother" are felt to exercise fascination or pressure. Not that there is no inconsistency, even confusion of thought. But with divergent thinking being banned from the surface of print, it may only move underground, consciously or unconsciously camouflaged. To speak again with Awad, "this is why Egyptian thinkers and analysts very often look more like apologists and commentators on things past, giving little direction for the present and little vision of the future."[49] Vision is a prerogative of men of power, not of visionaries.

We witness a supreme attempt, of pyramidal dimensions, to underpin a regime in all its stages and sustain its ideal image. Multitudes labored at it, by virtue of conviction, conformism or out of sheer necessity. It was a threefold attempt: to harness a religion to an essentially secular ideology, to inject a scientifism-oriented ideology into a people's mind by dictate and to interpret in its light a legacy of religion and culture.

Now that the era of 'Abd al-Nasir has closed, one is tempted to ask how Egypt's ideology has materialized in view of the circles drawn in *Philosophy of the Revolution*. At its heyday, in some respects even after 1967, the Arab circle policy was exclusive insofar as it presumed a role of national guidance and endeavored to impose one brand of socialism, or a semblance of it, on other Arab countries, which couldn't but fail. 'Iraq, Syria, South Yemen, Tunisia and Algeria pursue their own brands of socialism.[50] The experiment of the Federation of Arab Republics has yet to prove its compatibility.

At latest since the Suez campaign in 1956, Egypt's intra-Arab policy was also conspiratorial, to Egyptian spokesmen "revolutionary." In 1958, Egypt's President spoke of "one battle in which one and all hearts join from the (Atlantic) ocean to the (Persian) gulf and by this we shalll attain the supreme aim for which free men have been dying."[51] There is no Arab region — from Mosul to Aden and from Baghdad to Morocco — that has not felt Egypt's missionary fervor, in propaganda and subversive activities, by ancient or modern means. Nowhere has Egypt succeeded in gaining a solid hold, still less in implementing designs, but Egypt's exploits in Arabia did succeed in calling to mind Muhammad 'Ali's performance there in 1815-1840.[52] The "road to oil" was obstructed not only by Sa'udi Arabia. The road from 'Iraq southward is shorter, hence the claims could be made stronger. The Iranian factor, too, confounds the calculations. Furthermore, Nasserism faces a leftist ideology based in Aden.

The postulate of Africa circle proved to apply only in one point, namely, "the Nile draws its supply of water from the heart of the continent." The old regime strove to place the Sudan, on whatever basis, under one crown. Whether or not colonization aims there were harbored, considerations of living space through economic and cultural activities are not to be denied. But in renouncing her claims to the Sudan, various designs on Africa are not sealed.

In the war years debate on the future, Egypt's Africanism had been articulated, by some even given priority. On the basis of temporary conquests in the Nineteenth Century, down to Lake Albert in the South and Massawa or Zeila to the East, Italy's former colonies, Eritrea and Somaliland, had become, after the war, a sphere of acute interest.[53] 'Abd al-Nasir speaks of Egypt's "responsibility in helping, in every way possible, in diffusing the light and civilization into the farthest parts of the virgin jungle," which lends itself to interpretation. Notably since 1957 Cairo radio and the Voice of Free Africa turned their attention to East Africa. With the Congo fiasco, Nkrumah's demise in Ghana and the failure of Sukarno's "guided democracy" in Indonesia, the whole structure of "positive neutralism," meant to encompass Africa, seems to have collapsed. But the activities of the National Liberation Front of Eritrea, for obvious reasons supported only by Libya and Syria, are conducted with a view of making the Red Sea a mare nostrum of the "progressive" Arab countries. It would make it a vehicle in world politics.

The real test of Arab-African solidarity has also taken place in the Sudan, "Physically, culturally, and ethnically... a microcosm of Africa."[54] The northern Sudan is culturally and linguistically, in the main, Arab and Muslim. No doubt, the ruling North cherished, even tried to apply the idea of Islamization, hence Arabization of the African, animistic or Christianized South. As in the case of 'Iraqi Kurdistan, a special status or autonomy presupposes a political atmosphere of tolerance, a federalist outlook supplanting centralist rigidity, above all abolition of socially disguised military dictatorships. It is also conceivable that the South would refuse to be enmeshed in intra-Arab power politics. But in the Sudan is also African solidarity, namely the actual attitude to the quest of fellow Africans for self-determination tested. It is not carried to an international forum for discussion. The statutes of the Organization of African Unity bar interference in the internal affairs of member states, and yet Egyptian jets shelled the area of rebellion in southern Sudan with impunity. 'Abd al-Nasir's Africa circle proved an illusion.

In his *Philosophy of the Revolution*, 'Abd al-Nasir omitted what seems the main circle, namely the Egyptian one, related to the Egyptian personality *(shakhsiyya misriyya)*. Even at the heyday of 'Abd al-Nasir's triumphant march this issue was never completely glossed over. It is ever dormant.

At times of *examen de conscience*, notably after 1967, attention turned to it. It is the core of Egypt's problem. Regionalism *(iqlimiyya)* has become anathema, and Arab parties, all arguing for primacy of union, charge each other with it. And yet it represents the sum total of a people's experience in an Arab country, in geography and history. The argument that "Arab socialism" couldn't be implemented without Arab union has proved futile. Arab countries claim to implement various brands of socialism.

### Footnotes

1. A large body of traditions said to be transmitted from the Prophet's and his Companions' mouths.
2. See Edward Wakin, **A Lonely Minority; the Modern Story of Egypt's Copts** (New York 1963).
3. **Ibid.,** p. 172. Wakin speaks of "Nasser's political manipulations of Mohammed's message."
4. See **Encyclopaedia of Islam,** n.e., **s.v.** Ahmad ibn Hanbal.
5. **Haqiqat al-ishtirakiyya fi 'l-Islam** (The Nature of Socialism in Islam), **Majallat al-Azhar,** February 1962.
6. **Sawm Ramadan ishtirakiyya ruhiyya** (The Fast of Ramadan Is Spiritual Socialism), **ibid.**
7. Mustafa al-Siba'i, **Ishtirakiyyat al-Islam (Socialism of Islam),** series **Ikhtarna Lak,** 108, 1961. It is noteworthy that this work of a former Muslim Brethren deputy in Damascus has been given currency in Egypt.
8. **Al-Fard wa-'l-mujtama' fi 'l-Islam (The Individual and the Society in Islam,)** Cairo, n.d., pp. 10, 47, 64, 131.
9. 'Abd al-Hamid Jawdat al-Sahhar, **Abu Dharr al-ishtiraki al-zahid (The Ascetic Socialist),** Cairo, 1966. An extract is translated by Rene Jammes **(L'Afrique et L'Asie,** No. 75, 1966, pp. 46-50). Prefaced by Hasan al-Banna, founder of the Muslim Brethren, it was published in 1943.
10. 'Abd al-Rahim Fudah, **al-Mujtama' al-ishtiraki fi zill al-Islam** (Socialist Society in the Shadow of Islam), **Majallat al-Azhar,** February 1966.
11. **Ibid.,** March 1966.
12. **Ibid.,** June 1964.
13. **Ibid., February 1966.**
14. See preface to **al-Muntakhab fi tafsir al-Qur' an al-karim,** (Cairo, 1387), p. 6.
15. "Islam started a socialist revolutionary republic, but the Umayyads overthrew it and changed to a feudal caliphate." See Muhammad Iqbal, **al-Katib,** January 1964.
16. 'Abd al-Hafiz Rabbih, **Thawra wa-thuwwar (Revolution and Revolutionaries),** (Cairo 1962), pp. 7, 11. The author is in charge of "moral guidance of the armed forces."

17. Al-Khatar al-yahudi (The Jewish Menace), transl. by Muhammad Khalifa al-Tunisi, sec. ed. (Cairo, 1961). The translator still upholds, as in the first edition of 1951, his view that "democrats and Communists charge each other with crimes perpetrated not by them but by an international Jewish gang seeking a clash between the democrats and the Communists in a third world war to smash both forces and remove the obstacles to world mastery of the Jews" (p. 67). "There is a finger of Jewish fingers hidden behind any propaganda that scorns moral values" — a Jew, Karl Marx, is behind communism that "destroys morals and religions;" a Jew, Durkheim, is behind sociology that "tries to invalidate the effect of the family on virtues and morals"; and the Jew, or half Jew, Sartre, is behind existentialism that "affects the individual and the society with evil of despair and dissolution" (p. 83). Jews "manipulate the sciences of economics, society and comparative religion" and make them "corrupt morals, law, cultures and minds in all the corners of the world." (p. 82).

To Mahmud Muhammad Shabaka, **Qararat hukama' Sahyun ("Resolutions of the Wise Men of Zion"), Majallat al-Azhar,** May-June 1967, "these are secret documents in which the Jews drew their plans to take possession of the world and sought infernal ways to enable them to dominate all nations and states." In 1967, this periodical carried also articles like "Vices of the Jews as Described in the Noble Koran," and "Dregs of Unbelief Concentrated in the Sons of Israel."

18. See my **Aspects of Near East Society,** pp. 130-131.

19. Muhammad Ahmad Bazaniq, Muhammad Yusuf al-Mahjub, **Muhammad wa-'l-Yahud (Muhammad and the Jews),** series Ma' al-Arab, 4, pp. 138, 139, 140.

20. Anwar al-Jundi, **al-Fikr al-'arabi al-mu 'asir fi ma 'rakat al-ta 'rib wa-'l-ta 'biya al-thaqafiyya (Modern Arabic Thought in the Struggle for Arabization and Cultural Mobilization),** Cairo, n.d., pp. 396-397.

In 1969, al-Jundi links only Masonry to world Judaism or Zionism. Based on Hitler's **Mein Kampf,** the **Protocols** of Zion and Benjamin Franklin's statements (?), he warns of "the danger to humanity from mastery of Zionist influence over nations and peoples in an effort to implement the greatest project, namely a Jewish world government whose base is Jerusalem and its symbol is Solomon's temple." Another version: "To build a Jewish empire as a part of a plan of world imperialism and in co-operation with it" **(Majallat al-Azhar,** October 1969).

21. February 1966.

22. **Tariq al-insân al-'arabi al-jadid (The Way of the New Arab Man),** Cairo, n.d., pp. 166-189.

For "Jewish materialism" see also Muhammad Mukhtar Amin Makram's **Hawla al-ishtirakiyya al-'arabiyya (On Arab Socialism),** Cairo, 1966, p. 175. Here are also approvingly mentioned 'Abd al-Nasir's views on communism as presented in the preface to **Haqiqat al-shuyu 'iyya, op. cit.**

23. It is noteworthy that studies in political science, all drawing inspiration from the Charter, open and close by invoking Allah's name and help respectively.

24. March 1963; January, December 1964. See also **al-Majalla,** February 1964.

25. From an ideological encounter, **al-Katib,** January 1964.

26. Salah al-din 'Abd al-Wahhab, **al-Malamih al-falsafiyya li-'l-ishtirakiyya ("Philosophical Aspects of Arab Socialism"),** al-Majalla, January 1964.

27. Muhammad Tal 'at 'Isa, al-Nuzum al-diniyya wa-'l-ishtirakiyya "(Religious Systems and Socialism"), **al-Majalla al-Misriyya li-'l-'Ulum al-Siyasyyia,** April 1965, pp. 81, 82.
28. Salah al-din 'Abd al-Wahhab, **op. cit.,** February 1964.
29. **Ibid.,** April 1964.
30. A. S. El-Emary, **"Etude comparée du socialisme experimental en Egypte" (en arabe), L'Egypte Contemporaine,** January 1966, p. 142.
31. From his speech on the Day of Science, **al-Majalla,** January 1964.
32. Isma'il al-Mahdawi, **al-Ishtirakiyya al-'ilmiyya (Scientific Socialism), al-Katib,** December 1964.
In the two years before June 1967, Nasserism is still presented as apogee of revolutionism.

The three main aspects of the 23 July revolution are: permanent revolution; a national revolution of liberation; social revolution. With the expulsion of imperialism in 1956, the revolution begins to shoulder the tasks of revolution of union. With 'Abd al-Nasir's revolution ends the "metaphysical age" of unity, the dream evolves to reality.

"Permanent revolutionism prompts her to join the world forces of liberation that will end in final elimination of imperialism from the earth's surface."

What UAR does in Congo and elsewhere and her policy of non-alignment is "one of the dimensions of world revolution." Che Guevara complained to the author that the weak spot of Latin American revolution is that it started in a small country. 'Abd al-Nasir's revolution started in a big country. Added to this, 'Abd al-Nasir's "heroic command" of the revolution in whose personality "all the hopes, aspirations and grandeur" of the nation are crystallized, his "magic ability" to move the Arab masses and induce them to action and sacrifice. A historic precedent can be seen in Lenin. (Mazin al-Bandak, **Da 'wa ila al-thawriyyin al-'Arab** ("A Call to Arab Revolutionaries"), **al-Katib,** June 1965).
33. Al-Mahdawi, **al-Mawqif al-tabaqi min al-sahyuniyya** ("Class Position Towards Zionism"), **al-Katib,** April 1966, p. 95.
34. **Ibid.,** p. 96.
35. **Ibid.,** p. 107.
36. **Ibid.,** pp. 102-103.
37. Rabbih, **op. cit.,** pp. 103, 132.
38. A few popular **hadith:**
Obey though an Abyssinian slave be made your governor with a head like a dried grape!

Let him who dislikes the conduct of his **amir** be patient, for he who divides the Muslim community a hand's breadth shall die the death of a pagan!

After my death sayings attributed to me will multiply just as a large number of sayings are attributed to the prophets who were before me. What is told you as sayings of mine you must compare with the Koran. What is in agreement therewith is from me whether I have actually said it or not.

Against this:

He who speaks falsely on my authority is placed in Hell. Said al-Zuhri (Eighth Century): These princes have compelled us to write *hadith*. (Presently, it could be rephrased: These princes have compelled us to interpret *hadith*, namely to sing the praise of socialism.)

Ibn 'Awn refuses to credit traditions on authority of a known person because he had held office of governor under Mu 'awiya.

Of course, *hadith* could be used in a derogatory manner, allusively or overstressedly. Its humor, concealing more than revealing, and utter conciseness allow for varying interpretation. The reader is overawed by the very standing of the *hadith*. In Persia, maxims of 'Ali and popular saws are "very old devices for the dissemination of sage counsel in a manner as inoffensive as possible to suspicious censors." See H. Kamshad, **Modern Persian Prose Literature,** 1969, p. 19.

To Mohamed al-Nowaihi, "neither ... Muhammad himself claimed perfection, nor did the Qur'an claim it for him." He speaks of fabricating fables about the birth of the Prophet, of "certain exaggerations and outright inventions." "Such a claim is utterly blasphemous by the strict tenet of monotheistic Islam." See "Towards a Re-evaluation of Muhammad," **The Muslim World,** October 1970, p. 308.

39. Cairo 1966.
     In **Madhaib Wa-shakhsiyyat (Creeds and Personalities),** 1965, p. 19, Dr. Ibrahim Zaki al-Sa'i states that "Muhammad's first wife, Khadija bint Khuwaylid... whose ancestry goes back to Ibrahim... is named mother of socialism."
40. **Islam wa-'L-ishtirakiyya** ("Islam and Socialism"), **al-Katib,** March 1968.
41. Ahmad 'Abbas Salih, **al-Sira'bayn al-yamin wa-'l-yasar fi'l-Islam** ("The Struggle between Left and Right in Islam"), **al-Katib,** April 1965.
42. **Ibid.,** May 1965.
43. **See** R. Marston Speight, **The Muslim World,** October 1966, p. 284.
44. David C. Gordon, **ibid.,** pp. 285-289. Also Jean-Francois Kahn, **"Socialisme et Islam,"** Le Monde, January 7-13, 14-20, 1965.
     **Revolution Africaine,** the central organ of FLN, seeks to "bring the teachings of Islam and its creative potentialities into harmony with reason and economic imperatives." "Algeria, by virtue of her median and mediating position in the Arab world and in Africa ... doesn't cease to elaborate a doctrine in sense of humanism without nostalgia and without resignation." **See** Pierre Rondot, **"Vers une nouvelle inflexion du réformisme musulman en Algérie,"** L'Afrique et L'Asie, No. 75, 1966, p. 41.
     "The evocation of the Arab-Moslem cultural heritage... predominates over the aspect of political unity in President Boumedienne's concept of Arab unity... the theme of 'Algerian socialism' is never the signal of any lengthy ideological speculation." See Jean-Pierre Peroncel-Hugaz, "Algeria Ten Years After," **Guardian Weekly,** July 15, 1972.
     In an age of utter relativization of ideology it shouldn't surprise that a regime named socialist and serving a lighthouse of liberation movements in the world should resort to a traditional concept of Islam as a means of pre-

serving national identity. The recent coincidence of some policies of King Faisal and al-Qadhdhafi is a case in point. Recently both extended help to Uganda's Amin.

It remains to be seen how Qadhdhafi's fundamentalist concept of Islam epitomized in literal interpretation of the Koranic precept of cutting a hand for thievery is to be integrated with Egypt's concept of Islamic socialism, evidently under al-Sadat taking a turn toward conservatism.

Al-Qadhdhafi has recently been denounced 'in Habash's **al-Hadaf** is a "fascist tyrant." "Hundreds of intellectuals, lawyers, university professors and journalists are being physically tortured to near death in Qaddafi's concentration camps." **(New York Times, August 19,1973.)**

This fact could enlighten **al-Hadaf** about the treacherousness and double-edgedness of violence in political warfare.

45. Against this, in Sa'udi Arabia, once the standard bearer of the purity of Islam, socialism is shown to militate against religious tradition.
46. **Islam wa'usual al-hukm/ (Islam and the Principles of Government),** 3rd ed., 1925, pp. 35-36, 79, 103.
47. See the miscellany, **al-Hadara al-haditha (The New Civilisation),** Cairo, 1933, p. 151.
48. "Cultural and Intellectual Developments in Egypt since 1952," in **Egypt Since the Revolution,** ed. P. J. Vatikiotis (New York 1968), pp. 156-157.
49. **Ibid.**
50. In March 1963, on the Day of Union, proclaimed to commemorate the union of Syria and Egypt, 'Abd al-Nasir still held to the "right of rebellion" that takes no notice of borders. "I represent all the freedom fighters in the United Arab Republic and in every other Arab country." **(Neue Zürcher Zeitung,** March 12, 1963.)
51. **New York Times,** July 23, 1958.
52. In **The Muslim World** issue on Islam in politics (October 1966) we are reminded that "not far from Riyadh lie the ruins of the old Sa'udi capital city of Dariyah, destroyed by an Egyptian expedition, a monument to a harsh occupation, to the captivity and subsequent execution of Imam Abdullah Ibn Sa'ud... the invader, it seems to King Faisal, has returned by way of Yemen."

Modern warfare against Arabs culminated in bombing of places in Yemen, Sa'udi Arabia and South Yemen. (See **Times,** December 21, 22, 1966.)
53. **See** R. H. Nixon, "Egypt Looks South," **Spectator,** March 4, 1949.
54. Muddathir 'Abd al-Rahim, "Arabism, Africanism, and Self-Identification in the Sudan," **Journal of Modern African Studies,** July 1970, p. 233.

Chapter III

## CRITIQUE: FROM ADULATION TO SEVERITY

Critical examination, albeit still-voiced, of Egypt's ideology in Arab countries could be traced back to the 'fifties. From the start Ba'th would accept neither its personalism nor its Islamic underpinning. ('Aflaq elaborated the place of Islam in Ba'th ideology in terms of metaphysics or cultural legacy). 'Abd al-Nasir's authority had overshadowed the discrepancy in views. The debacle of the Anglo-French campaign in 1956, still more the first essay in Arab union in 1958, enhanced Egypt's standing. The ensuing disillusionment with the implementation of union meant rude awakening to both partners.

Having no power of coercion, the leaders of Ba'th could not avert splits; unionist seceders moved "leftwards," hereby staunchly defending 'Abd al-Nasir as a symbol of unionism without subscribing to the whole of Egypt's ideology. But the protracted war in Yemen could not but lessen his authority. The June 1967 war and Egypt's readiness for peace negotiations disenchanted militants of the new generation that fell under the spell of Leftism and its concomitants—guerrillism and anti-bureaucratism.

Egypt's excited espousal of fidq'ism has not mitigated the anger of the new révoltés. Being charged with hailing from the small bourgeoisie and promoting her interests, Egypt's ideologists had to exert their minds to prove their fitness to be accepted into the rising three-continental world.

The admissibility of the Islamic component in Egypt's ideology, to be precise, of the blend of Islam and socialism in it, has been questioned by traditionalists ranging from Sa'udi Arabian *'ulama* to the Muslim Brethren. Inside Egypt Marxists of various shades who saw or have been made to see light and joined the Arab Socialist Union glossed over this element in their new creed that strongly militates against their philosophical credo.

But the June 1967 war helped loosen the psychological grip of Nasserism and stimulated questioning of its elements. It is in Lebanon that critique of the implications or applications of contemporary Islam, to be sure not of its articles of faith, is relatively freest. It is a paradoxical situation, since in the past the tenuous power balance between Christians and Muslims there has tempted believers on guard or opportunists to seize upon any imaginary shred of transgress. But a new generation has come up.

The press is a clearing house for all shades of Arab politics (in part, materially committed). Sophistication and rationalization—a new version of *taqiyya* —in presenting views has reached extreme limits. Neo-Marxists, in part transcending communal bounds, are emboldened by the convulsions of the exclusive ideologies of the "progressive" Arab states. Pan-revolutionism swayed the minds.

In his speech at Cairo University, on April 25, 1968, 'Abd al-Nasir defines modernism as "renewal of authenticity *(asala)*."

What is this authenticity from literary viewpoint, asks the Lebanese poet Adonis, himself a Shi'i?

Is it belief in the infallibility of our literary legacy, the values it carries and the ways of its expression? This authenticity is synonymous with stagnation and barrenness. Strangely, it is this authenticity that dominates the Arab socialist countries, though socialism is not merely a political and economic transformation. It is primarily a cultural revolution (*inqilab*); without this, our countries cannot be truly socialist.

Likewise, religious authenticity.

Is it absolute upholding of the religious teachings and books as they are? How can a society that agitates for this be revolutionary or modern?... Societies attained modernity only after having rebelled against their history, their legacy and their values, after having rejected and doubted. How can our life be modern when no doubt is allowed, no rejection, no questioning in regard to our history and legacy, about what is dead in it and should be discarded, and what is living and should be inserted into the present?

Thus we slip into two shells: a shell of things perishing that no more benefit us, and yet we keep upholding them, and a shell of contemporary things made by others, which we try to imitate or borrow. We seem to strive not only to rescue our past but to revive it and extend into present and future. ... We seek to emulate the past with all its values, religious and secular. We should ask what in our religious legacy could benefit our present and future, not just accept and preserve it as inherited and examine in its light our life and problems. We should probe into the economic, human and political dimensions of religion. If it is deficient then it means that it is far from us, and it is right to move away from it.

There is no longer a problem that can be considered strictly religious. Allah himself has become an economic, racial and political problem, beside being a spiritual and mystical problem. Paradise, resurrection, hell and angels, no longer can all these be examined merely from the viewpoints of heaven and revelation. They have to be seen also from viewpoints of earth, hunger and war.

It appears that our childish clinging to the infallibility of the legacy is stifling our revolutionism. We believe that it is valid for all times and all places. This attachment is our first mental disease, it is embodied in our regimes, institutions — educational, cultural, political and social.

Perhaps this may explain why all we have done for the last fifty years were only stirrings on the surface and celebrations in praise of the weather. This childish clinging may explain our inability to make that basic leap toward raising a new Arab man, new Arab values, toward seeking a new Arab future.

True revolutionary culture is a culture that emanates from the future and its potentialities, a culture that prompts man in the direction of the future, frees him from submission in order to embrace the future; it directs man toward excellence in art, science and technology.

The Arab revolutionary faces a difficult dilemma: a revolution cannot work without relying on the masses, but the Arab masses are not on a level of revolution, on the whole they are moved by non-revolutionary thoughts and values. If the revolution surrenders to them, she betrays herself, if we give the masses up, she will die.

We have to adopt the masses and lead them, understand and raise them. Never in the whole history did the masses dream or think of revolutions, as the educated did. But never in the whole history did revolution come about by the force of the educated, but by the force of the masses.[1]

Intellectual ingenuity or sophistication knows no

bounds. There was much casuistry in the scholastic reasoning on Marxism in its classical period. True, this reasoning sprang from a creed then not over-diluted by implementation. Eduard Bernstein, charged with revisionism, tried to clear it up. The present neo-Marxist line of argument, bent not so much on re-evaluation of Marxism as on its "restoration to purity" of the golden age, adds a new layer of sophistry.

One can't help thinking that the intellectual scaffolding of Egypt's Arab socialism is an extension of the imaginative creativity as displayed in *hadith* making. and yet support is extended to it from unexpected sources.

At a conference on *pluralite' des mode'les du socialisme* in Cairo, R. Garaudy traces 'Abd al-Nasir's dictum that "socialism is essentially control of the means of production by the people" to Lenin's "great tradition" urging to "combat bureaucracy to the end, to a complete victory, which is possible only if the whole population takes part in conducting the affairs of the country." Forms of socialism are also linked to the "historical national, political and spiritual, traditions of each country."[2]

Garaudy, too, endorses the socialist inspiration from the Koran and *hadith* and urges the nonbelievers to reflect on the "complex role of religion, notably of Islam, in the national movements of liberation." Scientific socialism "can and should strike roots in the culture and civilization of each country." In the Arab countries, the great traditions of Islam "such as the utopian socialism of the Qarmatians, Ibn Rushd's rationalism, Ibn Khaldun's sociology could play in the development of scientific socialism the role played by Hegel, Ricardo and Saint-Simon.[3]

One would assume that a socialism immersed in religion, at that of basically unchangeable coinage, would impress Egypt's mind. But Louis Awad assures us of the "secular and humanistic character of the charter." Visible evidence notwithstanding, we are told that "unable to attack socialism openly because it was the avowed social philosophy of the State, the militant reactionaries declared that all the basic principles of 'healthy' socialism are to be found in religion ..." But the official interpreters of Egypt's socialism followed the same path and abundantly "invoked the authority of the Muslim patriarchs." Louis Awad upholds the view that "the Egyptian intelligentsia has been and will always remain predominantly secular."[4]

Even Muhyi al-din, one of the eleven founders of the Free Officers group, who faced vicissitudes on account of his Leftist views, upholds the myth of panrevolutionism.[5]

"The Egyptian Revolution is not Egypt's alone. It belongs to humanity, which looks upon the unique experiment with faith and respect... Nor does it belong to this generation alone. It is the sum total of the dreams and hopes of all past revolutionaries and those of the future."

Muhyi al-din speaks of the "Egyptian Revolution... expressing the hopes... of all Arab and African peoples," of uniting "all the Arab revolutionary forces" and of "the beginning of a new revolutionary war that will sweep Africa, Asia and Latin America."

Still, being Marxism-bound Muhyi al-din points to the class struggle in Egypt. The class composition of the National Assembly has changed in favor of middle groups. ... "The definition which puts directors of big companies in the category of workers, and owners of up to 25 acres... in the category of peasants, allowed seats intended for workers and peasants to go to the middle groups."

Lower and medium level organizations of the Socialist Union also suffered in this respect. A distinction is to be made between "productive middle groups which play a positive role in increasing production, such as those practicing agriculture, and parasites who play no part in the production process while they accumulate wealth by sponging on the public sector, through black marketeering and evasion of the laws."

Meanwhile, because of the inability of the public sector to find specialists, new social groups emerged — contractors, suppliers, and others. "They are trying to create difficulties in the public sector and to turn it, through bribery, into a source for their profit alone. . . . The old reactionaries . . . together with the new class of the wealthy form a united front opposed to progress." The need is felt for a "narrow party machinery that would encompass well-trained and cultured cadres, capable of rallying and leading the people" and of eliminating the "corrupt and parasitic elements."

In a bold "analytical study of 'Abd al-Nasir's régime," Yasin al-Hafiz, in 1964 expelled from Ba'th in Syria, applies Marxist and populist reasoning to Nasserism.[6]

"Positive characteristics of the revolution."

Patriotic revolution, hostile to feudalism, both political and social; revolution with a socialist outlook; Arab revolution.

"Arabdom is not merely politics, basically it is a civilizational and intellectual legacy. Egypt always carried the burden of this legacy. Islam was the womb that protected our nation from disintegration and prevented the differences of degree and quantity stemming from historical shifts in the life of the Arab peoples from turning to differences of essence and quality making dismemberment natural and intelligible. It is Egypt that carried the moral responsibility of guarding the Arab civilizational legacy. Al-Azhar was an Islamic (in consequence, Arab) fortress against factors of disintegration and weakness."

"Negative characteristics of the revolution."

The revolution is not a populist one . . . No party or "national people's front" has guided the revolution. Petty officers mostly belonging to the small bourgeoisie triggered it.

"It failed to install a revolutionary people's democracy... The revolution contented itself with rejecting old forms and began circling in a vacuum, chewing and repeating the progressive ideas of parliamentary democracy, which, though true in principle, became in the course of time demagogic claims to hide the failure of the revolution to build up a new people's democracy ... Notwithstanding its lofty traits, the result is personal rule."

"A change in the nature of personal rule should come as the crowning point of a people's democracy, starting from an organized popular base and evolving upwards to a revolutionary form of collective leadership."

Second result: a revolution that has no populist base... is always in danger. It has no active positive organization.

Third result: it totally relies on suppression as a means of struggle against reaction or other enemies of the revolution. It installed new instruments of suppression. At the beginning they were meant to be instruments of the revolution, gradually they separated from the revolution to be above its command, instruments to destroy the revolution...

These instruments moved in an infernal circle of undeterred moral decay—an animal force afflicted with what resembles sadistic anomaly.

Fourth result: no clear-cut attitude to reaction. The battle against reaction enjoins, if necessary, its complete destruction—political, social, economic and material.

Fifth result: the growing bureaucracy, both military

and civil, nearly becomes the heir of the exploiting classes.

In Egypt, the present bureaucracy is to a great degree an extension of the old bureaucracy, in mentality and psychology.

The cure of the sickness of bureaucracy will not come about without the elimination of the capitalist regime itself. Only a socialist order makes it possible to fight bureaucracy and open the way to uproot it.

The uprooting of bureaucracy is possible only... through revolutionary and populist organization and promotion of socialist democracy... 'Abd al-Nasir has not switched a populist revolution to a bureaucratic road, but he had not changed a revolution started by a non-populist tool (military) into a populist revolution... These are the limits of 'Abd al-Nasir's responsiblity.

Sixth result: slowness of progress.

Two conditions for swift and complete revolutionary action: a large and deep movement of the masses and a revolutionary élite to lead this movement. Egypt lacked these two conditions.

The second negative feature of the revolution is that it is a pragmatic revolution, whereas revolutionary action needs revolutionary theory.

The socialism of such an 'haphazard' pragmatic revolution set up only an understructure to the old society, whereas the superstructures remained cut off from the revolutionary spirit. The cultural sector is still in the grip of bourgeois reaction and education... it is still far from rearing generations believing in science as the only reality in life.

The Charter needs precision and clarity, intellectual and ideological solidity.

The revolution did not content herself with the elimination of the freedom of the reactionary classes, but abolished also the freedom of the masses.

The non-revolutionary median elements in the command of the revolution exploited the partial and not incompatible contradictions between the leadership of the revolution and the working masses to deprive them of their freedom, too.

... The commitment of the revolution to the masses assumed a form of paternalistic superiority; the relations between the revolution and the masses were relations of custodianship, so that not organized masses emerged, but fanatical, amorphous masses.

Reality is always revolutionary and always moral. Democracy allows reality to evolve. Democratic populist ideas cannot be implanted from above as a surprise gift of a ruler who is convinced that the masses have come of age. Democracy cannot be shelved today to be applied tomorrow when ripe; political maturity is in the first place a result of democratic practice, so that democracy today is a prerequisite to democracy tomorrow.

Real comprehension of a revolutionary movement makes it necessary to forge the spontaneous forces of the masses in an organization, to lend them power and maturity and, in consequence, open before them a chance of active leadership in the revolution.

Instead of doing this the Charter glosses over this briefly and superficially, whereas the problem of bureaucracy in Egypt is most complex and most urgent.

'Abd al-Nasir's régime plays a basic role in the general Arab struggle against imperialism and Arab reaction. Objectively this role is progressive.

Egypt's revolutionary experiment is not a pioneering one... 'Abd al-Nasir's régime is not a revolutionary exemplary régime. It is ideologically poor, lacks exact socialist goals, is steeped in bureaucracy. There is no populist scent in its methods and tools of structure.

The contradictions between the Arab progressive movements are real and inevitable. These contradictions stem from the characteristics of every movement, the degree of its maturity, from differences in ideological levels and also from the extent of the revolutionary populist spirit infusing it. Basically they are one of the results of dismemberment of the Arab homeland.

The problem of the relations between these movements is exact delimitation of the borders between right and error, which makes it necessary to compose the not incompatible contradictions from the point of the main incompatible contradictions. This scientific and revolutionary approach should dictate the political attitudes of Arab revolutionary forces between themselves generally and towards 'Abd al-Nasir's régime in particular.

Egypt's objective conditions make demolition of 'Abd al-Nasir's régime a kind of madness or political blindness (if not a direct commission of imperialism and Arab reaction). Demolition of 'Abd al-Nasir's régime will not bring a higher régime, but darkness and death ... a régime of pashas, agents of imperialism and Egyptian regionalists.

By contrast, Nasserism is made to stand the test of panrevolutionism. Mu-ta'Safadi, to J. Berque, a Syrian existentialist writer, bestows on it immense praise in an exalted style, steeped in flowery 'arabiyya. All trends and notions of revolutionism are deduced from or attributed to Nasserism.[7] A vision of the future is projected back into the present. The reader will notice the discrepancy between word and intent, in part a result of inadequate assimilation or rendering of foreign ideas.

The revolution of 23 July, 1952, evolved from a coup against a king's régime in one country to a "permanent revolution for a comprehensive change of the whole structure of Arab life." In this epoch of "historic transformation of the whole nation," Nasserism has leaped to the "forefront of vanguard revolutions of the Third World."

73

"The essence of Nasserism as an exemplary cultural revolution is born of living creative argument over the understanding and transforming of reality, over turning the thought of it to theory and directing it."

The six principles came to fruition after ten years, in a complete theory in the charter of the Socialist Union. "Revolutionary political and economic creativity was put to the service of Arab revolution — first in Syria, where it stumbled, then Algeria, Yemen, 'Iraq. . . . Springing from man's heart and forearm, Nasserism settled in the nation's heart and her forearm."

Nasserism faced various ideologies besieging Arab reality: utopian nationalism, brands of Marxism, religious metaphysical trends. "Deep objective understanding of utopian nationalism led Nasserism to adopt its human tendency toward unity of the Arab nation, its historical and cultural affirmation of the nation's existence and continuity." But Nasserism "transcended this utopian nationalism to proletarian or populist nationalism. . . . from mere repetition of slogans and indulgence in mystical thoughts" about "the paradise of Arab unionist future" to "forceful comprehensive activity that set in motion the underlying factors of revolution in every part of the Arab homeland."

The revolution was shifted "from a ruling élite to the large masses" —"a method of evolving a militant democracy by associating the masses in opinion and action."

Nasserism "moved from utopian nationalism to the real content of socialism and its natural concomitant — genuine democracy freed from the domination of capital and feudalism. . . . Nasserism has become the only historic movement representing the nationalism of the Arab nation in its modern aspects and progressive populist content."

"Nasserism, from its inception marked by the deepest

sincerity in understanding Arab reality and uncovering the possibilities of an actual revolution in its structure and the forces militating against it, has felt that Marxism —the revolutionary ideology most strongly equipped- —presents many scientific verities to guide any revolution, but there are things distinguishing the Arab revolution from any class revolution."

It is a "national populist or proletarian revolution, because it implies the unity of various Arab peoples in a combined struggle—liberation from imperialism in all its forms and liberation from backwardness in all its aspects, material and cultural." It is a "revolution of a rising nation... which, together with other rising nations, takes part in liberating the toiling working classes in bourgeois capitalist societies. Ridding all the rising nations of imperialism means that basic life will no more be subject to Western capitalism, which will collapse under the blows of the internal proletarian nationalisms. ... "

"Elimination of bourgeois and feudal pockets in the Arab world will follow the final elimination of imperialist influence from this area. Thus class struggle merges into national struggle through its populist socialist content."

The Arab revolution sets out to "create a third world composed of proletarian nations demanding real world peace, away from the great interests of the two blocks. World peace is a vital condition for their growth. . . and participation in creating a culture for the benefit of the absolute majority of the world population. Unity of the working classes in the world will be replaced by the unity of proletarian nationalisms. . . . "

The Nasserite revolution is "receptive to any scientific method of understanding and changing the reality. Of all the revolutions of this age. . . it comes closest to harmonize with the conditions of the new populist nationalisms. It occupies a leading position in regard to revolutions in Asia, Africa and South America."

"Being a populist national revolution, Nasserism cannot renounce the Arab nation's past; it is a rich legacy in the personality of this nation and even in her struggling present, Islam being the essence of the legacy ... Originally Islam was a great cultural revolution, and from this viewpoint Arab nationalism coincides with Islam ... Nasserism rejects all factionalism and communal strife within the nation.

Nasserism cannot invalidate the people and rely on an élite; unlike utopian metaphysical nationalism it cannot use dreams and slogans instead of real revolutions. ...

"This intellectual structure that matured in the midst of daily revolutionary experience, in the blaze of revolutionism, fed on possibilities and their obstacles alike, on victories and calamities, ... treated adverse reality with unique revolutionary realism. ...

"Nasserism was not exposed to most of the maladies of revolutionary schools, has not known struggle between syndicalists and evolutionists; artificial differences between ends and means did not fetter it. Victory has not kept it from marching towards a greater victory... It has planted new revolutionary ethics. ...

"Beside the national revolution against imperialism, and the socialist revolution, is perhaps to be placed highest the scientific cultural revolution that encompasses various fields of scientific knowledge as well as literary and artistic creativity in a form never known to the Arab nation, even at the peak of cultural past.

"By this Nasserism has anchored the principle of freedom of mind or thought on the basis of comprehensive knowledge, and not utter ignorance.

"Nasserism rises in the Arab world as the strongest

doctrine of contemporary Arab man, in which idea, action and belief combine in conditions of revolutionism, of cultural and moral creativity."

In his *Mawaqif*[8] *(Attitudes)*, the editor Adonis, as seen, a lucid and outspoken essayist, assembled some of the new ideologists of Arab revolutionism for a quest of *quo vadis*. Ba'th in its two strains is nearly ignored here; when mentioned, it seems to be a ghost of the past. To all Nasserism, once awesome, pointing to the main road of self-realization, has lost much of its drive. A few still hold fast, not unquestioningly, to its blessings as the main spring of Arab revolution. To some it served its purpose and is overcome, at best a passing phenomenon; to most it is retrograde in that it is upheld by a new military and technocratic bureaucracy that springs from the petty bourgeoisie.

Throughout the issue Nadim Bitar's stand is discussed. Himself a kind of meta-revolutionist, in the vein of Debray, al-Bitar presses the point of "tactical and strategic link to 'Abd al-Nasir and the 23 July revolution"—the "base of revolutionary unionist action," the "road to union." He who departs from this premise "falls prey to metaphysical or mystical thought." The efficiency of Egypt's régime, its superiority to other Arab régimes, 'Abd al-Nasir's political acumen—all warrant rallying around them.

To Hisham Sharabi, the Arab Left should hold 'Abd al-Nasir's and Egypt's cause in love and esteem ("but for them we would have fallen prey to American Zionist imperialism"), but not "at the expense of the present revolution." What 'Abd al-Nasir and the 23 July revolution represent, "finds realization and extension in the Palestinian revolution," the "real vanguard revolution in the whole Arab world."

Yasin al-Hafiz acknowledges Egypt's being "center of gravity—human, cultural, geographical,... historically a lever of the expected Arab renascence, its revolutionary focal point." But the concept of "base for revolutionary action is wider and deeper than that epitomized in the 23 July revolution." Al-Bitar maintains that the controversy over socialist and political content should be postponed until the realization of union. But to an Arab Marxist-Leninist, "union is not a mere national issue, it should be viewed from the point of liberation of the Arab masses." When struggling for the aims of the present "great historical" stage (elimination of reaction, capitalism, imperialism, partition and Israel), the "strategic axis of the action of revolutionary forces being union," one should at the same time "prepare the objective and subjective condition of the coming stage, to overstep and present stage dialectically." While struggling for union effected under the command of the petty bourgeoisie and under the banner of her median ideology, a Marxist-Leninist should struggle for educating and mobilizing the masses to open a "proletarian road" for Arab union.

Echoing the New Left and scathing in his critique of the Arab "petty revolutions of the petty bourgeoisie" is Jamil Kazim al-Manaf. Lenin, Che Guevara and Debray, Stokely Carmichael, Charles V. Hamilton and Black Power are called to witness. The inner workings of the Arab progressive states—the "traditional Left"—are severely presented. The petty bourgeoisie in the Arab countries turned the state into a source of her economic enrichment, a "vehicle of class-bound exploitation," of "monopolistic and exploitative relations, personal and collective." This corroborates many "stories of bribery, protectionism, association with smuggling, commission fees, contracts, licenses, concessions, export, import," and so on. In her struggle for power the petty bourgeoisie has sought to "monopolize the stages of evolution and social advance." In her revolution against capitalism and parliamentarianism she strained after offices, big and small, and 'having been politically entangled with socialist

78

slogans, she launched nationalization policies in which the public sector has the main part." Followers and members of the party that came into power seized the government offices, and "instead of enlarging the apparatus of production, they enlarged the apparatus of administration." The mentality of the petty bourgeoisie has no "industrial dimension." Her political era resulted in growth of prosperous bourgeois cities. Without political power she has no economic weight, and this is what explains her violent struggle for power. She is "marginal and parasitic in her economic structure, parasitic in her class composition, non-productive, dreaming, sophisticated in her thinking, operates with mechanical materialism in reality while elaborating things in moral or idealistic terms."

To Manaf, an air of despair spread in the 'sixties. This stage ended in "political crises, revolutionary adventures, splits, economic crises, intellectual anarchy, rise of material demands, social tension, class shifts as a result of commercial and administrative growth in the cities, psychological turmoil, spread of violence because of political animosities within the masses corroding all their revolutionism in a Byzantine argument."

Added to this: "betrayals and accusations raised by the political commands, causing the lies to multiply and criteria to be confounded so much so that Right became Left and Left more radical. . . "

The Arab petty bourgeoisie is a "cemetery of true re-volutionaries; in the university and in the office she teaches them moral practices and opportunism so that their minds are motivated only by material incentives. . . . Complete suppression of genuine moral stimuli" resulted in *embourgeoisement* of most fighters of the 'fifties and the 'sixties. It is the petty bourgeoisie that caused the June 1967 disaster. "The present objective condition is the armed *fidạ'i* struggle in Palestine, so that the revolutionism of the youth should be linked to it completely."

The petty bourgeoisie aims at "total despotic rule while feigning the opposite," putting up a "rationalistic, historicist" appearance and using analytical tools of historical materialism. Inevitably power will pass to new classes, forming a "revolutionary vanguard" — destitute paupers and "producing proletarians" in the cities, revolutionary students, intellectuals totally given to struggle, "romantics of socialist thought" and scientists motivated by moral stimuli.

To Al-Manaf, the New Left approaches the Cuban (Castro-Guevara) and Maoist thinking, but it is far from imitation and import of experiments and revolutions. It has not crystallized yet in organizational form.

To M. Kishli, an editor af *al-Hurriyya*, the petty bourgeois command of the Arab revolution was unable to generate a "real cultural revolution building a new Arab man." It is this bourgeoisie — professionals, shopkeepers, small merchants, small and medium landowners — that supplies hosts of educated to fill the present state apparatus, also military personnel. A military coup cannot effect basic changes in an "ideological set-up." The economic measures (agrarian reform, nationalization) are of a purely bureaucratic and administrative nature, with no changes in "super-structure," hence of no revolutionary nature. In line with Bettelheim in his *La Construction du socialisme en Chine*, Kishli asserts that the growing consumption of a minority — the ruling bureaucracy — precludes evolution of the productive forces and a degree of economic progress. In human terms, this means bureaucratic dominance of the state apparatus, notably with the change of ownership relations and the emergence of a public sector. From this dominance a new ruling class is formed.

"Only a vanguard party armed with a vanguard theory

can raise the political conscience of the masses. The parties and movements of the petty bourgeoisie present themselves as a vanguard, but they are vanguardist in a sense of fascist élite (a conscious minority representing unconscious masses following without understanding), not in Lenin's sense (in his *What Is to Be Done* ?), namely a vanguard party of the working class armed with a revolutionary theory." The petty bourgeoisie is revolutionary in terms of political slogans, but conservative in terms of ideology. Her ideology cannot "build a new m a n" this needs an utmost revolutionary theory — Marxism — "representing the interests of the masses that in their revolution have nothing to lose but their chains."

'Afif Farraj, one of the *al-Hurriyya* group, sees in the statement that Egypt's Socialist Union represents an "alliance of the working people's forces" a mere "misguiding slogan." It claims to be a substitute for a "one-class dictatorship," but in fact it covers up a reality of dictatorship of the small bourgeoisie and the administrative and military bourgeoisie exercising political and economic dictatorship. The salaries of the bureaucracy are fifty times higher than the minimum wages (4500 against 90; in the Soviet Union nine times, in Cuba, China and Vietnam three times).

Bassam Tibi, who draws from the Frankfurt school (Adorno, Jïorgen, Habermas, also Marcuse), professes to have a year ago been a Nasserite, considering 'Abd al-Nasir a model of a total Arab revolutionary. To al-Bitar, he who rejects "tactical and strategic commitment" to the personality of 'Abd al-Nasir and his movement, is "metaphysician, missionary, mystic" failing to understand "science" and "objectivity." No, contends Tibi. Bitar's attitude is "non-scientific," he is unable to explain the rifts of 23 July in terms of an "exact social analysis." Rejection of class analysis in interpretation of social phenomena means changing Marxism into "vulgar Marxism."

Commenting on *Mawaqif*, Muta' Safadi, now more temperate in his apologia, pleads for a "dialectical approach." One of the ailments of Arab thought is its shift from opposite to opposite, its "chronic emotionalism:" before the June disaster Arab revolutionaries saw in Egypt's revolution only her "first symbol," the leader's personality; after the disaster he was held solely responsible; "absolute vilification superseded absolute glorification." Egypt's acceptance of a peaceful solution is held a second disaster, hence a shift from the 23 July revolution to the Palestinian revolution. The "course of revolutionary practice" as well as the scientific materialistic method do not warrant seeing both revolutions contradictory. In the name of "scientifism and objectivity" is the Nasserite revolution both rejected or accepted. Safadi pleads for "freedom of experiment and practice—through coordination and cooperation—to all revolutionary forces in view of common aims, from the battle of destiny with Israel to progressive and unionist change in the whole Arab world . . . The weighty experience of the Nasserite revolution does not warrant its custodianship to every revolutionary upshot; sound sense should prevent the new revolutionary vanguards fathering those who preceded them."[9]

Anouar Abdel-Malek, an exile of the Marxist Left who went through the hard school of non-conformity, sounds secure on the ground of conceptual analysis and illusory remedying.[10] The military group "set up a totalitarian technocratic state in Egypt and industrialized the country . . . assured national independence, created a military power and put Egypt at the head of the Afro-Asian world." But the "basic contradiction" in Egypt today is:

On the one hand between the new, technically advanced working class . . . and on the other, the brutal, all-powerful machine; on one side between the army officers — the "new class" — who thus far have taken the country as their fief and intend to "preserve" the positions that they have gained, and on the other, the technicians, to whom more and more of the command posts in the economic, social and cultural sectors are being entrusted and who have won substantial representation in the new political apparatus; between the bureaucrats and the police on one side, and on the other, the Egyptian intellectuals, the guardians of revolutionary traditions...

The basic exigencies of economic and social development will *compel* a confrontation    time is on the side of the resurgence of the social dialectic.[11]

Abdel-Malek argues that "it is impossible to initiate a socialist revolution and to build a popular state in the absence of socialists."[12]

The evolution into socialism was supposed to occur without class conflict. Immediately the class-struggle organizations of the working class and peasants were destroyed ... The Left was enjoined to fuse into the single party, by way of the concentration camps; and the dissolved trade unions were reorganized by the state in the form of a single union for each craft or profession, their leaders were selected and appointed by the government.

... The leashing of the universities, the "positive" censorship of the press, the suffocation of any thinking except the government's brought on the "crisis of the intellectuals"... ; the official ideologists whipped the thinkers who balked at disgorging a philosophy for the new system... conformism was stifling originality... And night and day the voices chattered "socialism," though not once, in all the prattle of the apprentice ideologists, penitent careerists and sophists, was there a single Marxist voice that could call itself such and take part, independently, in socialist development in the name of revolutionary Marxism.[13]

In the last analysis, *everything* in Egypt will depend on the creation of a genuinely popular *Socialist party, equipped* not only with proper *means of action* but also with the power of *critical reflection* —not just in the cultural and aesthetic field, but above all in the domain of social science and political theory.[14]

This party of revolutionary Marxism is presumed to do away with the "pyramidal tradition" and "monolithism" that "stifles dialectic."

In 1971, before the upheaval of May-June, Abdel-Malek's views seem more conciliant, and yet no less doubtful. How is the *synthése entre l'autocratie et le populisme qui porte la marque de Gamal Abdel-Nasser* to be modified or replaced? He stipulates

> *création de formations politiques, dotées de l'autonomie idéologique et d'organisation, à l'intérieur et dans le cadre de la Charte et de son instrument de front national.. Il est temps que la nouvelle classe capitaliste d'État se démarque du prolétariat, que les fellâhs cessent d'être confondus avec les grands propriétaires fonciers, que les socialistes marxistes se distinguent des anticommunistes et de tenants de l'islam intégriste ... La clé de ce dispositif doit être la formation politique autonome du socialisme révolutionnaire, qu luttera pour concerter ... toutes les tendances du marxisme égyptien.*[15]

The experience of cohabitation within revolutionary Marxism makes Abdel-Malek's suggestion more than problematical. In practice, it would result in destruction of the whole edifice of Nasserism.

It remains to explain in Marxist terms Egypt's ideology in the shadow of Libya's al-Qadhdhafi.

For a merely factual critique we have to turn to a symposium on "Nasser and After." The observations presented may have been attuned to the range of interests of *Asian Affairs*,[16] or they may be within the main range of interests of the participants. Matters of ideology seem irrelevant.

Within these limits the views are divergent indeed. To Nevill Barbour "Nasser was entirely right in recognizing the position which geography and history have allocated to Egypt." Edward Lane and Ibn Khaldun are called to witness. To E. H. Paxton "the Arabs... are still waiting for their Bismarck, Cavour or Garibaldi. Nasser was the nearest to it so far." To J.M. Troutbeck, "The Egyptians are not Arabs. They are Egyptians." P. E. L. Fellowes sees 'Abd al-Nasir's "special tragedy that his great potential as a national leader should have been exhausted in the attempt to perform three tasks... —the regeneration of Egypt, the uniting of the Arab world, and the war against Israel." We are reminded of "the dichotomy in Egypt's personality as a nation... recently there were some small signs that her native genius was regaining her upper hand."

As regards positive achievements, Peter Mansfield cites "agrarian reform... the drive for industrialization, the Nile High Dam, desert reclamation, the health and educational program and... narrowing the gap between Egypt's masses and the élite." Against this, "his régime was authoritarian, although unsadistic, in character and... he never succeeded in creating a lively democratic political system with the participation as well as the consent of the people."

Some observers are unable to gloss over negative characteristics. Geoffrey Furlonge stresses 'Abd al-Nasir's "obsessive desire to dominate the Arab world ... his repeated attempts to subjugate Jordan, to the point of broadcasting incitements to its people to murder King Husain, ... his intrigues ... mainly responsible for the

85

dangerous confessional split in the Lebanon in 1958." Added to this, his intervention in Yemen's civil war and "tying up in a sterile commitment a high proportion of the Egyptian troops badly needed aginst Israel ... But his supreme failure ... was so to misjudge the Israelis as to precipitate that major Arab disaster, the 1967 six-day-war." Finally, "Egypt became a police state with a Nazi-like secret service ... It is widely held that he ('Abd al-Nasir) ordered the murder of his old comrade-in-arms 'Abd al-Hakim 'Amr ... Following a long campaign of subversion he poured arms into Yemen in 1962, hoping to start a train of revolution in Arabia; but the Royalist tribes checked his forces, and he won hatred in the Republic ... Day and night his radio made propaganda on behalf of Arabism, while his planes were smashing many a defenceless village. This culminated in the well-attested gas bombing of Yemenite villages, such as Jabel 'Iyal Yazid, remote from the fighting, with horrible civilian casualties ... When the moment of truth dawned ... Nasser's own defeat brought reactions ranging from the open jubilation of Yemeni tribesmen to the covert relief of many governments and individuals to whom Nasserite subversion was a far closer threat than Israel."

#### Footnotes

1. **Al-Adab** (Beirut), June 1968.
2. **L'Egypte Contemporaine,** April 1970, p. 6.
3. **"Le socialisme et l'Islam,"** **ibid.,** January 1970, pp. 38, 46.
   To Mahmud Isma'il 'Abd al-Raziq, Garaudy's "invention of a concord between Islamic thought and Marxism" is "arbitrary,... weak and baseless." Science and Marxism reject and Islam does not accept it **(al-Fikr al-Mu 'asir,** February 1970, p. 59).
4. **Op. cit.,** pp. 160-161.
5. "The Course of Egyptian Revolution and Its Future," **World Marxist Revue,** August 1966.
6. See the miscellany **Fi 'l-fikr al-siyasi (On Political Thought), II.** (Damascus 1963), pp. 26-97.
7. **Hizb al-Ba'th, ma'sat al-mawlid ma'sat al-nihaya (The Ba'th Party — Tragedy of Birth, Tragedy of End),** Beirut 1964, pp. 170-177.

8. **Li-'l-hurriyya, wa-'l-ibda' wa 'l taghyir (For Freedom, Creativity and Change),** Beirut, January 1969.
9. **Thawrat 23 Juliu fi mahkamat Mawaqif** (The 23 July Revolution at the Court of Mawaqif), **al-Adab,** January 1970.
10. **Egypt: Military Society** (Random House), New York, 1968.
11. **Ibid., pp.** 382-383.
    In 1966, in a review of this book, **al-Hurriyya,** an organ of ANM, still believed that the "Nasserite experiment" is capable of "resuscitating social dialectic. 'Abd al-Nasir's personal leadership appears a basic factor in realization of this development." See the issue of August 29.
12. **Ibid.,** p. XXXIII.
13. **Ibid., pp.** 379-380.
14. **Ibid.,** p. XXX.
15. **"L'Avenir de l'Egypte," Le Monde,** April 8, 1971.
16. N.s. vol. II, part 1, February 1971. See also **Times,** December 21, 22, 1966.

Chapter IV

# THE END AND A START

In retrospect, 'Abd al-Nasir appears a rather tragic figure, in a way a victim in the "procession of history." In spite of being a "supreme conspirator"[1] and "a master propagandist whose radio stations, teachers and military missions in the Middle East have been orchestrated with great skill,"[2] also "a master of political timing," he failed in his attempts to make his grand political designs prevail. He lost three wars (Israel, Yemen). He backed the wrong faction in South Yemen. His essays in effecting some Arab union failed. He saw the policies of "positive neutralism" and "nonalignment" end as an experiment in futility and its pillars crumble (Nkrumah, Sukarno, also Sihanouk). What is more, he made foreign bases reinstalled in Egypt to be dependent on them for her very existence.

It was President Nasser who encouraged the Fedayeen raids into Israel from the Gaza strip which led to the Israeli riposte in 1956. It was he who, nine years later, was largely responsible for the Six Day War with its disastrous results for Egypt and other Arab countries.

It was he who launched the imperialist Egyptian invasion of the Yemen which probably caused the loss of one hundred thousand Arab lives, although it is impossible to calculate it exactly. It is ironic that it was on June 5 and 6, 1967, when President Nasser was calling for Arab unity in the Six Day War, that the Egyptian Ilyushin bombers were dropping poison gas bombs on the villages of Immad and Bua in the Eastern Yemen and also destroying crops, cattle and wells in that area.[3]

This note may help to a discriminative appraisal of 'Abd al-Nasir ("a very attractive personality. As a politician we can admire him, but certainly not as a statesman"). Here we are also reminded that in an interview published in the *U.S. News and World Report* of May 20, 1968, President Bourguiba of Tunisia described President Nasser as the "evil genius of the whole region even for the Egyptian people."

Arguably, it is intangibles that prevail here. 'Abd al-Nasir himself spoke of dignity valued in Egypt; foreign observers repeatedly stressed the self-respect restored to the Arabs or to the people of the *ra'is*. In matters of dignity, its meaning and manifestations, views may differ. No doubt, his flamboyant oratory excited the masses. To quote admiring foreigners, his "good nature," "manners and affability" were disarming; one of them is captivated by his "courage, integrity, incorruptibility, imagination, eloquence, patriotism, modesty."[4] The Bedouin or fellah may have seen in him the redeemer, the avenger, the liberator, a new hero in the image of the mythical Salah al-din. And a hero is to be glorified not only at his height, but also at his demise, when the masses feel orphaned.

Closer scrutiny would probably show many levels in the voice of 'Abd al-Nasir, hence the ambivalence in his appraisal. One's concern is not always mannered speech making one sound to anticipate the listener's view or sweeten the bitter pill of exhortation. When he branded Tshombe as a murderer, he may not have thought of his

Voice of the Arabs rejoicing at the murder of Qasim in 'Iraq or appealing to get rid of King Husyan, or regularly calling Sir Roy Welensky a pig, a dog, and a Jew. It is his sense of vocation in the Arab Near East and in Africa that may have blinded him to myopic behavior.

There was a streak of the tragic in his inner policies, too. Speaking at length to Humphrey Trevelyan, British Ambassador in Egypt (1955-1956) about his struggle with Naguib, 'Abd al-Nasir remarked: "The story has not ended yet, and I wonder how it will end.'*

Trevelyan sees Egypt's "basic problem" as that of "a dictator trying to give the appearance of a parliamentary system, but at the same time keeping the power firmly in his own hands."[5] Nowadays we know better.

As early as 1967, Hasanayn Haykal knew of two forces menacing the "Revolution"—the "instruments of government" and "power concentrations" that seem to serve, respectively protect themselves, not the "Revolution." "Strengthening of democracy" is the remedy against "power groups" stifling it. "Freedom of thought and expression" is one half of democracy, "freedom of the written and printed word" is the second one. "In the oncoming era democracy can not be realized save through participation."[6] In 1969, Haykal, complaining of the "chronic resurgence" of pressure groups, maintains that already in 1967 an "important part of power" escaped 'Abd al-Nasir.[7]

Perhaps an irremediable failure in internal policies were the essays to ensure a base of social and moral cohesion for the régime under varying names—Liberation Rally, National Union, the Arab Socialist Union as a "socialist vanguard."[8] Union not party was the aim, to mark the régime off "party dictatorship" and give it a na-

*Strangely, Qasim's premonition is not much different. "You think the situation in 'Iraq will change. I wish to emphasize to you (oil companies) that this is a chain that has no end."

91

tional coloring. Built up through selection and appointment from above, not unlike the party structure in popular democracies, it could not but further self-serving and group interests, stifle criticism and inhibit self-criticism.

Having no voluntary mass party nor democratic institutions to control power interests, 'Abd al-Nasir had to cope with army plots in 1965 and in 1966 and let power slide to the uncontrollable security services. In fairness, given the realities of a régime with no public control he must have become a victim of his own making. In the plot of Marshal 'Amr, vice president and commander-in-chief, on August 25-26, 1967 — were implicated the former ministers of war and interior and the chief of intelligence service. It is noteworthy that Muhammad Fawzi, the then new commander-in-chief, later on jailed by Anwar al-Sadat as a plotter, helped 'Abd al-Nasir subdue the 'Amr plot. 'Amr's death remains a mystery.

Finally, it may be asked what was 'Abd al-Nasir's part in the body of theory called Nasserism (nasiriyya). He presented the National Charter to the Congress of Popular Forces — an agglomerate of maxims to be treated as near articles of faith. They were not to be questioned, but interpreters were allowed to exercise personal judgment (ijtihad) — primitive or intellect-bound — with various degrees of sophistication: identifying the moral and social code of socialism and Islam, making them co-extensive, co-existent, sometime ignoring postulates. Except for a few official marxisants, Marxism-bound theorists were never admitted into the corridors of power; intermittently, with the tactical shifts of power between conflicting groups, in some sense more moderate or more radical, hence in the process of gambling, they were given more or less leeway to exercise their power of reasoning in the highbrow periodicals, especially in the field of socialist theory. No doubt, the National Charter could not but be a Damocles sword over the interpreters, often making for opportunism or elusive sophistication.

> The difficulty of blending all these tendencies (of the Charter) into a systematic whole is reflected in the large number of schools of thought with divergent interpretations of the same text. Underlying these differences are conflicting material interests, political and religious affiliations and honest philosophical convictions...
>    ... It might be tempting to say "let a thousand flowers bloom" were it not for the ideological confusion, intellectual opportunism, and religious obscurantism which contribute neither to efficient production nor to the quality of cultural and social life.[10]

The scrutiny of 'Abd al-Nasir's personality will go on and, as usual, obscure more than reveal. In a great part it is self-interpretation of the authors, an urge to present one's flight of imagination, an essay in originality. Geoffrey McDermott assembled a few externals and labelled 'Abd al-Nasir Egypt's Gaitskell.[11] To Tom Little, "he had courage, strength, tenacity of purpose, dedication, idealism, but all flawed in the end by the complex of power allied to an innate distrust in his dealings with people."[12] And who will take Haykal's dicta, 'Abd al-Nasir's *alter ego*, for golden coins?

In his *The Game of Nations*, Miles Copeland finds him "one of the most courageous, most incorruptible, most unprincipled" leaders he ever met. And yet an ideology was named after and built around him (*nasiriyya*).

In his *Nasser*, Anthony Nutting maintains that Nasser never really understood the Arabs he tried to lead, "he was trapped in the role of the Arabs' champion, to which destiny and his own success had called him, but he might have done still more for Egypt's welfare and prosperity if he had not tried to secure her supremacy in the Arab world."

Finally, a statement by Ahmad Kamil, Chief of Egypt's Intelligence until May 13, 1971, serves to corroborate P. J. Vatikiotis' assumption that the crisis of 13-14 May "was the result of the confrontation between Nasser's *apparatchiks*, allied temporarily with 'Ali Sabri, and the new President Sadat over power." Ahmad Kamil's testimony

> shows clearly what was always suspected: the fact that all political organizations and structures which were formed after 1953, or which emanated from such ideological formulations as the National Charter of May 1962, or the Political Reorganization Programme of 30 March 1968 were — and are — no more than additional venues and agencies of central political regimentation, coercion and control.
>
> The question. . . . : Who was to govern Egypt . . . never arose while Nasser was alive; for he was the sole ruler of the country. Scribes, paid conspirators, propaganda purveyors and court sycophants assisted him in his task. They inevitably also benefited from, if they did not share in, his power. But they did not challenge it, or question his right to govern (*Survey*, Spring 197).

Official or inspired pronouncements are at best one-sided. Even if the "horrible things" Anwar al-Sadat spoke of at the National Assembly on May 20, 1971, are by no means an overstatement, a final verdict is to be shelved until the accused are allowed to speak freely. A free court would have to ascertain whether a majority, as far as it could have a decisive voice, or a minority of the Central Committee of ASU supported 'Ali Sabri and, given the framework of the régime, what were the President's constitutional powers *vis-à-vis* the ASU. But much of the moral background of the régime is to be deduced from

Edward R. F. Sheehan's *Who Runs Egypt.*[13]

At the National Assembly Anwar al-Sadat spoke also of "the rectification effected by the people against the deviationists of May 15" and he terms it a "return to the alliance of the laboring people's forces." He envisages a permanent constitution "rooted in the soil and mores of Egypt, based on the message of faith and maintaining the moral values against the horrible wave of materialism." "Social liberty and political liberty ought to move *au pair*" (unlike 'Abd al-Nasir's dictum that social liberty has to precede political liberty). Free elections "from the base to the summit" of the ASU are promised.[14]

The May 1971 upheaval could by no means be appraised in terms of "left" and "right." The *marxisants*, still less the unrepenting Marxists, are not to be identified with the "plotters" around 'Ali Sabri. Khalid Muhyi al-din, detained for a short while, was speedily released. Lufti al-Khuli, removed from *al-Tali'a* under 'Abd al-Nasir in 1970, is reinstalled as its editor. Probably to placate the Soviet ally, some Marxist leftists were admitted, in spite of thorough screening, to the People's Council. A few loyal Marxists had been admitted to the leadership of ASU and two into the government. Still, *al-Tali'a* betrays some confusion and uneasiness. Given the erratic nature of Anwar al-Sadat, it may have a hard time of ideological equivocation ahead. Dictatorship, whose power ultimately resides in the army's support, makes even principled theorists pliable, at best elusive.

In line with Sadat's dicta, a "new stage" and "new principles of the July 1952 revolution" are extolled. The writers of *al-Tali'a* nurse some cult of al-Sadat. The "police methods inimical to democracy" are condemned, also the "new class" dominating the country's vital apparatus, the "centers of police and administrative, political, social power" that sought to "remove the multitudes of the people from real participation in determining the country's destinies." Hence the "constant failure to create a political masses 'structure capable of supplying masses' heat to the revolutionary command," to "restore a democratic and populist spirit to our revolution."

Thus the Egyptian revolutionary experiment enters a new stage, opening its era with comprehensive elections to all political, trade unionist and social apparatus and crowning this transormation with a permanent constitution.[15]

Said al-Sadat: "We don't begin from void, we begin from the glorious July legacy."[16] Al-Sadat calls for a "democratic method, public, clear, open in confronting our problems." In the name of this method the ranks of the trade unions are purged of "opportunists and deviationists."[17]

Meanwhile, the trumpets of *al-Tali'a* blow the praise of democracy, and, as was to expect, elections to the ASU, in July, and to the People's Council, in October 1971, produced bodies loyal to the régime.[18]

The new era of "liberalization," of loosening the economic grip of the régime, heralds virtual, if tacit, denasserization. The modest opening to the weaker left can by no means offset the larger opening to the stronger right. Even under 'Abd al-Nasir had "the strong sections of parasitic capitalism deriving their wealth from contracting and speculative business succeeded to make their voice within the national alliance and their influence within the Arab Socialist Union the strongest."[19] To this should the voice of the thriving class of bureaucracy be added.

The slogans of "rectification," "rectificational revolution" and "renewal" raised by al-Sadat since May 14, 1971, had come to documentary fruition in the new Constitution. It stresses the supremacy of the law, vaguely modifies the relationship between the "national alliance" and the Arab Socialist Union, ensures "personal freedom," freedom of opinion within the limits of the law. By way of "rectification" the right strives and achieves more living space for private initiative. The left, envisaging "Arab socialism" accommodated within a mixed economy, is aware of the chasm between paragraphs and practice. It is aware of the contradiction inherent in the "national alliance," of the "element of struggle in unity" and its social roots. While resorting to homage to al-Sadat and taking comfort in world revolutionism, it cherishes no illusions about Egypt's present. The reins of authority are somewhat loosened, but there is no illusion about the identity of the ultimate arbiter.

It was a short spell of freedom-dreaming. Egypt's part in the events of 1971 in the Sudan, her oncoming merger with an already "federated" Libya, whose leader attempts to crusade in Morocco, Syria, Lebanon, Yemen, the Sudan, and Uganda against "communism, imperialism and Zionism," finally the eviction of Soviet advisers, all this has helped speed up the process of deideologization. Meanwhile President al-Sadat armed himself, for the sake of national unity that "comes from the Koran and the holy books," with new draconian powers restricting freedom to "protect and guarantee freedoms."

The immense ideological output of Nasserism is gradually being petrified to a new pyramid. Socialist parlance is still adhered to, but the infatuation with revolution is gone.

It was to be expected. Given the World War Two background of Anwar al-Sadat, his career as Secretary of the Islamic Congress in the 'fifties, it shouldn't have been difficult to imagine him reverting to his original attitude. There came the loosening of the ties with the Soviet Union, preceded by the strengthening of the ties with Libya and Sa'udi Arabia. In fact, both the flowering and the withering of socialist ideology have coincided with the degree of closeness to the Soviet Union. There came the great purge of men of integrity and intellect from the

Arab Socialist Union and seizure of Communists and unrepentant leftists. Economically and politically Egypt's régime definitely turned toward the past. There may be turns, even sharp twists in policies, but Nasserism has definitely passed away.

### Footnotes

1. **Times,** September 30, 1970.
2. C. L. Sulzberger, **New York Times,** November 2, 1963.
3. Lord Colyton, "Nasser's Bequest to Arabs," **Sunday Telegraph,** October 17, 1971.
4. **Asian Affairs, op. cit.**
5. **The Middle East Revolution** (Boston 1970), p. 88. This book fully vindicates its seemingly ambitious title. It is a personal account of a close observer, in a way an outside actor, hence more of an inside story. We see individual and mass psychology at work, the former decisively conditioning events.

   The author does not apply himself to ideologies, nor does he try to distill patterns of behavior. But in the name of these ideologies slaughtering takes place; frenzied mobs respond to calls pro and contra and multitudes of ignorant soldiers are turned by their superiors against each other. This violence revolves, in the main, around socialism (Ba'thists **contra** communists and Qasim and vice versa in 'Iraq, Flosy against NLF in South Yemen, Ba'th within itself). No doubt, at the base the historical setting of each country, unleashed instincts and uncontrollable power stimuli, should be sought.

   Trevelyan sees in 'Iraq a "succession of unstable rulers holding their power by military dictatorship."
6. **al-Ahram,** December 8, 1967.
7. **Le Monde,** June 24, 1971.
8. Launched in 1953 with the slogan "Unity-Order-Work," the amorphous Liberation Rally was abolished in 1956 and superseded, in 1959, by a National Union, in 'Abd al-Nasir's words as a "means through which we can realize a socialist, democratic, co-operative society... without civil war... not by class war, but by love and brotherhood." This body, infiltrated by "reaction," "opportunists and foes," had become, again in 'Abd al-Nasir's words, a mere "organizational façade" and was dissolved in 1961. In November 1961, the idea of "unity of the people's forces" was launched – a kind of revolutionary populism – and a Congress of People's Forces convened as a means to "reorganize all the national forces on a democratic basis and make the people itself steer the revolutionary movement." The Arab Socialist Union, set up to comprise "the forward stirring people's forces in the framework of national unity," was definitely established, after many attempts since 1962, in 1965. Whatever its organizational manipulations – from above to below and from below to above – it is a pyramided body patterned after a unity-party.

   Since June 1967 the idea of a "new political vehicle within the framework of the Arab Socialist Union" has been elaborated with a view of setting up a "socialist vanguard party." —See **al-Tali'a** ("Vanguard"), November 1967.

This should be a "party of **doctrinal** cadres, a party whose basic support are workers and fellahin." (**al-Katib,** September 1967.)

In practice, this idea, meant to curb the "power centers" and the powerful bureaucracy of the Arab Socialist Union, couldn't but become perverted. The Vanguard Organization was placed under Shar 'awi Jum'a, Minister of Interior. (See P. J. Vatikiotis, **op. cit.**)

9. See Eric Rouleau, **Le Monde, sélection hebdomadaire,** February 8-14, 1968.
10. See Fauzi M. Najjar, "Islam and Socialism in the United Arab Republic," **Journal of Contemporary History,** July 1968, pp. 184, 189.
11. **New Statesman,** October 22, 1971.
12. **Observer,** June 11, 1972.
13. **New York Times Magazine,** November 29, 1970. To Sheehan, it is argued that only a tiny minority of the Arab Socialist Union is active and "they are bound by their privileges to the bureaucracy."
14. See Roland Delcour, **Le Monde,** May 22, 1971. According to Jean-Françcois Chauvel (**Le Figaro,** July 28, 1971), the Central Committee of the A.S.U., inspired by 'Ali Sabri, the vice-president, insisted on knowing the details of the negotiations on the planned federation. Al-Sadat asked not to raise questions at this stage and was supported by four out of 140 members. Al-Sadat decided to break the "pressure group" and dismissed 'Ali Sabri on May 3. On May 13, Sabri's friends submitted their resignation, after having tried to involve the army in this affair. To al-Sadat, the affair of federation was only a pretext, since the plotters decided to act in February, after Sadat's decision to open the Canal against partial retreat of the Israelis. To J. F. Chauvel, the plotters invoked the principle of collective leadership decided upon in September 1970, after 'Abd al-Nasir's death.

A seemingly Marxist analysis by Anouar Abdel-Malek (**Le Monde Diplomatique,** September 1972) terms 'Ali Sabri and Shar'awi Jum'a "leaders of the Nasserite Left" and sees the old liberal bourgeoisie around Mahmud Fawzi aligned with the state sector bourgeoisie around 'Aziz Sidqi against the "Marxist Left." It ignores the tangle of non-ideological motives—personal, opportunist, tactical. Abdel-Malek complains of the decisive weight of the armed forces high command around General Sadiq sustained by the apparatus of the ministry of interior. In October 1972, General Sadiq, who ensured Sadat's victory, was removed.
15. **al-Tali'a,** August 1971.
16. **Ibid.,** July 1971.
17. **Ibid.,** September 1971.
18. H. G., **Neue Zürcher Zeitung,** October 29, 1971.
19. Hilmi Yasin, **al-Tali'a,** January 1972.

## Chapter V

## GENESIS OF BA'TH

Young men launched a movement aiming at their nation's resurrection, national and social. Fired by lofty ideas from the West, they soon tended to believe their movement indispensible, furthermore exemplifying the very process of resurrection, still more, identical with the nation's destiny. Theirs is the nation's vocation! They are soon to realize that words, however solemn and reverberating in Arab lands and animating educated youths, may remain a voice crying in the wilderness. They grope for tangible influence; temptations of power follow suit. Finally, they reach for power embodied in a party.

The party sets out to claim freedoms — a "constitutional parliamentary régime" — to do away with external and internal coercion. Obviously, political freedom entrusted to native custodians, men of traditional and economic power, may be perverted to coercion, too. Having simultaneously stated that its "main objectives," namely realization of Arab nationalism and socialism, "cannot be achieved except by means of revolution" — a term in its ambivalence reaching down to the soul and up to naked violence — it may be convenient soon to despair of ever being able to fulfill a vocation by ballot. It impatiently looks around for allies — especially after having merged in

1954 with the group of al-Hawrani — a weather-beaten politician — and finds a potential ally in the army. A vocation-minded party in collusion with a faction-ridden army is hardly a guarantor of freedom.

Meanwhile an essay in union with Egypt — 1958-1961 — fails. The new generation within Ba'th is no more given to romanticized nationalism and vague socialism presented as an educational process or a pragmatic performance. "Reality" and "objectivity" of Marxism captivate the minds. And violence, as extolled in theories of guerrilla warfare, in Fanon's call and exercised in national liberation fronts, seems the only way of salvation.

It will be remembered that in the 'Sixties violence had been elevated from an element of alleged dire necessity of reconstruction, an evil *per se*, to a level of morality, purging and enhancing, so much so that art and social science, as carried by a vocal segment of the new generation of intellectuals, fell prey to it.

Thus the way is open to naked violence of a *coup d'état*, of course in an ideological guise. Not only violence against "colonialists" and native "reactionaries," also against other "progressives" challenging the exclusive validity of Ba'th vocation and between two factions within Ba'th vying for prevalence, again in ideological guise. Finally, coercion within and between the civilian and military wings of both factions, the military, that is the strongest groupuscule that strikes first, having the upper hand. The victors try to make ideological sense out of it, to the vanquished it is counter-revolution. But a dispassionate observer would hardly glean much sense from senselessness. Of course, the story is much more tangled.

The loss is incalculable — in human life, by wasting the country's resources, by sowing enmity within the nation, by barring the way out of a dictatorship of a tiny minority. But fascination with power carried on the tips of lances and vindicated by a vocation-centered ideology or by a new trend in its interpretation — needn't stand to reason.

In *A Summary of Talks to a Group of Youth*,[1] in its autobiographical immediacy a rare piece of Arab pamphleteering, elements of Bitar's and 'Aflaq's initial intellectual gropings are to be discerned.[2] Allowing a degree of rationalization, this work does shed light on the genesis of the early Ba'th. The reader might detect some affinities with the dawn of any movement.

In 1928, as schoolboys, they saw the national problem only as a struggle between nation and colonialist. There were persons and governments, called reactionaries and traitors, subservient to and cooperating with the colonialist; and others, called nationalists, demanding independence and upholding the country's rights. Later, as students in the West, they found sympathy for the Arab cause only among some socialist and Communist deputies of the French parliament. They discovered socialism—a "new solid interpretation grappling with all the political and social problems the world in general and the Arabs in particular complain about." A group of Western writers and thinkers of noble aspirations, "scolding their governments for crimes of subjugating weak peoples under pretense of civilization and enlightenment," fascinated them. Theirs was a vision of a society in which peoples and individuals would be allowed to develop their potentialities, to "purify life, embellish it and fill it with good and happiness."

It was an attitude of youths "sighing from two deep wounds"—a "national wound" caused by foreign rule and a "social wound over the decay of a society steeped in ignorance, stagnation, deceit, subject to exploitation, slavery of thought and soul." Some of their writings published in their years of "Westernization" and sometime after "genuinely express their state of mind, their intense sorrow and naive hope, their vagueness of view and need of thought." When they left for the West, they carried with them a bit of their country and looked at the West's thought and culture through their "national sorrow and social needs," grasping from the West only that which would "help to relieve this sorrow and to meet these needs." Upon return to their country, "they carried with them — imperceptibly — something of the West, which made them look at the problems and needs of their nation through the West's problems and needs." Naturally, critical revision and conciliation with their milieu took several years.

From the West they adopted a socialist persuasion upholding two goals: struggle against foreign rule and against "internal reaction in all forms." To be "genuine, comprehensive, useful," the struggle against the colonialist has to be a people's struggle. The class then representing the national movement could not, however genuine its intent, rise above its economic interests, "clannish selfishness" and "greedy mentality," in consequence, could not persist in a lengthy struggle. "To succeed, an intellectual revolution changing old barren notions and intensely shaking souls is indispensable, a revolution to recover freshness of perception of life and create a new serious moral outlook manifested in personal and general behavior."

The Communist party in Syria comprised a few open-minded youths, daring in their fight against colonialism and oppression. "Having no ties with them," 'Aflaq and al-Bitar yet viewed them with sympathy. It never occurred to them that this party was soon to be a meeting ground of "dissidents, enemies of Arabdom and a pillar of the pillars of colonialism."

Even when in the West they never relished a "narrow Communist mentality." They gained insight into socialism by way of "free thinking writers, noble of soul," such as André Gide and Romain Rolland. Their sympathy for this idea has not barred them from seeing right in an opposite idea. In their teaching and writing they tried to instill into the mind of the new Arab generation the ideas of Nietzsche, "the greatest enemy of socialism," for which they were scolded by the communists.[3] And yet communism had a two-fold use: in dealing a blow to foreign colonialism and in violently shaking the old and stagnating Arab thought.

This situation lasted about three years. In 1936, after the electoral success of the Communist and socialist parties in France, the Communist party in Syria was legalized and consequently grew. In spite of "old promises and artificial sympathy," these parties "did nothing serious" for Syria's rights to freedom and independence. The Syrian Communist party became a tool of the French Communist party and of the French government in general. It began to lure racial and sectarian minorities, "everyone alien to the nature of the nation and her national aims, all who are inimical to the Arab movement."[4] This party "made truce" with the French imperialists and began to divert the people from its real enemy to "distant or imaginary enemies"—Franco, Chiang Kai-Shek, Mussolini, Hitler, Japan, *i.e.*, the enemies of France and Russia. It also allied itself with political and social reaction. Russia pursues realistic and independent policies and defends her national interests, while making use of world communism to further them. Why should not the Arabs, still "taking the first steps of their awakening," make their policies independent?

A "deep spiritual and intellectual crisis" made them abstain from writing and action for two years. "We are not politicians donning robes for every situation, resorting to sophistry to make changes palatable... We always strove to elucidate in our souls and in our nation what is deeper than politics: Arab soul and Arab thought."

These reservations notwithstanding, their affinity for the socialist idea was "genuinely deep," a chance to show their "leanings to good and justice." However, as a result of this crisis, a basic change occurred: "We became aware that what we cherished in a foreign land and in foreign ideas is to be found on our own soil, in our own ideas and history." The "gnawing distress" that befell them proved that the Arab soul "could feel security and freedom, be innovative and creative only when it regained its vocation." Was not the destiny of the Arabs at this stage to find a way to themselves and their own nature, "after having been in touch with what is alien to them, to make them keenly feel their own substance and understand their own reality and need?" "German philosophy helped to direct our thought to what is deeper than material phenomena and economic relations in the interpretation of history . . . It reduced the impact of materialist philosophy and spared from being deceived by the abstract theory on which socialism rests, namely utter rejection of nationalism."

In 1943, 'Aflaq and al-Bitar saw themselves "representing the movement of Arab Ba'th in the new generation," "not forming a political party."

In a proclamation of June 15, 1943, the "new generation" is called to vote for Shukri al-Quwwatli, leader of the National Party, "a man known for his integrity and uprightness." A distinction is to be made between "the national movement emanating from the new Arab generation and the present political constellation in which the old generation is still strongest in influence." "Before the Ba'th movement has expanded to encompass the nation, the new Arab youth, still growing and unable to assume sole leadership, has to co-operate with the fittest persons." "Our idealism is not utopianism ignoring reality, it is practical idealism that enters reality to set it in motion and change it." "The Arab Ba'th movement is to stay a militant movement for many long years; neither the movement nor the men representing it should participate in the government or take up posts." They seek "neither reward for past struggle nor road to ministry and position."[5] They take part in the elections, because parliament is "an assistant in the struggle."

We know that by this attitude we benefit without profiting, strengthen others without gaining in strength. In this attitude there is some self-sacrifice, to be appreciated only by those who feel that the nation's interest is not merely a word of boast ... but a deep truth to which the heart beats and the inmost soul shakes.[6]

## The Founding Fathers

### I. 'Aflaq

In a lucid but somewhat condescending essay,[7] as befits a young man rebelling against a "fathers" ideology, Tarif Khalidi fails to trace the *evolution* of 'Aflaq's thought; and evolve it did. Unfortunately, we have no access to the magazine al-Tali'a, considered Communist by some and "leftist" by others, where 'Aflaq's first offerings had been published. But two of his collected essays date back to 1935 and 1936.[8] In the first we are told that "heroism is not always attack, it means also patience and perseverance, and courage is not only in fighting the external foe, but also — especially — in fighting the internal foe, *i.e.*, despair, softness and love of ease." A "patriotic person" has also to be human, "virtuous of soul, noble of character."[9] In the second, 'Aflaq feels fortunate not to be one of the "men of politics choosing streets and meetings to diffuse their propaganda and addressing themselves to narrow minds and tepid superficial emotions." He invokes the "calm, serious mind and deep, genuine feeling." He deems it unnecessary to invoke socialism from Marx's and Lenin's writings. "Socialism is the religion of life, the victory of life over death. It opens the door of work for all, allows all the gifts of men and their virtues to develop and to be used, it upholds the fortune of life for life, so that to death are left dry flesh, decay, bones."[10]

In 1941, he discards "theoretical belief in the Arab idea because it is within easy reach of all." He points to the individual's "practical belief" in "the rightness of his idea, in the genuineness and force of his soul and its secure final victory, his belief that all these properties are with his leaders in whom his idea is represented.[11] Individuals and generations will pass our long road."

The password is not a scientific theory nor an exercise in constitution. It is a characteristic that marks man at any age and in any country... it is spontaneity that distinguishes genuineness from deception. This spirit of spontaneity is fed by experiments and refined by thought and inquiry, but not produced by experiments or science and thought.[12]

'Aflaq envisions a future in which Arab Ba'th, *i.e.*, Arab revolution (*inqilab*) materializes—a "life integrated, free, socialist," a "Ba'thist life" in which "social differences, regional barriers and communalist dissensions, any trace of slavery, private interest, ignorance and imitation disappear." The future is not distant, not "time to come," it is a "level of soul and thought" to be reached "in a second"; "we can realize it immediately, own it and with it own eternity."[13] These notions may seem in part inspired by Tolstoi or Gandhi. But the concept of leaders representing ideas betrays the then current fascination with the idea of leaderhood as glorified in Europe.

In the first Ba'th era, when appeal to sentiment prevails ("we the new Arab generation carry a message not politics, belief and conviction not theories and words")—'Aflaq's style, though often involved, is vibrant, somehow exalted, even cadenced.

The new generation believes in itself because it believes in its eternal nation, believes in its eternal nation and her ability to defeat her decay, because it believes in itself; as long as it issues from her she is able to depart from herself, as long as it rises above her she is able to rise above herself; as long as it secedes from her she is able by its work and impact to depart from herself, from her decayed rotten self, to return to her genuine essence, to become the eternal Arab nation.[14]

This train of thought could hardly be a guideline in practical politics. Later on, when the urge to enlighten and win gives way to political argument, 'Aflaq's world of ideas, ways of argument, not to speak of terminology, are European. For some measure of self-discipline and clarity combined with solemnity, he seems to be indebted to French schooling.

Is Ba'th's claim to ideological autarky vindicated in 'Aflaq's writings? References to foreign authors and sources are very scarce. Only once is Hegel mentioned ("communism is linked to Germany through Hegel's philosophy"), also Marx who "breathed into communism from his vengeful Jewish spirit." From Tolstoy's and Dostoyevski's works 'Aflaq gathers that "communism is linked to Russia's national spirit," a "mixture of Russian mysticism and European science."[15] 'Aflaq himself maintained in 1963 that he had lost contact with the trends of Western thought since the beginning of the Second World War, "devoting the best part of my time to the practical tasks of my party."[16]

We have seen men professing some enchantment with communism having given way, after 1936, to disillusionment with the French Popular Front government for having dimmed the hopes of Syrian independence. A menacing factor then emerged in Europe — German National Socialism — and considerations of an imminent war could not but be paramount in Europe. The idea of a symbiosis of nationalism and socialism, combining glorification of the past and a cult of the hero, of might rested in the élite, swayed minds everywhere. Furthermore, National

Socialism set out to eradicate capitalism, imperialism, Marxism and communism identified with Judaism and Zionism.[17]

It is argued that 'Aflaq fell under the spell of Alfred Rosenberg's *Der Mythos des 20 Jahrhunderts* —possibly a new revelation to a disillusioned but impressionable mind. Rosenberg's dictum that *"Schicksal and Persönlichkeit stehen nach germanischer Auffassung in steter Wechselwirkung"* [18] is worth remembering while reading 'Aflaq's writings of the early 'Forties.

> When an individual awakens to its destiny he departs from a state of superficial life and enters the course of passionate strong life, and when this awakening to destiny goes along with its acceptance, his life takes a direction and is marked by manhood.[19]

One is tempted to look for landmarks leading to Sorel, at least to collate their respective writings for affinities. For instance, Sorel's views on social revolution in *Réflexions sur la violence* call to mind 'Aflaq's obsessive deliberations on *inqilab*.[20] ("The Party of *Inqilab*," 1949; "The Arab Ba'th is *Inqilab*," 1950; "Revolutionary Organization," 1950; "Time and Revolutionary Movement," 1950; "The Link Between Arabdom and Revolutionary Movement," 1950; "Meanings of *Inqilab*, 1950; "On *Inqilab*, Destiny and Freedom," 1950; „The Link Between Organization and Revolutionary Work," 1957,[21] and "For an Arab Revolutionary Conscience," 1957.[22])

Just as Sorel's theory of minority or élite revolution enhanced by the myth of masses' motion is not conceivable without violence, at least as a mythical force, 'Aflaq's theory of revolutionism of Ba'th had to lead to bloodshed (in the case of neo-Ba'th bloodshed against the "old" Ba'th). Likewise the stress on heroic struggle (*nidal*), on the dangers of struggle, on a burning vision. Furthermore, one might confront Sorel's *"L'humanité contre la douleur"*

*in his Introduction à l'économie moderne* with 'Aflaq's dicta
on suffering.[23]

'Aflaq's fascination with Bergson is self-confessed: *Les deux sources de la morale et de la religion* may have inspired 'Aflaq's *In Memory of the Arab Messenger* (1943),[24] where Islam is presented as an experience and constant preparedness, as renewal of Arabdom and humanism, and *The Problem of Religion in Arab Ba'th* (1956).[25] Furthermore, Bergson's *L'énergie spirituelle*,[26] where emphasis is placed on "*l'élan de conscience, qui manifeste l'élan de vie*" couldn't have escaped 'Aflaq's attention while writing "Meanings of *inqilab*"[27] and "The Arabs Between Their Past and Present" (1951),[28] notably "The Future" (1950).[29]

But easiest to identify in 'Aflaq's deliberations are the elements of Fichte's concept of nation, though no mention is made of him. One recalls Fichte's notions of the function of pain, his stress on "serious struggle" and continuance of struggle, on the evil of self-seeking, the primacy of education (as upheld at the initial stage of Ba'th), the near-mystical attitude to the people "in the higher meaning of the word" (comparable to *al-sha'b* in Arabic), the "eternal people" that "forms itself in accordance with its own peculiar quality," people as a "totality that arises together out of the divine under a certain special law of divine development," and whose greatness is "filled with awe and reverence in the face of dark and mysterious fate... mindful of the ever-rolling wheel of destiny." Likewise Fichte's call for "the devouring flame of higher patriotism, which embraces the nation," an "all-powerful love of the nation", a "totally new order of things" and a "fashioning of an entirely new self," his fervent appeal to the "new generation," his overestimation of the significance of the German language in identifying all German-speaking people as the German nation, finally, the "lofty universal mission as regenerator and recreator of the world," the "message of eternal life" (Ba'th's *risala khalida*), "people and fatherland as a support and guarantee of earthly eternity." 'Aflaq's rhetorics must have also drawn heat from Fichte's solemn, exalted style.[30]

Unlike the "metaphysical" elements in 'Aflaq's philosophy, his views on Arabdom and its "eternal mission" as well as on all-inclusive nationalism have been upheld by the Leftists or neo-Ba'th. Only dissidents and breakaway groups questioned some of them. In practice, these views mean cultural and political uniformity enforced on countries of diversity, some, like Syria, extremely heterogeneous, some, like 'Iraq, teritorially bi-national. Under the Ba'th rule, both "Right" and "Left", such views are being translated into policies of denationalization (some Kurdish areas in 'Iraq, the northeastern oil-bearing Kurdish edge of the Jezira in Syria).[31]

'Aflaq's concept of self-centered nationalism fails to notice the same drive for self-realization in others. To him, since the Arab conquest, the element of racialism is no more a hallmark of Arabdom. The Arabs had "experienced the meaning of racialism, of injustice." Nor is Arab nationalism religious; "religion is no link of a nation, on the contrary, it divides a nation." It is not historic, "since Arab nationalism does not reject, that is, does not conflict with the non-Arab historic legacy." "It comprises various cultures that entered it and co-operated with it—the Egyptian, Assyrian, Babylonian, Phoenician and others."[32] As to the Maghrib, "the Berber race blends with the Arabs completely... since the Arab conquest until today it became one country, one religion, one culture, one language, one present interest."[33]

'Aflaq fails to mention the Sudan, where the four million strong non-Arab population in the South claims the right of self-determination—a real test of Arab-African solidarity. As for the Christian minorities, "no one is preventing them from observing their religious ritual and their Christian culture within the general Arab culture." "Arabdom is humanism, Arab nationalism we understand to be true humanism, sanctification of other

112

nationalisms, of these feelings in any other people. We do not believe in internationalism... , we consider the humanism of the Communists artificial, since internationalism is an attempt to make every people lose its personality. ... The first to deviate from it, on national grounds, is Yugoslavia. She is socialist, but does not wish to lose her personality."[34]

As late as 1955 the Kurds were told "no one prevents them from studying their language, on condition that they obey the state laws and are no danger to the state. ... Why do the Kurds or a part of them fear Arabdom? Most of this fear results from imperialist propaganda that started fifty years ago, when the British and the French entered the Arab East. For centuries the Kurds have lived with the Arabs, fought and excelled in defence of Arab lands. ... Some leaders with feudal interests apart, the Kurdish people do not wish more than the Arabs themselves" — "noble happy life."[35]

'Aflaq maintains that "there are no oppressed minorities and communities, there is an oppressed people, i.e., the Arab people, and there is an oppressing minority of plotters with imperialism. He who does not oppress a Muslim Kurd does not oppress a Christian Arab, a Kurd, a Berber, an Assyrian, a Muslim, a Christian, a Druze, etc. ... There are exploiting classes plotting at the peoples' expense, and once exploitation is eliminated there will be no difference between compatriots."[36]

In 1960, 'Aflaq envisages "revolutionary peaceful solutions" "to 'Iraq and her racial minorities, especially that great Kurdish minority... and Lebanon whose structure has given doctrinal and religious differences a meaning of cultural divergence." These solutions are to "preserve for Arabdom all parts of its land and people and bring about spiritual unity, mutual understanding and harmonious integration of all, instead of solutions emanating from despair. ... "[37]

In Lebanon it is imperialism that feeds the Christians with "false thoughts."

It is our duty to explain to the Lebanese that the Arabdom we work for is the very thing they demand and strive for behind their flight from Arabdom. Arabdom bars religious pressure. They flee from it, because they maintain that Arabdom — in their view, Islam —- does not allow the building of a society that preserves human dignity and keeps pace with the modern evolution of the world. Due to their geographical position, their links with the West and foreign missions, they enjoyed Western culture more than any other Arab country and experienced the value of personal freedom — the most precious thing in Western culture. Having attained some of this freedom, they fear to lose it when integrated in the Arab whole.[38]

In 1960 'Aflaq's argumentation sounds more attuned to the vogue of "progressivism." He rejects the division of Lebanon's population into two – for and against Arabdom. "By national revolutionary criteria all are far from it, in various forms and degrees." The problem of Lebanon and Arabdom is only a problem of "Arab progressivism." Lebanon "has a basic role to play in clarifying, deepening and perfecting the revolutionary Arab movement, even if those who oppose Arabdom do not intend to rectify their inimical negative attitude. New Arabdom is presumed to be able to accept this challenge and respond to it with further clarification of its progressivism and a deepening of its belief in freedom and humanism."[39]

It remains to be asked how Ba'th élitism leading the masses could preserve "personal freedom" and "human dignity" and face the burden of history making for Lebanon's uniqueness. The succeeding events provided an answer.

By sheer force of reasoning, 'Aflaq seems impelled to stress a positive effect of Zionism.

114

The imperialist states established Israel to prevent Arab renascence and Arab unity, but this act itself was a very great factor in awakening our nationalism, in raising the level of our consciousness and our struggle (1957).[40]

The catastrophe of 1948 in Palestine was a "historic occasion to endow Arab consciousness with such depth, clarity and comprehensiveness as to enable it to carry the heavy burden of the national cause" (1956).[41] Of course, it is only a side effect.

Israel is also an expression of the power of world Zionism... Imperialism makes use of Zionism, but world Zionism is able to make use of imperialism itself ... in consequence, another struggle should go along with our struggle against imperialism, it is our struggle against Zionism.[42]

One is tempted to speculate on the course of Arab nationalism without the mental pressure of Zionism. The evil of Zionism is absolute, beyond argument is the historical, religious and cultural background, and the national stimuli to a movement of renascence — linguistic, cultural, social — that wouldn't have materialized without the creative exertions of four generations, nor, furthermore, without a strong socialist movement.

Zionism aside, the ban on freedom of expression is implied in 'Aflaq's deliberations on Ba'th as a vanguard party.

One of the characteristics of a revolutionary phase is a minority holding the command of a people's movement, for if the people's majority were able thoroughly to grasp the evils of the conditions and properly to organize its ranks... the nation would have no need for a revolution in her life.[43]

(It is a). . . minority of a special kind, conscious of its nation's reality, believing in the country's cause and in its people's rights, completely identified with the people's deep needs and aspirations. This minority proceeds to represent the people before the people entrust it openly with this representation.[44]

Here are the intellectual seeds of future upheavals planted. The indispensability of Ba'th is taken for granted. In 1957 it has not yet occurred to the author that other revolutionary minorities from within or without may claim the right or some right to representation.

Being a national movement in the sense that it arises "from within the nation," Ba'th "enjoys great freedom because it draws its thought and plans from the Arab people's needs" and is "always much nearer to integration with the nation's soul" (1957).[45] A guardian of the "eternal Arab mission," it could not cease to exist, as it was asked and has agreed to in the short-lived United Arab Republic. Two salvation-minded bodies — the Arab Socialist Union and Ba'th — could not co-exist in one state. True, in its infancy, being harshly treated, Ba'th could not but plead for civic freedoms. Subsequently, it gained some foothold in a government issuing from a coup or in a coalition government. Finally, having no chance to gain power by ballot, it resorted to a coup via army officers (February 1963). In a way, not unlike the all-Russian Communist party, the logic of exclusiveness was to lead to mutual elimination of ideologists of exclusiveness, when a faction of so-called neo-Ba'th overpowered, again via the army, the ruling Ba'th faction (1966).

A "national philosophy" that admits the primacy of a revolutionary minority can at best be ambivalent about "freedom" and "democracy."

Revolution and awakenings that work to create a new man, of independent personality, of free thought, capa-

116

ble of creating, inventing, and bearing responsibility, should not apply Machiavellism that relies on lies and attaches no weight to morals (1960).[46]

The "national philosophy" of Ba'th... rejects the capitalist régime and the Arab democracy that gave birth to capitalism, rejects communism as a régime, and leaves free scope for a genuine revolution... in which means and ends are harmonized.[47]

One of the three pillars of Arab nationalism that assumed "realistic revolutionary content" is freedom from the "imperialist foreigner" and from "tyrannical rule" within. The second pillar is

... socialism for the people as a whole, independent socialism that does not follow a definite school and is not a doctrinal tool of factional partisanship and rivalry, but benefits from all theories of peoples and is keen to harmonize them with the nation's spirit, her conditions and needs.[48]

The third pillar — unity — "needs a generation believing in it, fighting for it, pursuing its message on sound bases, on democratic and socialist principles." 'Aflaq envisions a "socialist democratic populist unity."[49]

The first essay in Arab unity proved a hard lesson to votaries of unity. In its "superficial optimism," writes 'Aflaq in 1962,

Ba'th hoped... that the union should be able to resolve the basic conflict between the applied policies of the two countries, namely the conflict over freedom and democracy, and that people's cooperation between the two regions of the federal state and between this state and the militant movements in other parts of the Arab homeland would bring about a fast evolution of the personal régime in Egypt toward democracy. (1962)[50]

The Egyptian revolution was a "military revolution, it had not started from the people, nor with an idea or a theory," but after some time her characteristics came to light. It was a "genuine true revolution," it "overturned Arab history," it "affected the life of the age and the whole world," and the birth of UAR was a "beginning of new history as regards the Arabs and the world."[51] True, for some time "old separatist trends" animated Egypt's revolutionary government, and until 1954 her rulers used to say "they don't mind Syria uniting with 'Iraq or with Turkey." But Arab "revolutionary dialectic" worked its way—the Palestine problem, the Zionist menace showing that imperialism and Zionism are one thing, the internal reforms "augmenting confidence and audacity on an Arab and a world scale." At the Bandung conference in 1955, 'Abd al-Nasir perfected the "new dialectic" that Syria's people had pursued for years.[52]

In 1956, 'Aflaq vaguely envisioned a union or federation (*wihda* or *ittihad*) between Syria and Egypt, by virtue of its "revolutionary dialectic" open to other parts of the Arab homeland and carrying the seeds of its "human message": "realization of actual freedom to individual and community, to Arabs and the world, and of free cooperation between free socialist peoples."[53] In 1962, in a *post-mortem* on the short-lived UAR, 'Aflaq suggests that from the beginning of 1956 Ba'th strove for "one federal state not a federation of two states,"—a régime that provides "safeguards against domination and selfish regional reactions, also conditions that take into account the present differences between Arab countries and allow their sound evolution toward integration."[54] Hardened by experience, a clearer concept is presented: a "régime in union preserving its national meaning and preventing it from deviation toward regional domination." A "federal régime" is to "implement the power and strength of the Arab nation, build her renascence and culture and safeguard her independence," and "remove fears and doubts and whatever residue there may be of regional leanings and divisiveness, while attending to local differences and the special circumstances of each region." 'Aflaq speaks of "fruitful cooperation between the associated regions in devising a policy of one state."[55] The dangers of "regional tyranny" are clearly stressed.*

## II. Salah al-din al-Bitar**

Bitar's cast of mind is pragmatic, hence his simple, near-utilitarian idiom. He was the practitioner in Ba'th politics. In terms of a country with no democratic control, pragmatism is bound to end in limitless opportunism. The era of military, economic and political dependence on the Soviet Union, since 1955, had to be somehow ideologically underpinned: communism became *salonfähig*, and the approach to Marxism more "broadminded." The failure of the first essay in Arab union, in 1961, set off dissensions within the party. The second generation took to "scientifism" and classbound slogans drawn from the Marxist-Leninist arsenal. Exigencies of implementation and intra-party strife may account for some shift towards opponents, hence more sobriety of style, even in 'Aflaq's later writings.

To be sure, Bitar's key attitude to communism remained unchanged. In 1950, he unreservedly rejects communism, its social achievements notwithstanding, for "being oppressive and barring individuals from evolving their

---

*In August 1971, a high security court in Damascus had condemned 'Aflaq, al-'Aysami, former secretary general of Ba'th, Amin al-Hafiz, president of the Republic overthrown in 1966 and two others of the "Rightist clique," to death **in absentia**. The reason — "plot against the revolution and the Ba'th party" (**Le Monde**, August 5, 1971).

President al-Asad commuted the death sentence to life in prison.

** After the new Ba'th coup in 1966, he fled his country. In January 1969 he was condemned, **in absentia**, by a supreme security court, to forced labor for life.

faculties." He envisions for the Arabs an "original social order doing away with exploitation, but without murder or terror." In 1959, he still believes in Arab nationalism realizing the unity of the Arab countries and "giving the world a fine human example of national entities resting on the basis of freedom, democracy, socialism, brotherhood of peoples and world peace." A "national socialist Arab society is to stand on a basis of equivalence of the individual, social justice, dignity of the individual, freedom of opinion, people's rule — a real democracy."

To al-Bitar, four are the enemies of Arab nationalism: "reaction, imperialism, Zionism, and Communists." Communists militate against Arab unity that is bound to eliminate foreign influence in Arab countries and build an "Arab democratic socialist society," so that their existence might have no more justification. Al-Bitar appears to be a reform socialist, he stands for distribution of land, just wages, social security, people's sovereignty by democratic rule and exercise of political rights, "general freedoms" and freedom of elections. But he also speaks of a "conscious vanguard," of "leaders in the people's vanguard."[56]

In 1965, Bitar's stand on problems of nationalism and socialism seems hardly changed. But in contending with the new generation he yields some ideological ground.

Nationalism is permanent revolution. The Arab revolutionary doctrine is not Marxism that denies national revolution, it is the doctrine of Arab revolutionary nationalism.

National spirit is origin and source, it appears in the life of all nations, even those which adhere at the beginning to the Marxist-Leninist doctrine. This national spirit manifests itself today in the doctrinal difference between the Soviet Union and the People's Republic of China.

. . . Marxist logic has infiltrated the minds of certain

"Ba'thists" who act as if this logic were absolute verity and substitute it for the Ba'th doctrine, without forgetting to season it with salt of Arabdom... as if Arab nationalism could be grafted onto Marxism, so that this fusion would constitute an Arab revolutionary ideology, not an imported one.

To say that only Marxism is scientific and define it as "scientific socialism" is contrary to the scientific spirit; the revolutionary character of Marxism cannot detract from the revolutionary character of Arab nationalism — the source of Arab socialism and of Arab revolutionary doctrine.

... Neo-Marxism has views larger and more comprehensive than Marxism. In Asian and African countries liberated from colonialism a socialist spirit is born emanating from all the sources of socialist thought, particularly from the traditions and civilizations of these countries, and this will enrich world socialist thought.

... Socialism is one of the elements of the Arab revolution... Marxism contains socialist principles that life's constant progress has sanctioned. It opened new horizons to Arab thought and particularly offered economic options, without a part of which a national socialist revolution cannot be implemented. But to adopt Marxism as a global philosophy capable of resolving all problems of life, for both society and the individual, under the pretense of being "scientific" socialism, would mean to place oneself in contradiction with the Arab revolution. Surely socialism borrows from Marxism, but it also borrows from other socialist doctrines.

... It is no accident that since its inception our party was named Party of Arab Resurrection (Ba'th) and much later the epithet "socialist" was added...

Socialism cut off from Arab nationalism, be it Marxist or non-Marxist, could not be qualified as revolutionary. In fact, it is nationalism that gives birth to authentic socialism; it is Arab socialism, Arab revolution.[57]

There is still an air of exclusiveness in Bitar's identification of Ba'th with Arab unity, but it is being mitigated. A tribute to new times is his assertion that "the ideology of Ba'th is scientific" and that a dialogue with other "nationalist revolutionary movements" is feasible.

> He who says Arab unity, says Ba'th party... It is the Ba'th party that has always placed the cause of unity at the head of its tasks of struggle, but it is equally true that it has linked this cause to many others, notably those of liberty and socialism, maintaining that they constitute a living unity embodying Arab revolution and renaissance.
> ... The necessities of evolving life are stronger than the doctrine and it is they that, through interaction with the ideology, bring about renewal, transformation and correction. But there is a great difference between the fact of renewing a doctrine and that of replacing it by another in the name of revolution.
> ... True Ba'th recognizes that there are other Arab nationalist revolutionary ideals and other movements in the Arab homeland and one should have an open mind so that they might fraternise and engage in a dialogue.
> ... A part of Ba'th let itself be dragged into folly, asserting that nationalism is retrograde and revolution can only be socialist... The Ba'th ideology, scientific and revolutionary, is the ideology of the Arab nation, and the original Ba'th remains the loyal guardian of this ideology.

Al-Bitar speaks of a regional "separatist spirit" of the revolutionary régimes themselves.[58]

At the unity talks held in Cairo, in March and April 1963, al-Bitar spoke of a need for a "government by the people" and 'Alflaq added "by the working people, *i.e.*, the peasants and workers, who are in the (Ba'th) party." 'Abd-al-Nasir's "impression was that Ba'th democracy as defined in its constitution is bourgeois." Al-'Aysami admitted that "the concept of democracy was initially affected by the mood of the times, hence was perhaps Western in color. The nature of this early struggle may have enjoined a concept of democracy for all classes. But now, with the legacy of bitter experience and of conflicts with reaction, capitalism, and imperialism, Ba'th is tending to view freedom as properly belonging to the working classes and to other socialist-minded bodies. It may, therefore, be finally forced to adopt a single-party system as its policy."[59]

In fact, the equivocal attitude of Ba'th came to the fore in the early 'Fifties, when it embarked on collaboration with the army. Ba'th may have been motivated by the consideration that by a democratic process it would never be able to fulfill its vocation. It is a far cry from participation in bourgeois governments to a single party rule.

*The Constitution of Ba'th\**

The Ba'th constitution of 1947, reaffirmed in 1954, may have affected the Ba'th practice more than all the ideological writings. In theory, its postulates retained their validity with all the warring factions. Ambiguities or inconsistencies lend themselves to interpretation, so that future developments could be vindicated. They sound like articles of faith and some could be made true only by violence.

---

\*According to Leonard Binder's English version, **Middle East Journal**, Vol. 13, 2, 1959.

Article 7. The Arab national homeland is that part of the earth inhabited by the Arab people and which lies between the Taurus mountains, the Zagros mountains, the Persian Gulf, the Arabian Sea, the mountains of Ethiopia, the Sahara desert, the Atlas range and the Mediterranean Sea.

These borders may involve the Arab homeland in ceaseless friction with Iran, Turkey, Ethiopia, not to speak of Israel.

The First Principle:

1. The Arab homeland is an indivisible politico-economic unit. It is impossible for any of the Arab regions to perfect the conditions of its life in isolation from the rest.

This principle ignores the historical background and the individual characteristics of the constituent parts of the Arab homeland. The first essay in unity between two socially minded Arab countries came to grief because of differing historical and present-day realities.

Ba'th centralism is enhanced by an authoritarian and formal approach to human issues of subtler nature (language, ethnic distinctness, traditional communalism and confessionalism, majority-minority relations) and disregard for sensitivities emanating from them.

On one side:
The Third Principle:

The Arab nation is characterized by an eternal mission which manifests itself in the form of a complete regeneration through the stages of history, leading to the reformation of human existence, the advancement of harmony and cooperation among nations.

. . . The Arabs will extend a brotherly hand to the other

nations and will cooperate with them in bringing about the rule of justice, guaranteeing to all peoples peace, well-being and moral and spiritual elevation.

On the other:

Article 10: An Arab is anyone whose language is Arabic, who lives in the Arab homeland or aspires to live therein, and who believes in his connection with the Arab people.

Article 11. Whoever agitates on behalf of or is connected with a racial group opposed to the Arabs, or whoever immigrates into the Arab homeland, for the purpose of colonization, will be expelled from the Arab homeland.

Article 15. The national tie will be the sole (social) bond existing in the Arab state. It will guarantee harmony among the citizens and it will guarantee their fusion in the crucible of a single nationality. It will combat all other denominational, factional, tribal, parochial or regional loyalties.

It is a primitive and crude concept of nation and nationalism. It augurs intolerance and arbitrariness.
In 1963 and again in 1968, Ba'thist governments launched campaigns against the rebellious Kurds in 'Iraq.

As against this:
The Second Principle:

... Freedom of speech, of association, of belief, and of science are sacred, and may not be limited by any government whatsoever.

Article 14. The system of government in the Arab state will be representative and constitutional. The executive authority will be responsible to the legislative authority, which is to be directly elected by the people.

Article 17... The party will strive to enact a constitution for the state which will guarantee absolute equality before the law to Arab citizens; which will guarantee the complete freedom of the expression of their will and the choice of their representatives in honest elections; thus organizing for them a life of freedom within the limits of the laws.

But Article 41 grants and denies at one breath: "There will be freedom — within the limits of Arab nationalist ideology — in the establishment of clubs, the formation of associations, parties, popular organizations, and institutions for travel... "

Strangely, nowhere is democracy made mention of. Instead, Ba'th populist notions are evident. "The Party is populist, believing that dominion belongs to the people, that they alone are the origin of all government and leadership, and that the value of the state derives from the will of the masses, even as its sanctity is in proportion to the extent of their freedom in choosing the government" (Art. 5). And yet "the Party is revolutionary, believing that its principal goals of reawakening Arab nationalism and building socialism cannot be achieved except by revolution and strife. The Party believes that dependence upon gradual change and contentment with superficial (because) partial amelioration will defeat these ends (through faintheartedness and loss of opportunities)" (Art. 6). The Party decides to "rebel against existing evils affecting all intellectual, economic, social and political aspects of life." (*ibid.*)

The constitution seems to have opened the door to all eventualities and to warrant them.

## Minorities Versus Majority

It has become a near axiom, no doubt inflated by opponents, that the Ba'th régime is a minorities régime. To A. Hottinger, an open-minded observer of a scholarly bent,

... a small group of Baath-indoctrinated, nearly always Alawite army officers together with their fellow travelers, constituted the core of the régime. In the absence of a real echo from the people to their socialist slogans and nationalist war theses, they began, with the troops loyal to them, to form a nucleus of power; their principal task seemed to be to defend the privileges which the government had seized by the bloody coup of February 1966.[60]

This view, differently presented, is also upheld by Rondot. To the dissident 'Alawis,* Isma'ilis, Druzes and non-Muslims, the tolerant laicism of Ba'th meant a kind of liberation from the socio-political preponderance of Islam and from the tutelage of their own communities and chiefs.[61]

In a somewhat high-flown essay, Viennot asserts, without corroboration, that "by establishing a radical difference between western Christianity (which, according to 'Aflaq, accepts and defends the capitalist imperialist régime) and eastern Christianity, Ba'th seeks to prevent the Arab Christians from falling into the trap of sympathy for the Christian imperialist West." Again, as if self-explanatory, Ba'th unites in its midst members of all confessions "sans qu'aucune d'entre elles puisse être considérée comme prépondérante ou majoritaire."[62]

Édouard Saab attacks this problem from a startling sociological angle, somewhat flavored with revolutionary semantics. He speaks of an emerging "new class," a "formidable leap of the proletariat, represented by the federation of workers unions of Khalid al-Jundi** and the

---

* The relationship between the 'Alawis and Islam is of a controversial nature.
** Isma'ili leader of the Workers' Militia. A corrupt parvenu, soon to be removed from his position.

revolutionary peasantry represented by the army of General Jadid."

> *Que cette nouvelle classe se recrute dans les rangs d'une communauté, qu'elle rallie plus particulièrement les minorités alaouite, ismaélite et chrétienne, ou qu'elle soit le produit brut de la campagne syrienne opposée aux villes nanties et prospères, ce ne sont là que des constatations qui confirment l'etat de fait, plutôt qu'elles ne dénoncent une discrimination sectaire ou la dictature d'une minorite' ethnique.* [63]

Dr. al-Razzaz, co-founder of Ba'th, finds it "natural" that the percentage of minorities in Ba'th is higher than their percentage in the population at large. The countryside, where these minorities live, was exposed to feudalism, so that it responded to Ba'th ideology "deeper and faster" than the city. As to the army, the number of Ba'thists in it was small, so that after the "March 8 revolution" all the Ba'thist reserve officers, also some officers linked to families and tribes of the "leaders of revolution," were called up. Added to this, many of the officers who supported the secession were "reactionaries" and town dwellers, and with their dismissal the percentage of the Sunnis in the army dwindled. Thus began the sectarian strife in the army.[64]

The main reasons as to why have members of minorities come to the fore under the Ba'th régime seem to be:

1. Minorities in Syria make up a third to 40 percent of the population. Under the former Sunni-led régimes, sustained as they were by land-owning and merchant families and professionals allied with them, the political influence of the minorities had been negligible.

2. The minorities have a long tradition of autonomy, be it confessional (Christians) or based on religious secretiveness combined with territorial isolation (Druzes,

'Alawis, Isma'lis). There were also concentrations of national entities (Kurds in the Jezira, Circassians). The new régime provides a new avenue of self-assertion, a kind of inverted freedom. What is being won through participation in a dictatorship's régime, in terms of imagined heightening of self-respect — in a way more than symbolic reveng — 8is offset by the loosening of community bonds and the loss of a semblance of "inner freedom" under previous régimes.

3. The 'Alawis and Isma'ilis are preponderately downtrodden communities of an agricultural proletariat, working the land of town-dwelling Sunnis. The cities in the 'Alawi province have a Sunni majority. The 'Alawis have been spilling over the boundaries of the Sunni areas.

4. Since the end of World War I minorities, especially Circassians, 'Alawis and Druzes, were strongly represented in the security services. Being socially superior, the Sunni town-dwelling youth was less drawn to military service. No wonder the 'Alawis and Druzes rose to senior positions in it. Since 1958, the Syrian officer corps has been recruited, by selective screening, almost exclusively from the urben proletariat or the peasantry. In the neo-Ba'th leadership the rural milieu was strongly represented (Latakia, Homs, Hama, Salamiyya, Jezira).

5. Ba'th's apologetic attitude to Islam may have helped attract non-Sunni youth. But in this respect Ba'th is now not exclusive.

All the sects and confessions — Sunnis, 'Alawis, Druzes, Christians and Isma'ilis — were represented in both camps of Ba'th. Before 1966, the national Command counted among its members, beside 'Aflaq (a Christian), al-Razzaz, al-Bitar and al-Hafiz (Sunnis), 'Umran ('Alawi), Mansur Atrash (Druze). Among the younger leaders in the regional Command the non-Sunnis were more conspicuous: Jadid, al-Asad, Makhus ('Alawis), Hatum and 'Ubayd (Druzes).

Under the neo-Ba'th régime the part of the Druze

leadership markedly dwindled. Mansur al-Atrash was jailed. Salim Hatum, the real leader of the coup of February 1966, who had led the assault on President Hafiz's residence, rebelled in August 1966, fled to Jordan and, on return with the outbreak of the June 1967 war, offered his services and was put to death. His co-plotters, Abu 'Asali, Fahd al-Sha'ir and most of the other officers, were Druzes.[65] 'Ubayd was one of the opponents of the authors of the February 1966 coup.

To speak with Jubran Shamiyya, "a great proportion of Ba'th partisans, especially in the army, are members of minorities." Some of them may uphold the Marxist doctrine, but the greatest part are "moved by confessional sentiments clad in socialism." Political differences hide behind a doctrinal shield just as in ancient Islam they assumed a religious color. Since the riches had been in the hands of the Sunni majority of the towns, *eo ipso* also political power, the villages have nothing to lose from virulent socialism. On the contrary, they are bound to gain political and economic power from confiscation easy to justify. Hence the "natural union" between economically weak minorities and socialist doctrinaires.[66]

Finally, the majority versus minorities problem is only one aspect of relations between parties or within one party. No doubt, within Ba'th relationships, hence also contention, have evolved between Sunnis and non-Sunnis as well as between members or groups of minorities and within each minority group. Here social, be it confessional or tribal, and individual psychology interact. In South Yemen, tribal loyalties affected the relationships between the officers groups, often even conditioning their ideological affinities. Zaydi or Shafi'i allegiance in North Yemen had fed the ideological cohesion of contending officers groups. The genesis of the rivalry between al-Asad and Jadid, two 'Alawi "strong men" in Ba'th, is well worth detecting.

A Ba'th application of communalism in politics is presented by Muta' Safadi.[67]

"Perusal of the names of overseers in institutions of terror such as the political branch of the intelligence service or the National Guard, etc., shows that nomination from among some communities was by no means incidental. All those jailed, interrogated and punished keep mentioning the names of their torturers, how most of them and the most violent were from certain communities. Moreover their methods of punishing and vilification were 'sectarian.'

"Hundreds of those jailed at al-Mezze after July 18, 1963, including myself, cannot forget the superintendent of the jail nor the torture and interrogation team. The hundreds of nights of whipping and electrocution, blows, abuse of belief with the most slanderous words... And yet the conscientious among the prisoners shrank from hating every 'Alawi, Christian or Druze just because the superintendent of the jail or the head of the torturers' unit and most of his assistants were 'Alawis, displaying their 'Alawidom in denigrating the belief of the victims, or because a Christian was the rudest legal investigator the cellar of al-Mezze has ever known, or because two or three overseers torturing day and night were Druzes.

"The communalist planners among the Ba'thists eagerly planted heads of the intelligence sections and their branches in the provinces. By this means communalist strategy was pursued. In provinces with numerous Sunni groups the supervisors of Ba'th "security" were 'Alawis first, Druzes second, Isma'ilis and Christians third. It was so in Damascus, Dar'a, Homs, Latakia, Aleppo.

"Groups of new 'officers' chosen from high school graduates or teachers or petty officials — members of the minorities — were tempted by 'doctrinal' planners with military posts, so much so that some of them were raised by a number of ranks above active officers from the old real 'Syrian' army. They were tempted by a doubled salary apart from military and party 'authority and dignity.'

"As against this, hundreds of officers from the big cities, especially Sunnis, were dismissed. Services, such as the air force, the navy and the armored force were deprived of their chief officers. Whole brigades with their staff officers and soldiers were reserved for certain communities (for instance, the seventy fifth brigade). The doors of military colleges and various military schools were closed to youth of Sunni cities. Entire classes of these colleges were dismissed before graduation...

"As to administrative and ministerial posts, the Ba'th problems were more difficult. To fill an important administrative position one needs certificates and certain abilities. Important ministries were placed directly under military or intelligence jurisdiction whereby the communalist quota was observed.

"The ministry of information became a fortress... under the command of an active officer. The ministry of education, its offices and schools, surrendered to intelligence authorities and the National Guard; naturally, the ministry of the interior was handed over to the security services. Communalism became a criterion of an official's fitness to be promoted and to occupy principal posts.

"The Ba'th planners shunned no means to fan a secret war of community against community, a war fed by daily provocations in every sector, in the army, in government, in schools, in quarters, factories, villages... between mountain and valley, between countryside and town, between province and province... to destroy the country's bases of natural life... and standards of civilized life."[68]

### Footnotes

1. al-Qawmiyya al-'arabiyya wa-mawquifuha min al-shuyu'iyya (Arab Nationalism and Its Attitude to Communism), 1944, 64 pp.
2. 'Aflaq and al-Bitar greatly differ in their mental dispositions, one being of a reflective, even visionary bend of mind, and the other more given to pragmatic reasoning. Both shared one political fate, namely being discarded by the victorious wing of the party they initiated.

3. As shown later, Fichte's **Reden an die deutsche Nation** had been a great source of inspiration.

   Unfortunately, no mention is made in this **Summary** of their confrontation with the forward marching alternative in the 'Thirties — German National Socialism.

   In 1941, Ba'th sent a message of support to the **coup d'état** government of Rashid 'Ali. See **al-Wathba**, a collection of depositions published in Baghdad during the rebellion.
4. Later on, when in power, Ba'th was charged with excessively harboring minorities and affording them undue influence.
5. In 1947, at the first Ba'th conference, the Ba'th party was formed; inevitably it embarked on power politics.
6. Translated from a leaflet.
7. "A critical study of the Political Ideas of Michel Aflaq," **Middle East Forum**, XLII, 2, 1966.
8. **'Ahd al-butula** ("Era of Heroism") and **Tharwat al-hayat** ("Richness of life,") in **Fi sabil al-Ba'th (Toward Resurrection)**, 3rd ed., (Beirut 1963).
9. **Ibid.,** p. 22.
10. **Ibid.** p. 26.
11. **Ibid.,** p. 28.
12. **Ibid.,** p. 30.
13. **Ibid.** (1950), p. 35.
14. **Ibid.** (1943), p. 75.
15. **Ibid.** (1944), pp. 195, 196. Hegel's impact on 'Aflaq's thinking is discussed in Michael W. Suleiman, **Political Parties in Lebanon** (1967), pp. 148-149; also by Khalidi, **op. cit.,** where 'Aflaq's pet idea of the "eternal Arab message" is regarded as "no more and no less than the Arab version of the other 'eternal message' of Mazzini's Italy, the Slavophiles' Russia and Revolutionary France."

   To A.H., an observer well-grounded in Arabic culture as well as in the contemporary history of the area, 'Aflaq seems to have become acquainted with Hegel and the "more or less mystical theories derived from him by European nationalists . . . about a people representing something **gotgewolltes**, a kind of collective creation, that has to find itself to develop further and further according to dialectical laws." — See **"Doktrin und Taktik der Baath-Partei," Neue Zürcher Zeitung,** April 21, 1963.
16. Eric Rouleau, **Le Monde Diplomatique,** September 6, 1967.
17. **Ibid.** Here we are also told that Zaki Arsuzi, an 'Alawi and originator of Ba'th as an old-new idea and name, considers 'Aflaq an "opportunist" and charges him with setting up the Committee of Aid to the pro-Axis revolt in 'Iraq in 1941 with the encouragement of the Vichy authorities in Syria.

   Arsuzi cherished ideas of his own on Arab resurrection, notably on pre-Islamic **(jahiliyya)** values.

   To Michael H. Van Dusen, **The Middle East Journal,** 1972, p. 133, n. 43, he "became a kind of intellectual father to those 'Alawi officers who dumped 'Aflaq and al-Baytar in 1966."
18. 1932, p. 401.
19. **Op. cit.,** p. 47.
20. **Inqilab,** as here conceived — inner transformation, also revolution — was later

supplanted by **thawra**. Depending on one's viewpoint, **inqilab** may also be applied to a coup (Za'im's **inqilab**). As against this, Bakr Sidqi's coup in 'Iraq in 1936 was extolled as **thawra**. Nadim al-Bitar, an exponent of Debray's idea of revolution in revolution, repudiates the externalized meaning of **inqilab**. But the mystique of **thawra** is hardly to be overcome.

21. Op. cit.
22. **Ma'rakat al-masir al-wahid (The One Destiny Battle)**, Beirut 1963, 3rd ed., pp. 170-172.
23. **al-Jil al-'arabi al-jadid** (The Arab New Generation), 1944, in **Fi sabil** . . . , p. 72; also al-'Uruba wa-'l-alam (Arabdom and Suffering), 1956, in **Ma'rakat** . . . pp. 103-105.
24. **Fi sabil** . . . , pp. 50-61.
25. **Ibid.**, pp. 129-136.
26. **Paris** 1919, p. 161: conscience signifie d'abord mémoire . . . conservation et accumulation du passé dans le présent.

    Mais toute conscience est l'anticipation de l'avenir . . . L'avenir est la; il nous appele, ou plutôt il nous tire a lui . . . Toute action est un empiétement sur l'avenir (pp. 5-6).
27. **Op cit.**, pp. 176-181.
28. **Ibid.**, pp. 83-91.
29. **Ibid.**, p. 35.
30. Quoted from **Addresses to the German Nation**, translated by R. F. Jones and G. H. Turnbull (1922).

    Fichte's views are pragmatically expounded by Sati'al-Husri in **Muhadarat fi nushu' al-fikra al-qawmiyya (Lectures on the Evolution of the National Idea)**, 1951. An ardent nationalist and apologist of 'Abd al-Nasir, al-Husri denounces 'Aflaq's "delusion and boast" ("we the carriers of the eternal Arab mission") about "the destiny that loaded us with this mission and also entrusted us with the right to command and speak by force and act in harshness." To 'Aflaq, no other party is capable of calling for a revolution such as was called for by Ba'th and "our movement became the destiny of the Arab nation at this age." Al-Husri finds similarities with "medieval scholastic thought" in phrases like "the basis of our eternal work . . . is belief" and "the destiny of our nation and our legacy, her spiritual value and her human essence willed that this belief finds expression within a community of youths very much removed from politics and license of politics." See **al-Iqlimiyya, judhuruha wa-budhuruha (Regionalism, Its Roots and Seeds)**, Beirut 1963, pp. 215-225.

    In fairness to 'Aflaq, these views of al-Husri had been voiced after Syria's secession from the UAR, furthermore, could be applied to Egypt's ideology, too.

    Husri's concept of secular nationalism stimulated the Arab Nationalists Movement at its initial stages.

    'Aflaq's rather confused positive and, in part, unhistorical concept of Islam didn't prevent opponents from reproaching Ba'th with heresy.

    A few excerpts from his **Fi sabil al-Ba'th:**

    "Islamic religion is part of the Arab personality and entity, not an addition to them. There is a deep link between Arab personality and Islamic personality, between Arab culture and Islamic culture, so that it is difficult to distinguish between them.

"In this area Islam is linked to the masses and never was divorced from their basic causes. By this it contrasts with the usual kind of religion in Europe, where the church was linked to feudalism, one of its strongest pillars. There it resisted potentialities of social, scientific and intellectual evolution and was a tool of coercion and terror and a form of intellectual stagnation.

"The Arab road to socialism views religion in its metaphysical aspect from the point of freedom of belief and respect for personal convictions. As to its social aspects, it does not try merely to establish relations of peaceful co-existence, if one may say so, as is the case with leftist parties in France and Italy. It benefits from religion as a 'positive legacy,' as a militant force not to be disregarded in many of the problems of liberation and unity."

31. See Ismet Chériff Vanly's pamphlet **The Persecution of the Kurdish People by the Baath Dictatorship in Syria**, which reproduces a "National, social and political study of the province of Djazireh" by Muhammad Talab Hilal, a Ba'th functionary.
32. **Ibid.**, p. 104.
33. **Ibid.**, pp. 98-99.
34. **Ibid.**, p. 98.
35. **Ibid.**, pp. 97-98.
36. **Ibid.**
37. **Fi sabil**, pp. 281-282.

Exigencies of the intermittent wars with the Kurds in 'Iraq seem to have made 'Aflaq change his views. In 1969 he helped the Ba'th government toward reaching an agreement with the Kurds that should "enable the Kurdish people to exercise their full national rights and autonomy" by uniting "administrative units shown by a census to have a Kurdish majority... into a single province." Of course, a census is to be correctly held and its results justly interpreted.

Hasan al-Bakr speaks of the project of decentralized administration as a "peaceful democratic solution of the Kurdish problem within one people and one homeland," to enable the Kurds exercise of their national rights **(al-Jumhuriyya,** January 1, 1970). "Educational rights" will make the Kurds and Turkomans a "cultural creative force." "The revolution believes in the ample place of the Kurds and other minorities in the progressive thought of the revolution." **(Ibid.,** February 12, 1970).

The agreement of 1970 still awaits implementation in main points, namely delimitation of the Kurdish area and real participation in government. As long as supreme power is vested in the Revolution Command Council, that is, in the Ba'th controlled army, Kurdish partnership in the government is illusory, and a "national charter" or "constitution" are to remain a smokescreen.

Meanwhile the tension between 'Iraq and the planned Federation of Arab Republics seems to have some bearing on Kurdish policies. Barzani's appraisal of the situation appears still valid:

As long as military dictatorships succeed one another in Baghdad, no solution of our problem is possible. The national rights of the Kurds and the integrity of the state of 'Iraq will be safeguarded only the day genuine democracy will prevail in 'Iraq. And democracy will be realizable only when all political formations agree to work in the interest of all components of the 'Iraqi nation (Éric Rouleau, **La deuxième révolution blanche, Le Monde,** August 2, 1968).

To Thierry Desjardins **(Le Figaro,** April 10, 1972), in the Kurdish view Baghdad had tried to make Barzani assassinated and intensely arabicizes the oil-bearing region of Kirkuk. True, the government made in the North a considerable effort on the economic plane, but, in spite of the National Front, the Ba'thists alone wield the real power. Barzani maintains that the country is ruled by the police under orders of Vice-President Saddam Husayn. It is he who wanted to liquidate him. The authorities expelled from the South 40,000 Kurds who had lived there for two or three generations under the pretext of being Iranian spies. There are no Kurds in the Revolution Command nor in the general staff or in the security forces. Enticed by the oil of Kirkuk and the Gulf, Moscow supports the worst of régimes.

By the end of 1972 relations between the régime and the Kurds worsened up to the verge of a civil war. In 1974, a full scale war is waged against the Kurds.

38. **Ibid.,** pp. 96-97.
39. **Ibid.,** p. 282.
40. **Ibid.,** p. 343.
41. **Ma'rakat** . . . , p. 76.
42. **Fi sabil** . . . , p. 340.
43. **Ibid.,** p. 186.
44. **Ibid.,** p. 187.
45. **Ma'rakat** . . . , p. 53.
46. **Fi sabil** . . . , pp. 111-112.
47. **Ibid.,** p. 112.
48. **Ibid.,** p. 110.
49. **Ibid.,** pp. 113, 114.
50. **Ma'rakat** . . . , p. 199.
51. **Fi sabil** . . . , pp. 272-273 (1958).
52. **Ma'rakat** . . . , p. 78 (1956).
53. **Ibid.,** p. 79.
54. **Ibid.,** p. 195 (1962).
55. **Ibid.,** p. 207.
56. See **al-Siyasa al-'arabiyya bayn al-mabda' wa-'l-tatbiq** (Arab **Politics Between Principle and Practice),** Beirut, 1960, pp. 32-33, 138, 142.
57. **Orient,** No. 36, 1965, pp. 163-167 (from **al-Ahrar,** October 27, 1965).
58. **Orient,** No. 37, 1966 (from **ibid.,** October 28, 1965).
59. See **Political and Social Thought in the Middle East,** ed. Kemal H. Karpat, London 1968, p. 292.
60. "Syria; War Psychosis as an Instrument of Government," **Swiss Review of World Affairs,** August 1967.
61. **"Quelques remarques sur le Ba'th,"** Orient, No. 31, 1964, p. 15.
62. **"Le rôle du Ba'th dans la genèse du nationalisme arabe,"** ibid., No. 35, 1965, p. 75.
63. **La Syrie ou la révolution dans la rancoeur,** Paris (Julliard), 1968, p. 248. See also Éric Rouleau, **"La Syrie Baasiste ou la fuite à gauche:** III, La revanche des campagnes," **Le Monde,** October 16, 17, 1966.

On the social motivations in the adherence to Ba'th in the 'Alawi region see M. H. Van Dusen, **op. cit.**, pp. 132-134. "There is little evidence that religious and communal factors entered into Ba'th Party politics or ideological commitments of 'Alawis until the 1960's. 'Alawis tend to believe that this issue did not become important until the 1960's and was not a factor until 1955."

64. **al-Tajriba al-murra (The Bitter Experiment)**, Beirut, 1967, pp. 158-159.
65. A.H., **"Syrien am Rand des Palästinakonflikts," Neue Zürcher Zeitung,** October 26, 1969, states bluntly that "Syria, **i.e.,** the Sunni majority is now ruled by officers from the 'Alawi minority."
66. See **al-Hayat,** February 26, 1966.
67. **Op. cit.,** pp. 338-340.
68. To Munif al-Razzaz, **op. cit.,** after the 1966 coup 'Alawi officers in power pursued a policy of pensioning non-'Alawi officers or transferring them to remote areas.

Some enlightening observations are to be found in Ayad al-Qazzaz's comparative study, "Political Order, Stability and Officers," **Middle East Forum, XLV, 2,** 1969.

Chapter VI

# TWO COMMANDS AND TWO WINGS

A natural source of dissension have been the relations between the national (all-Arab) command and the regional (Syrian) command of Ba'th. It seems impossible to untangle the strife of generations, the regional command representing more the younger generation, from personal rivalries and volte-faces. With the Ba'th coup of March 8, 1963, Damascus and Aleppo, ever since the focal points of power, had to share more and more of their power and representation with provincal towns (Latakia is an 'Alawi center, Salamiyye an Isma'ili and self-evidently Jabal Druz).[1] Faced with problems of implementation, the younger elements pressed harder for nationalization and vocal pan-Arab dynamism, which, in turn, bred intolerance, hence the much scorned "regionalism." But behind the ideological strife of civilians there simmered the strife of the military wing with the civilians and within themselves.*

On December 20, 1965, the national Command dissolved the regional Command and substituted itself for it by "adding to it a certain number of comrades from the Syrian region." The government headed by Zu'ayyen re-

---

* Elections to command in a secretive party could easily be manipulated. Added to this, with every split the commands doubled.

signed, and a few days later al-Bitar formed his fifth government.[2]

This is what 'Aflaq had to say on December 19, 1965, on the eve of the neo-Ba'th coup against the Ba'th régime of Amin al-Hafiz:

At this very moment when the crisis worsens and endangers the party and the people, we have come to ask you to restore order and apply the rule. We have historical responsibilities and the burden of a people threatened with extinction, of a cause and a party with a past of sacrifices ... In these circumstances, how could we deceive ourselves, pretend not to know or refuse to recognize a crucial truth: the infraction of our internal laws that the regional Command has not ceased to commit since its inception up to now? How could we be silent one second when this Command tramples our party's constitution? I don't accuse any one and do not want to renounce my friendship to any one, but the facts show that this Command today rules the party and the country and pretends to act lawfully, whereas it infringes a law laid down twenty years ago ...

... I feel that the party is threatened with destruction and that the revolution is coming to an end. In these circumstances one can not take recourse to half-measures. Only revolutionary solutions should be adopted; not for love of revolution and for sacrifice to fashion, but because only revolutionary measures can save us today ...

... The national Command has to assume historical responsibilities lest the disaster experienced in 'Iraq repeats itself, and the Arab people loses its faith in our party. The national Command can rise to the height of its historic responsibilities if it wishes to. Only the national Command can adopt a solution that will restore dignity to the party and hope to the citizens. Only the national Command can employ revolutionary means and punish the deviationists who have committed mortal errors, taking lightly the people's sacrifices and establishing an artificial structure which we oppose and which has no support. I am convinced that it falls within the duties of the national Command to take up its responsibilities at this grave hour and dissolve the regional Command, to punish the responsible ones and remove from leading positions those who may injure the party and the country.[3]

On the face of it, it was a normal procedure. Says Sulaiman al-Khish, minister of information, on December 21, 1965:

... power in Syria is held by the ruling party; all the political set-up of this country normally derives from the will of this party.

The party is organized in two commands: the national Command and the regional Command. The national Command solves all the questions concerning the party, because it is formed of representatives of various sections of the party in all the Arab countries. The regional Command, in every Arab country, executes the policy decided by the national Command. From the regional Command, acting in consultation with the national Command, emanate the state council, the cabinet and other political formations. When the revolutionaries of March 8, civilian as well as military, undertook their action against the secessionist government, they merely executed the will of the party communicated to them by the Command. It is for this reason that the movement of March 8 was called a revolution and not a *coup d'état*, because a *coup d'état* is a military action taken by some officers against the established power, whereas the military who brought about the movement acted on the orders of the party; consequently, they were revolutionaries and not authors of a *coup d'état*.

Since March 8, the party has not ceased to exercise civil and military authority. Whenever the national Command undertakes some changes in the government or in the party in Syria, foreign trumpets resound. The situation in the country is described as a state of tension between the warring military and civilians, within the military, or between the national Command and the regional Command. At this moment the national Command has deemed it necessary to effect some changes in the command positions of the party ... All the changes occurring in Syria within the party and the régime under the shield of the party in power and the national Command, are to be seen occurring within the normal frame of their competence.[4]

This version is to be contrasted with another statement. On February 18, 1966, 'Aflaq elucidated to a party audience in Damascus the meaning of the strife between the civilian and military wings of the party in terms of contention over power.

... The crisis in the party goes back to the first months of the March revolution (1963). We then felt strange things at our regional and national conferences, a tactic laid down, before the revolution, by the military commmittee. We do not deny that it had borne the brunt of the burden, but power dragged them into pitfalls remote from party morality. Some of these comrades conspired with second rank members of the Command in charge of organization after the revolution. They nurtured in them thirst for power, to leap to command posts. They involved them in a plan to beat the old Command and pervert the past of the party and its legacy, to enable the members of the military committee to get into the party command. These second-rank party men who had neither sufficient moral strength nor long experience to resist temptations set out to subvert organization and elections. But responsibility falls on those military men who had power in their hands and played on weak points of those young men, knowing that these young leaders are no obstacle on their way, easy to get rid of. This actually happened; less than one year after the revolution this group that believed to be able to lead the party was removed.

It is not true that we asked the military comrades to vote against the regional Command at the emergency conference of February 1964. We had no power over the military men nor over the civilians ... Circumstances facilitated their undertaking as well as our self-deception: the revolution in 'Iraq collapsed, which greatly affected the situation in Syria; added to this, those 'Iraq comrades who ruined the glorious revolution in 'Iraq came to Syria to cooperate with the regional Command — an extension of their faction-mongering — to destroy the revolution here. Surely, they came to ease their crime, to infiltrate the party and cure their bitterness. In those complex circumstances they were like bad children, incapable of responsibility; inevitably one had to stop their ruinous work.

When the regional emergency conference assembled — in this atmosphere — the military comrades asked for an enlarged part at the conference. Out of good will we had not quarrelled much, so that we faced a block with definite positions. Many closed their eyes for fear that the revolution would perish; they took advantage of it, got the lion's part (seven to fifteen) in the regional Command, and put through the list they wanted to. When we became aware of this error — with no malice — we thought they may be excused, fear lest the revolution perishes may have induced them to increase the number of the military in the Command. We sensed that such a great number of military in the Command constitutes a deviation and that differences among the military could be a grave danger to the revolution.

It began with ignoring the national Command and neglecting its decrees and instructions. What would you do if you were in the national Command's place? The revolution in 'Iraq perished, the reaction in Syria took courage anew, and you remember the troubles in Hama. There was only one means: advice and warning for fear of seeing reproduced in Syria what had happened in 'Iraq.

You wonder why the secretary-general left the country ... I left for Bonn not to plot with imperialism, because I felt that the only solution was to hold a national conference outside Syria, beyond the reach of the government ... and I returned when the national Command became convinced that the crisis should be exposed. We deliberated at length, took decisions, but we faced a rebellion on the part of the government ... I do not say the regional Command because this became the government.

The national Command is the true party command, because Ba'th is a unionist party and its only command is the national command epitomizing the supreme interest of the Arab nation and only in so far as the regional commands obey the national command is their existence legitimate. The national Command has its defects, and yet it is more farsighted and worthy of leadership; therefore it should be respected and obeyed. To doubt this amounts to ruining the party and is an inexcusable crime.

... Some of our military comrades slid into pitfalls towards factionalism and dominance over the party and the people, through opportunism and nepotism, which nearly put an end to the revolution. We do not deny their struggle and their part in the revolution, but we should not sacrifice the party nor the revolution

144

because of their past services to the party and the revolution.

How is the situation in the army to be remedied? How is the army to be barred from meddling in politics? How is the interference of some comrades, of which the vast majority of the military comrades is innocent, to be stopped? When we speak of removing the military from politics, there is no question of setting up a barrier between the army and the party and political action. On the contrary, we want to strengthen the link between them, deepen the ideological consciousness and retain the strongest elements in their belief in the party ... We seek to rectify the function of the army in a revolutionary society led by the party. The army is a people's army, in which there are strugglers linked to the cause of the masses, members of the party like others — workers, peasants or intellectuals. They have the right to live the life of the party to the full ... As others, they have full right of criticism and self-criticism. What we want to avert is a plurality of military activity and leadership in the party and in the government: when the party appoints one of the military comrades to direct the party, this comrade should not retain his military capacity, he becomes a party man and a people's leader. There is no true revolutionary government in the world whose chiefs, formerly military commanders, remain in their units ... Against this, in the dissolved regional Command some of the seven military members still command military units and others retain their military rank and their connections with the army while being in the Command and in the government. When an officer is simultaneously in the Command and in his military unit he is no party leader nor people's leader, his language is not that of doctrine and of objective party dialogue, but that of force and arms ... Clearly, it means that real power is in the army, in army units not in the party Command. What is, then, the rôle of the formations of workers, peasants, students and women?

... Ours is a genuine Leftist party. But individual judgments vary in a doctrinal socialist party, absorbed as it is in trials and battles and facing unexpected events and circumstances. Some persons lean, if slightly, to what is called moderation or some rightism, depending on the circumstance ... It is inferred that some ministers hail from certain circles, and theirs is not a mentality of the toiling class. Do you know why this matter was not discussed in the party plainly, audaciously and objectively? ... The reason is that the would-be leftists distorted leftism by their opportunist designs and reckless infantile minds. When the party sees that the allegations of the left are due to opportunism, love of dominance, recklessness and are a menace to the revolution and the country's independence, it is obliged somewhat to refrain from moderation ... Some persons in the government have intellectual arguments and convictions, but this opportunism made it impossible to discuss them or some Rightist inclinations persons may some time display. Leftism is not extremism, incitement, nor impudent exaggerations, or slander; it is realistic analysis, objective scientific mind, not influenced by passions, ambitions, passing impressions; it is dominated by a scientific spirit, impartiality and integrity ...

You know what the Communists did in 'Iraq in 1959, their atrocities and beastly crimes in Kirkuk and in Mosul, their alliance with 'Abd al-Karim Qasim. You know the nature of this anti-national (shu'ubi), dictatorial era. We were convinced that reaction of the masses against the Communists is inevitable and that the reactionary and rightist forces would make use of it to wage a war of extermination against the Communists, to strengthen the rightist ideas and positions.

The national Command deemed it its duty to caution the party in 'Iraq not to get influenced by the conservative and rightist circles in 'Iraq and be dragged into vengeful battles with the Communists. True, the Communists were corrupted and they did what they did because of great and grave perversion, but one perversion can't be remedied by another. ... As for those who committed crimes, they should be brought to court after the elimination of 'Abd al-Karim Qasim's era.

We sent a message to this effect two years before the Ramadan revolution (1963) but the regional Command in 'Iraq was unanimously resolved on execution, which they did over nine months. Every month they executed a number of Communists — a hundred and fifty and a hundred and twenty — in view of the whole world. It was a fools' work, because they immediately incurred the enmity of three quarters of the world to the Ramadan revolution. 'Abd al-Nasir, too, was against it.

... Progressive circles in the world branded us Fascists and agents of imperialism. ... Of course, we know that 'Abd al-salam 'Arif and some military men from reactionary and conservative circles didn't understand the spirit of the revolution ... In view of the crimes of the Communists, they sought revenge and suggested those actions to the Command. Was the command of the revolution weak to such a degree? We don't put the blame for this misdeed on 'Abd al-salam 'Arif, a conservative Rightist wooing religious circles, nor on reactionary Rightist vengeful military men. We blame the Ba'thists who scorned the instructions and warnings of the national Command.

This case was submitted to the regional conference in Baghdad and to the sixth national conference. When the revolution in 'Iraq was thwarted, these infants who had slaughtered Communists jumped towards communism and, to cover up their crimes, pretended to have become Leftists. This is opportunism. They were also against 'Abd al-Nasir to the utmost. But, after having ruined the revolution, and out of resentment against the party, they started making advances to 'Abd al-Nasir and came closer to him.[5]

According to another version of this speech, the military men "succumbed to temptations of power to form themselves as a new ruling class with unlimited privileges." They prevented the national Command from passing on instructions to the party cells and sections in Syria. The special services of the army were used to conduct a campaign of denigration against the "historical chiefs" of the party.

... This situation ... is a result of a preconceived plan. They wish, under the cover of Ba'th, to transform the ideology, politics, organization and ethics of the party. They accuse the old militants — calling us *dépassés* — of immobilism. Never were we against rejuvenation of the ranks. Our first publications attest to this. Our ideology is not rigid; it evolves ... 95 per cent of the militants are ignorant of the party's past, its ideas, its programmes.

The military committee makes the army subject to its dictate in the name of the party and the party in the name of the army. Leftism is only a pretext. Not by "outbidding, demagoguery and unreasonable proposals" is one's socialist consciousness proved. At least a number of these who boast of being more Leftist than the old militants live as "princes" since the party came into power. The most extremist among us, a comrade from 'Iraq, lived far more comfortably than the "right wing deviationists." Sumptuous cars, palaces, remunerations, nothing was missing at the table. Regionalism threatens the national unity of Ba'th.[6]

On February 23, 1966, a military junta seized control of the government, ousted the president, Amin al-Hafiz, after having wiped out most of the hundred-man Bedouin guard and demolished his house. The junta appointed, in the name of a Provisional Command of Ba'th, Dr. Nur al-din al-Atasi head of the state and Dr. Yusuf Zu'ayyen premier. The party press charged Salah al-din al-Bitar, the ousted premier, with having contemplated the denationalization of industry. His statement about Vietnam is said to have shown secret sympathy for American imperialist aggression.[7]

### Declaration of the Provisional Regional Command

Toiling masses of our people, comrades combatants everywhere in our great Arab homeland.

The revolution of March 8, 1963, came to be an authentic revolution against backwardness and dismemberment, a war against imperialism and reaction, a victory of the will of the toiling masses against their exploiters and an implementation of the Arab nation's aims at unity, freedom and socialism. The Arab Socialist Ba'th party that generated this revolution and, to protect her, launched hard battles against the people's enemies, expected those enemies to infiltrate its ranks and make use of those who rode the revolutionary tide with no conviction or belief, by way of domination and personalism — waverers, cowards and those who are intellectually and historically connected with political trafficking.

The forces of reaction and backwardness tried to penetrate the heart of the revolution, to turn it from its definite way and lead to an abyss of monolithic power, haggling and tumbling. These forces were able to penetrate the party by way of the personalism of Amin al-Hafiz, the feebleness of Muhammad 'Umran,* the

* Assassinated in Tripoli, Lebanon, in 1971.

149

rightism of Salah (al-din) al-Bitar and the egotism of Michel 'Aflaq. In the last months they dragged this party to the verge of disintegration and ruin. The party that protected its revolution against all its enemies, was aware of their plotting. Having repeatedly warned them and employed means authorized by the constitution, it decided to do battles and wipe them out — a reminder to those who think of hurting the party or destroying the revolution from inside or out.

During those two months the party exercised patience, warning them, presenting memoranda from all branches of the party — both civilian and military — but they paid no attention. They were asked to call a regional conference to deal with what they have undertaken, but they refused and threatened to expel from the party all those who would attend that conference. They were asked to call a national conference, the highest authority of the party, or an emergency session of the national Council, but they refused ... They continued plotting more and more. For all their strong incompatibility, al-Hafiz and 'Umran both favored sectarianism, tribalism and regionalism in the army; they set off factions and made alliances with the enemies of the revolution so as to ruin the revolution and her commanding party.

'Aflaq and al-Bitar plotted and ruined the party on both political and popular level ... sowed dissension in its ranks and stretched their dirty hands to every cheap opportunist or plotting enemy, seeking their support against the party and its revolution ...

... 'Aflaq and al-Bitar thought that al-Hafiz's and 'Umran's militarism would be able to protect them and they could shield al-Hafiz and 'Umran with the party ...

He who betrays Ba'th inevitably betrays his own people; he who despises the party and its organizations will one day despise the will of his people and waste the

150

potencies of his fatherland; he who fears the application of democracy in his party and shrinks from facing its conferences is not able to implement democracy for his people.

Amin al-Hafiz thought he could, by way of his secret services and a handful of mercenaries, destroy the party and set up a régime of military dictatorship. But he forgot that the party that believes in collective leadership is able to destroy any individual who wishes to install a personal dictatorial régime ... it will never permit a new 'Arif (of 'Iraq) to appear ...

Masses of our Arab people, the Ba'th party, ever since an enemy of personal régimes of any kind and military domination of any kind and guise, maintains that the army in backward countries can either be a professional force used by foreign or local monopolies to strangle the people's aspirations, or be changed by revolutionary movements into a popular force adhering to the people's interests. The experiment of an ideological army is the only way to transform an army into a combative vanguard whose mission is to implement the objectives of the Arab nation and her masses, thereby preserving its military character and discipline. This can be accomplished only by tying the army to the party organically and definitely, demonstrating a new revolutionary concept of discipline based on belief rather than fear of death ...

As to Muhammad 'Umran whom the party had earlier convicted and exiled for conspiring against the revolution and the party and disrupting the unity of the army, they brought him back, out of eagerness to defy the will of the party and its combatants and to carry out — they by his agency and he by their agency — the designs of the enemies of the party and of the revolution, the people's enemies ...

After the splits that obstructed the party's struggle and disrupted its historical march, this mentality reverts to eliminating the party in this region after having struck it and its revolution in 'Iraq ...

... this 'Aflaq mentality tried to set up barriers between the party organizations in the Arab homeland and use them against each other.

Today ... we confirm our adherence to the national unity of the party and to the legality encroached upon and abused by the 'Aflaq mentality.

Masses of our Arab people: The Ba'th party, proceeding from the decisions of the national and regional party conferences, announces that the revolution is with the toiling deprived classes against their exploiters, with the unionist forces against the reactionary secessionist forces, with the revolutionary socialist forces against the Zionist imperialist forces ...

The regional Command, assuming the leadership of the revolution, declares:

1. It fully adheres to the resolutions of the party's national and regional conferences, to the phased program and to the policy declaration of the previous government;

2. It will call to account all those who caused harm to the revolution and the people;

3. It will cite the arrested before a special supreme party court;

4. It will promptly deal with the economic situation, compromised by the disputes which rent the command of the revolution, by consolidating and developing the socialist measures based on scientific foundations;

5. It considers itself a temporary command until the convening of the first regional conference, whose date will be jointly set by the heads of the civil and military sections of the party;

6. It will invite the representatives of the party or-

ganizations in other Arab countries to call a
national conference . . .[8]

A speech by Nur al-din al-Atasi, head of the state, on the
anniversary of Ba'th presses new notions (scientific
method, intellectual or theoretical premises, strategy of national action), but the "eternal mission" is present, too.
The coup was a "movement" to restore to Ba'th its "true
nature."[9]

The movement of February 23 was a historic necessity
not only in the life of the party. Actually, it restored to the
party its true nature, confirmed its intellectual premises,
enriched its experience, solidified its confidence in its
future and uncovered the ability of the party militants to
fulfill the tasks they avowed. It was a victory of the
eternal mission they had decided to fulfill. The ninth party conference was living evidence of the solidity of the
party's national unity, a definite proof of its constant
ability to develop. Moreover, the conference showed the
beginning of a road to a clear future. At this conference,
the party set forth a strategy of national action from
theoretical premises and defined the dimensions of the
present Arab struggle, assuming . . . that the people's
war of liberation is a scientific method to launch the next
battle. The conference confirmed the necessity of collaboration between the Ba'th revolution in this region
and the struggle of all the comrades in the rest of the regions of the Arab homeland, considering this struggle
mutually complementary.
    . . . The plot of September 28 (1966)[10] was the best
proof of complete coordination between imperialism,
Zionism and reaction.

The background of the movement of February 23, 1966, is
further elaborated by Malik al-Amin, member of the post-
coup national Command. It sounds a belated answer to

'Aflaq. It is revealing in its phrase-mongering as well as in intimations of facts. The cadres of Ba'th, both civilian and military, had to resort to arms "before the crime to the party, the revolution, the republican practices, the liberation movement and the national progress of the Arab nation is consummated." We are told that "a revolutionary movement is endowed with constant innovating vitality and active capacity to evolve in width towards comprehension through clear vision and in depth toward solid positions and attitudes grasping the reality of the authentic problems." Both characteristics "enable the movement to march towards crystallization of its aims and delineation of its strategy and tactic to implement them."

This is not to be achieved by a mere "genuine spontaneity" or "revolutionary theory." It is "dialectically linked to the social composition of the revolutionary movement and to an adequate method of combat," in line with a "comprehensive scientific analysis of the actual data of the rising and successive stages of struggle." Without this link "revolutionary theory (theory of revolutionary speech) becomes a screen of rightist backward hesitant attitudes lacking revolutionary control and a clear method of struggle" —in fact, "an ugly screen to a counter-revolutionary movement."

The first stage in the rightist project of confrontation was the attempt to obscure the theoretical premises decided upon by the sixth national conference, in October 1963. From the beginning till the end of the seventh national conference, in February 1964, the cadres in all the party formations had to face those who joined the party for personal motives, "groups of traditional careerists, of feeble-minded waverers, professional renegades and plotting infiltrators, of collapsing weaklings, of leftist impostors."

Then and later (from February 1964 up to February 1966) the party cadres had to face a "petrified Rightist mentality" fearing open confrontation and "trying to put it off by trickery and by feigning conformity with the party cadres."

Meanwhile a number of genuine members became victims of treachery and despair. At all the stages, these groups pursued one aim: plotting against the party as a "historical movement," disfiguring the party, and "malice against the party's living cells."

When the premises of the sixth conference were made public, under persistent pressure, the Right, having failed to fasten the party thought from behind, tried to push it backward by way of Razzaz's "doctrinal report," presented to and rejected by the eighth national conference in April 1965.

To keep the command positions for another confrontation, this time aiming at the party structure and its institutions, the Right gave in, only to take "fast illegitimate measures" contrary to the party statutes. It dissolved the party Command in the Syrian region, named new members to the Command who had no confidence of the cadres at the elections and, to serve their "dubious murderous schemes," began to make arrangements in the party, the state and the armed forces.

They refused to call a regional conference or a national conference. Clearly, their aim was to do away with the party and the revolution for the benefit of colonialism and imperialist monopolies and their agents.

On September 8, 1966, a plot of collusion between the Right and reaction, headed by a malicious plotter, was foiled. On June 10 (1967) the plotter came back equipped with instructions from the "nests of reaction to reap the fruits of aggression." Salah (al-din) al-Bitar had no objection to financial dealings (by checks) with nests of reaction. "Comradely spirit" again brought together Michel 'Aflaq with the master of apostasy (saffah al-ridda) of 18 November in 'Iraq, after having taken part in a decision to remove him from the party.[11]

The events of February 23, 1966, are further elucidated in a declaration of the post-coup national Command. Here psychology is the main tool of analysis. "Mentality" is the source of evil.

To return to al-Amin:

On that day — an historical turning point — the cadres of Ba'th moved to stop the Rightist deviation that tried to raid the party from within and strike the deepest Arab revolutionary movement for the benefit of the imperialist.

Ba'th is the first organized doctrinal movement that analyzed Arab reality scientifically and devised (at its first conference in 1943) a revolutionary answer to its challenges. The scientific answer offered by the first conference of the party (in 1947) was the ennobling slogans of the contemporary Arab revolution — unity, freedom and socialism . . . Ba'th took a basic part in establishing the union of 1958, in toppling the reactionary régime in 'Iraq, in the battles of South Yemen and in supporting the Algerian revolution . . . This struggle was crowned by the revolutions of February and March in 'Iraq and Syria.

. . . But the alien rightist personalist mentality deprived the party and the masses of many chances of victories. The party cadres uncovered it long ago and fought to check it and avert its harm, to correct some of it or eliminate it.

This oscillating mentality used methods and political manoeuvers, factionalism and personal loyalties to evade confrontation with the party and observation of the resolutions of conferences and the internal statutes.

. . . It continually tried to exercise personal and paternalistic (fawqi) rule, hamper and ruin the efforts of the party cadres to solidify the bases of a democratic revolutionary mass movement, indispensable for the existence and success of any real centrism and true collective leadership. Owing to its subjective deficiency, it was unable to grasp and pursue the deep aspirations of the masses to implement a comprehensive unionist socialist revolution. It worked to change the party to a political block to be used in the market of political maneuvers and struggle over power with certain reactionary and bourgeois factions.

On account of its social, intellectual and political make-up, it was unable to lead an organized revolutionary mass movement whose élite represents the party, so that it made various efforts to distort this historical movement and stifle it in a morass of reformist phased policies, to turn it from a historical movement representing the will of large masses and their hope for liberation to a passing phenomenon, like other barren movements in our contemporary history, were it not for the intellectual ingenuity of the party and its genuine interpretation of the laws of contemporary Arab unionist revolution and the strength of will of its fighters and their organic link with the toiling people's masses . . .

In 'Iraq the deviations of this mentality created proper conditions for a successful counter-revolution. They deepened the struggle and conflicts with progressive forces and through collusion with the right wing brought about downfall.

In Syria this mentality tried the same role. Its deviations made their mark on régime and party. Lastly, when things seemed ripe, it tried to hit the party with a reactionary leap and called for an opening to exploiters and opportunists and enemies of the masses.

Inevitably, this mentality bared and compromised itself, since the party cadres in their conferences (sixth, seventh, and eighth) laid down ideological and organizational principles that made it difficult to use the party apparatus for its dubious maneuvers.

The party's task is to mobilze the toiling masses in the region, to attack the reactionary interests and monopolies and to meet with progressive forces to generate an Arab revolution and march in the frontline of the world struggle of liberation.

The task of the revolution is to make the Syrian region a revolutionary base radiating on both Arab and world areas.[12]

On the fifth anniversary of the Ba'th coup in 'Iraq, Malik al-Amin throws some light on the course of events since the overthrow of the monarchy in 1958. "Persuasion," he says, should have been applied to other "progressive forces" as well as "self-persuasion,"that is, self-criticism. In fact, "unity of progressive forces" has been a slogan ever since. But a common front of all "progressive forces," all aiming at the elimination of non-progressive forces, implicitly a common front of various army factions, would presuppose some genuine democratic process of decision making and governing, a civilized relationship between "majority" and "minority." "Self-persuasion" was not applied even with regard to the factions within Ba'th. The men of the Ba'th government, overthrown in February 1966, are referred to as a "treacherous Rightist gang" given to "domination, exploitation, and opportunism."

It is a classical piece of veiled argument vaguely recalling that of al-Hajjaj. Added to this, verbalism bound to submerge even a revolutionary idiom. A mind, enshrined as it is in an originally mindful language, serves a state of near-mindlessness.

The revolution of February 8, 1963 (in 'Iraq) is the first mass movement in the Third World in which civilians—workers, fellahin, students, women, revolutionary intellectuals—joined the people's army sector under the command of a doctrinal revolutionary militant party. It had a great part in putting an end to the criminal secessionist gang in Syria on March 8, 1963.

From the start some progressive forces, extending the errors of the past, have forgotten sound logic and ignored the main conflict between the forces of liberation and progress and the forces of imperialism, regional and capitalist reaction, and treated the revolution inimically. After a short while the revolution, driven by a temporary reaction, succumbed to the same error, forgot the main conflict and turned to the elimination of those progressive forces, whereas scientific analysis requires a just attitude to those forces, through persuasion and self-persuasion, fully comprehending the people's forces that have any interest in the revolution and the forces that threaten the destiny of the revolution by resenting all the progressive forces and exploiting all the toiling people's classes, forces that are linked to extorting imperialist monopolies and sustain the backward and shabby social, political and economic conditions.

Why were children buried alive, women's stomachs cut open and fellow citizens skinned in Kirk ık, why were martyrs of Umm al-Tubul* put to death, why were massacres perpetrated in Baghdad, Basra, Mosul before the revolution of February 8? The same reasons made some progressive forces inimical to the régime of February 8 that was unjustifiably marked by continuous violence against these progressive forces. These reasons boil down to one basic reason, namely ignoring or forgetting or leaping over the main strife between two real poles in Arab society in general, and in 'Iraq in particular ... This struggle between progressive forces in 'Iraq at different stages was unnatural, resulting from a dubious plan of agents who infiltrated the ranks of progressive forces.

These two revolutions of June (1958) and February

---

*In the Mosul area a site of massacres of alleged pan-Arabists at the hands of partisans of Qasim after the al-Shawwaf rebellion in 1959.

(1963) failed mainly because of the strife between the progressive forces.

The Arab Socialist Ba'th Party has announced that the rightist gang that slipped into its ranks at the stage of preparations for the revolution and at preceding stages, the dubious elements which rode the crest of the masses and infiltrated the National Guard as well as official and party institutions after the revolution, exploited the circumstances and the facts of struggle between progressive forces to deprive the revolution of natural pillars. By continuing its dubious actions and by its ugly behavior, this gang distorted the image of the party and of the revolution ... in the minds of the masses ... This gang, now spit out from the party, once its identity and interests that conflict with those of the people's toiling masses had been exposed, stirred up a bloody artificial struggle inside the party and between the party and the progressive forces, in keeping with the interests of its masters in the oil companies and plotting imperialist circles, and with its aspirations for domination, exploitation and opportunism.

True, in its short span of life and under the circumstances, the revolution could not accomplish any of her phased program worth mentioning. True, the revolution committed grave strategic and tactical errors in her dealings with progressive forces and in her confrontation with the natural enemies of the revolution inside and outside. But the decisive factor that doomed the revolution to failure is the dubious Rightist plot of notorious Rightist elements and elements seemingly fitting the party who passed through her gateways ...

Inside the party it was a struggle between a deviant treacherous Rightist gang and opportunism boasting verbal Leftism, totally ignoring party organs and neglecting the party structure within the military sector, so that the noble combatants among the military comrades were tossed between eagerness to enhance the standing of the party and the revolution and the faults and allegations of plotting deviationist elements in command of the party and the régime.

The progressive forces in 'Iraq are called upon to uncover in their ranks all the opportunist and scheming elements that provoked bloodshed between the progressive forces after the revolutions of June 14 and of February 8. The cadres of these forces and their masses that fought Nuri Sa'id, the Baghdad pact and all the imperialist plots, should meet in militant brotherhood in view of the unity of their real enemy and of their real interests.

A front of all revolutionary and progressive forces and elements is a decisive factor in moving 'Iraq to serious participation in steering the course of contemporary Arab revolution against imperialism, Zionism and reaction, in our present battle and the coming battles with imperialism and its political, military, economic and social bases in the Arab homeland, in the Third World and in the world as a whole.[13]

On the twentieth anniversary of the party, "basic principles" are elaborated. Ardor of adepts of a new creed conjures up ironclad panaceas. The idiom is that of proselytes of "revolutionary Marxism." There is no "scientific" precision or consistency of presentation, but the gap in the ideology of the two wings is made wide indeed.

Fusion of the national struggle and the class struggle is the way to build an Arab socialist society.

The national party organizations and their combatant cadres are the vanguard in the struggle of the masses against reaction, dismemberment, imperialism and Zionism.

Scientifism and revolutionism are two basic hallmarks of the party's ideology.

... Our national ideology is a scientific ideology.

Naturally, a scientific mind is always alert to reality, feeds on every experiment and rejects preconceived patterns.

Only the scientific character of this ideology enables the Arab people to rid itself of its medieval mentality. ... The simultaneous national and socialist struggle requires the implementation of three revolutions at once: scientific revolution on an intellectual plane, economic revolution to change feudal and semi-capitalist relations to socialist relations, so as to create a material base for serious economic expansion, and revolution against dismemberment and its dregs on all levels.

... The scientifism of our ideology makes it possible to confront all aspects of backwardness in the cultural, social and economic life of the Arabs. The scientific mentality alone is capable of making the contemporary Arab revolution a total one, so that revolutionary changes in all levels and aspects of Arab life will accompany each other.

Only an incisive scientific critique and a profound analysis of all aspects and traditions of Arab society can prepare the conditions for uprooting all negative, ugly and inoperative aspects in this society ...

The second ideological characteristic of our party is revolutionism. The method of national socialist scientific thinking in social and economic analysis is a dialectical one; it proceeds from acknowledging the existence of a collision in national society and of class struggle marked by a tendency toward simultaneous realization of two goals: national unity and elimination of exploitation. This conflict will not be composed automatically or end by the good will of benevolent reformers, nor by accumulating partial reforms within the society we are fighting against.

Transition from one social régime to another, especially in backward countries, has to come about by one specific leap (not gradual) that eliminates the rotten economic bases of society and its political, juridical, social and cultural structures.

Ba'th ideology rejects, unhesitatingly and decisively, reformist opportunist views of drawn out and slow gradualism in social change. By no means can partial and secondary reforms lead to the complete transformation of the present framework of Arab society and its economic, social and cultural content. Again, a reformist trend makes a negative imprint on the composition of a revolutionary party and slowly moves it towards the traditional framework of the present society, so that the party submits to it . . .

Revolutionary ideology is the natural and sole solution to the problems of backward countries.[14]

### Footnotes

1. See Marcel Colombe, **"Remarques sur le Ba'th et les institutions politiques de la Syrie d'aujourd'hui,"** Orient, No. 37, 1966, pp. 59-60.
2. **Ibid.,** p. 63.
3. J. Jabale, "**La crise du Ba'th," Cahiers de L'Orient Contemporain** (from **Ra'y al-'Amm, Kuwayt, January 12, 1966).**
4. **Ibid.** (from B.B.C., December 23, 1965, **al-Ba'th**, December 22, 1965).
5. **al-Hayat**, February 25, 1966.
6. Edouard Saab, **op. cit.,** pp. 225-228.
7. Thomas F. Brady, **New York Times,** February 27, 1966.
8. **J. Jabale, ibid.,** (from B.B.C., **al-Ba'th**, February 24, 1966).
9. **al-Thawra**, April 8, 1967.
   Another version: "imperialism and its reactionary and bourgeois agents punctured (the union) so that the tragedy of the detestable secession took place." — **al-Ba'th**, April 7, 1967.
10. The affair of Hatum, **infra.**
11. **al-Ba'th**, February 23, 1970.
12. **Ibid.,** February 25, 1968.
13. **Ibid.,** February 9, 1968.
14. **Ibid.,** April 7, 1967.
    For the background of events see Gordon H. Torrey, "The Ba'th — Ideology and Practice," **Middle East Journal,** Vol. 23, 4, 1969.

Chapter VII

# REPERSONALIZATION OF POWER

The story has not ended, only the course of *reductio ad absurdum* in point of politics has quickened. One is tempted, at a risk of over-simplification, to trace the conflagration within neo-Ba'th mainly to one source, namely to power rivalries between Salah Jadid, secretary adjoint of the regional Command, and Hafiz al-Asad. Jadid's career is well worth pursuing back to 1965, when he was ousted by Amin al-Hafiz from the post of chief of staff in September and took up his activities in the civilian wing of Ba'th. The relationship between Jadid and al-Asad, both "strong men" and 'Alawis, may have stimulated their views to the point of an ideological superstructure.* In the heat of violent argument over issues like "regular" and "popular" war, economic priorities, relations with countries of "Arab reaction," attitudes, not unbridgeable, had moved more and more apart. It should be added, that the civilian wing under Jadid controlled also the al-Sa'iqa, a Ba'th sponsored Palestinian formation.

On February 28, 1969, al-Asad placed his tanks at

---

* Ideologically motivated violence didn't spare Jadid's family. Salah supported the "liquidation of his brother Ghassan," an officer belonging to the Syrian National Social Party (see M. H. Van Dusen, **op. cit.**, p. 134).

strategic positions in Damascus, while the fourth regional Ba'th conference, in its majority favoring Jadid's views, discussed the differences between the two factions. 'Abd al-Nasir, too, made an effort to bring about reconciliation. A compromise solution left the post of secretary adjoint in the hands of Jadid, whereas Premier Zu'ayyen and Makhus, foreign minister, were removed from the government. Al-Asad held tightly his dual position as minister of defense and chief of the air force.[1]

In November 1970, the tenth national conference of Ba'th denounced, at its extraordinary session, the "dualism of power" exercised by al-Asad "for the benefit of military organs and to the detriment of the party," thus "sabotaging the leading role of the party in the army," and demanded "abolition of all the privileges enjoyed by the minister of defense." Al-Asad and Tallas, the chief of staff, were called to "give up their present work for another in the party and in the revolution." The conference also voiced opposition to a political solution of the Israel-Arab conflict, to be resolved only by a "people's war." On November 13, al-Asad and Tallas, in collusion with their partisans in the army, overthrew the government. "Irony of history wanted that the same men who relied on the army in their plot against the old civilian command were in their turn overthrown the moment they sought to free Ba'th from the tutelage of the army."[2]

What happened sounds like a variant of events in the history of the caliphs. The setting is modern: unlike February 1966, the famous 70th Tank Brigade, stationed near Damascus and commanded by 'Izzat, Jadid's cousin, served to shield al-Asad from the would-be revolutionaries or, depending on one's view, from the leftist constitutionalists.[3] 'Izzat Jadid was lured to Damascus and taken prisoner. The recent role of the Sunni officers in the army ought to be clarified.[4] Added to this, the attitude of al-Atasi, president conciliator since February 1966, who, at times of crises, would retire to his native Homs and here, shielded by 500 to 1000 armed partisans at his disposal, wait for emissaries from Damascus asking to devise a compromise.[5]

The artificiality of the very existence of the party organs, whose composition is manipulated by the men in power, was once more demonstrated through Asad's arbitrary appointment of a "provisional regional Command" of the party. The considerable following of the hard-liners in the cadres counted for nothing; the "base" is hardly capable of resistance. Al-Asad broadened the base of the government by including members of the Arab Socialist Union, Socialist Unionists, Arab Socialists and two Communists.

Asad's actions had been crowned by his being elected President of the Arab Syrian Republic for a seven-year term by 99.2 percent of the votes. In the religious and social context of Syria, a president of 'Alawi descent may prove an ominous innovation. The President had also become Secretary-General of the national Command of Ba'th.

An appointed People's Council of 173 members comprises eighty-seven Ba'thists, eleven Arab Socialist Unionists, eight Communists, seven progressists, five independent Ba'thists, four Socialist Unionists, four Arab Socialists of al-Hawrani's tendency, three former Ba'thists, two independent Nasserites, three of the Muslim clergy, three merchants, thirty-six representatives of the General Peasants' Union.

While Ba'th remains the "leading party," al-Asad points also to "popular unity as essential to the progress of Syria."

The new participants in the government seem to harbor sober thoughts about the new venture. Whereas Ba'th conceded to other parties a 49 percent share in the Progressive National Front, it retains the army and the school as its exclusive domain of activity.[6] Jamal Atasi, leader of the "Nasserites," points out:

We supported general al-Asad not as a dictator in power but to promote the movement of the masses and resolve our problems with Ba'th. Our strategy is to make a piece-meal overture, without challenging the power of Ba'th, which could make Ba'th withdraw into itself and put us back into a vicious circle in which we have been moving for years.[7]

To Khalid Bagdash, leader of the Communist party, "Ba'th is inclined to think that participation in the government and the People's Council is by itself a true united front." This is a "static manner" of reasoning. The Front should function organically and be present in every city, every borough, every factory. This is the only way to mobilize the population. All the "progressive forces" should be able to express themselves freely. He marvels at a paradox that the communist party has two members in the government whereas her publications are clandestine.[8]

While al-Asad was seizing power, the above mentioned national conference decided to form a commission that should "call to account those who enriched themselves, took advantage of their positions and wronged fellow citizens." The republican formations and the party militants "face a military rebellion and fight it to restore power to the party and the masses." Hafiz al-Asad is charged with petty bourgeois aspirations.[9]

The national Command of Ba'th speaks of a "military rebellion of a handful of adventurers," "vestiges of rightist rotten mentality" and "dissident seceders from the sacred cause of their nation and homeland." They intend to impede fida'i work and eliminate it; to abolish the progressive achievements in the political, economic and social fields; to ruin the development projects, especially the experiment of national oil production. This "treacherous rebellion" is to end in failure.[10]

On November 16, the national Command expelled al-

Asad and Tallas from the party. "A clique seized the command of the Syrian army against the elected party commands and the resolutions of the tenth national conference in its extraordinary session." The Command points to the "hidden motivations" of the rebellion, its "link to imperialist projects," "emptying the revolution of the party of any progressive and masses content," to "elimination of the movement of Arab liberation and linking the Syrian region to areas of imperialist influence by way of throwing it in the midst of reaction and oil monopolies." To serve "liquidatory solutions" to the Palestine problem, the strategy of the party was not carried out. The regional Command elected at the extraordinary fourth regional conference is considered legitimate. The so called "provisional regional Command" appointed by the rebellious military clique is illegitimate.[11]

Against this, Hafiz al-Asad does not see in the recent events what the world press calls a coup. It is a "natural development and change" in a party. No shooting took place, no military units moved about. It was not a contention between military and civilians. It took place within all the cadres of the party, civilian and military.[12]

Al-Asad sees the new government and the People's Council solidifying the inner, progressive front. The tasks of the people's organization are "practical command of the socialist transformation, people's control of the state apparatus and participation in perfecting the popular democracy." A corner stone of this structure is the citizen's freedom and dignity.[13]

The Asad-appointed "provisional regional Command" condemns the "commandeering maneuvering mentalities" that split the party by "demagoguery, forgery, hiding behind unbelieved slogans." The movement of February 23, 1966, turned against "retardedness and tutelage of commandeering rightist mentality." Now again a kind of "domineering and maneuvering mentality uses a new method to put out the flame of struggle."This "dictatorial mentality" (another version: personalist) operates by "intellectual terror" against the cadres, by "personal self-seeking relationships" and violation of the decisions of the extraordinary regional conference of 1969.

The Command will work toward forming a progressive front under *qiyada* (meaning command or leadership) of Ba'th. "Man being the goal of every genuine revolutionary movement and his most precious thing being freedom and dignity, we will make every effort to preserve the citizens' freedom and their dignity."

The Ba'th régime in 'Iraq is termed "the Rightist mentality that dominates our people in 'Iraq."[14]

By comparison, President Hasan al-Bakr of the old Ba'th in 'Iraq has adopted an ultra-revolutionary idiom. "The Ramadan revolution (1963) welded the revolutionary people's forces of both civilian and military sectors. Its victory against dictatorship and deviation brought off the first fruit of the fruits of organized people's struggle resting on revolutionary principled bases." "The ensuing errors and negativism — a natural result of circumstances that allowed vestiges of reactionary Qasimite tyranny to set up a dictatorial régime — do not depreciate the value and significance of the revolution in regard to the people's struggle."[15]

Hasan al-Bakr's phraseology seems to outstrip Asad's version of Ba'th in Syria. He speaks of the "students masses organically welded with the toiling people's forces — workers, fellahin, revolutionary military," of "people's work resting on the arms of fellahin, workers, soldiers, revolutionary intellectuals," of "the interests of the toiling classes whose vanguard is the working class."[16] Al-Bakr sees in the attempted coup — on the night of 20-21 January, 1970 — of "some traitors and agents that sold their conscience to imperialism and reaction a plot against your (the masses') revolution that became a torch lighting the road to the militant peoples in the area in their just struggle against imperialism, reaction and Zionism." "Their plans collapsed just as the previous attempts collapsed."[17]

The demise of Nasserism and fida'ism, the plight of the Leftist Ba'th and its dilution in Syria, have tempted the ruling Rightist Ba'th in 'Iraq to resurrect the past and assume a leading role in Arab revolutionism. Its Arab Front of Liberation, said to be active since 1969, aims to "join Arab fighters from all regions under the banner of a revolutionary ideology" and "methodically effect Ba'th concepts of armed struggle . . . against the plans of Zionism, imperialism and reaction." No doubt, it is also a tribute to the present close collaboration with the Soviet Union.[18] But the relativity of trends is easily deduced from the fact that 'Iraq took a stand for the pro-Communist "plot" in Khartum whereas Syria had sent its vice-president three days later to congratulate General al-Numayri on his victory.[19] 'Iraq also espoused the cause of South Yemen against North Yemen. This revolutionary role purports Ba'th to assume in a country riven ethnically, religiously and politically.

The bare skeleton of events in Syria conceals as much as it reveals. To Diana Howard, "doctrinaire quasi-civilian rule by a party élite (al-Atasi, Zu'ayyen, Makhus, so-called progressives, now imprisoned) has been transmuted in a barely disguised military oligarchy under the pragmatic and charismatic leadership of Lt.-General Hafez el-Asad."[20] To the victors, the vanquished had exercised virtual dictatorship, economic and political; their doctrinaire intransigence in economic policies and negativism in regard to relations with the West, the states of "Arab reaction" and political struggle with Israel, had isolated the country and brought it to the verge of collapse. The victors purport to have awakened the country by economic and political "liberalization," in their idiom *tashih* (rectification). To a foreign observer, "draconian rigor" is replaced by "realism" and "moderation."[21]

171

One can't help asking: Why? Why is the history of a party championing renaissance (*Ba'th* and *inbi'ath*), unity and solidarity and fighting divisiveness a history of violence and suppression — within and outside the party? In 1972, Shibli al-'Aysami of the old guard, now adjoint secretary general of the Ba'th party in 'Iraq, still upholds classical and modernized postulates: "Dialectical" and "organic" link between unity, freedom and socialism; scientifism and revolutionism in the ideology, thereby honoring the spiritual values linked to the Arab nation's history and cultural legacy; receptiveness to revolutionary world trends and movements; comprehensive, nay total (*shamil*) revolution in "all spheres of life — intellectual, economic and social"; condemnation of racialism and chauvinism; armed struggle — regular and popular.[22] Many of these injunctions sound inherited from the dis-inherited neo-Ba'th.

In 1972 three Ba'th parties celebrated the silver jubilee of Ba'th; to mention are refugees of "historical Ba'th," in 'Iraq and Lebanon and militants of neo-Ba'th from Syria and 'Iraq in jail or exile. One tries hard to detect the differences in their ideological jargon. Even Hasan al-Bakr of 'Iraq speaks of "pure moral authenticity" of Ba'th. To him, Ba'th fights the "pockets of secession, opportunism, personalist dictatorship," "regionalist concepts, mentalities and methods, factors of division, submission and ignorance."[23]

The recent attempt at a coup, in July 1973, from within Ba'th in 'Iraq, proves that uncontrollable power breeds intrigues that cut across "wings" or alleged "left" and "right." Men of opposing persuasions or various motivations may combine or acquiesce in implementing a design of a coup. In the recent coup are implicated: the head of the security service, a real torturer and bloodshedder (saffah), who masterminded the liquidation of thousands of communists in 1963 and, since 1968, of multitudes of dissidents — Kurds, communists, Jews, Nasserites; the head of the military wing of Ba'th and, strangely, a member of the ruling "triumvirate," "theorist of egalitarian and humanist socialism."

A lesson on limitations of ideology provides the fact that since 1968 the communist party lost over three thousand militants (detained, disappeared or "repentant") and yet the relations with the Soviet Union grew stronger.

In 1972, the cultural bureau of the national Command deliberates in a pamphlet on democratic centralism of a vanguard party that "chooses to represent the historic interests of the toiling social classes."

The monster of violence conjured up by Ba'th rule seems to have frightened the remaining rulers into conceding democracy "to the parties in coalition" (communists and Kurds).[24]

In Syria, forty-two army officers were executed following an attempt to assasinate President al-Asad in July 1973.

This plot was preceded by riots of Sunnis in Homs, Hama, Aleppo and Latakia.[25]

### Footnotes

1. Eric Rouleau, **Le Monde**, November 15-16, 1970; Édouard Saab, **ibid.**, March 4, 1970.
2. Édouard Saab, **ibid.**, November 18, 1970.
3. According to **al-Tali'a** (September 1971), al-Asad "succeeded to seize power from the former command of Ba'th."
4. Arnold Hottinger, **Swiss Review of World Affairs**, June 1971.
5. Paul Balta, **Le Monde**, November 15-16, 1970.
6. Thierry Desjardins, **Le Figaro,** June 29, 1972.
7. Paul Balta, **Le Monde**, March 23, 1971.
8. **Ibid.**
9. **al-Raya** (Beirut), November 14, 1971.
10. **Ibid.**, November 15, 1970.
11. **Ibid.**, November 19, 1970.
   The Command of the Lebanese Ba'th formation is more explicit about Ba'th strategy whose aim is "liberation of Palestine through armed struggle and people's war of liberation."
   The party's achievements in Syria are praised: it made itself a "revolutionary vanguard vehicle;" it "leads the revolution on the road of socialist transformation and lays a material and human basis to national liberation and construction of socialism." In its relations it "pursues a clear revolutionary

method: open to Arab progressive forces and forces of socialism and progress in the whole world."

12. **al-Thawra**, November 27, 1970.
13. **al-Ba'th**, December 5, 1970.
14. **Ibid.**, November 17, 1970.
15. **al-Jumhuriyya**, February 2, 1970.
16. **Ibid.**, January 16, 1970.
17. **Ibid.**, January 23, 1970.
18. **Ibid.**, April 7, 1972.
19. **Le Monde**, August 5, 1971.
20. **New Middle East**, March-April 1972.
21. Thierry Desjardins, **op. cit.**
22. **al-Jumhuriyya,** April 7, 1972.
23. **Ibid.,** supplement.
24. **Le Monde,** July 19, 20, 21, 1973
25. **New York Times,** August 30, 1973.

Chapter VIII

# APPRAISAL OF BA'TH

Jamal Atasi, one of the founders of Ba'th, subsequently joined the ranks of "unionist socialism." In his *On Arab Socialist Thought* and *The Myth of Particularities* [1] he ventured to discard an article of faith of Ba'th (for that matter also of Egypt's ideology) on the uniqueness of Arab socialism. A somewhat similar issue was fiercely argued out in pre-revolutionary Russia between populists and Marxists. The concept of German socialism, epitomized in National Socialism, was meant to undermine the original socialist movement, so that it immediately assumed a nationalist or racist coloring. The controversy over "socialism in one country" in the Soviet Union somehow repeated itself in regard to socialism in one Arab country. This heresy about "the myth of particularities" was daring indeed. Here Arab socialism is reduced to a bare frame. Atasi, a lucid exponent of his concepts, contents himself with pointing to an "Arab road of struggle for socialism." Recent trends tend to discard "Arab socialism" altogether. The particularities of its implementation may account for it.

... Class struggle moved from a regional plane to an (all-) Arab plane ... which left behind two forces claiming progressivism and socialism: the first, a regional trend that believes in the possibility of implementing socialism within one region, and in a capitalist, patriotic (*watani*) stage;[2] for this purpose it entered alliances that plunged it into opportunism ... it is secessionist socialism. ... The second force, although believing in world revolution and in recent years beginning to believe in the reality of Arab nationalism, ... also upheld the rôle of patriotic capitalism (the Communist party).

... The basic principle of Arab socialism is the necessity to place the struggle for socialism in its national frame and to link the socialist demands to the national demands of liberation and unity. But ... before long some started giving it a mystical content and separating it from social, class and human factors. They started talking of Arab socialist theory, its specific Arab philosophy, Arab characteristics and original merits distinguishing Arab socialism.

... Possibly these emotional premises in socialist and national thinking were warranted in the past, when the Arab national movement had to emphasize the national mark of liberation before emphasizing its socialist character, when the Arab national attitude was rejected by local communism and political movements of a religious bent.

... Such socialism arouses in socialist and Western states doubts about our ability to devise a new scientific method in our socialist thinking.

... No doubt, the Ba'th movement overstepped the terms of its 1947 constitution, at least as regards socialism, and in the last ten years or so the writings of many of its members moved in the direction of scientific socialism and rejection of private property. But the myth of peculiarities and an outright negative attitude to Marxism as well as emotional and spiritual tunes in thinking still dominate many of the Ba'thists.

... We believe in Arab nationalism, that is, in the

Arab peoples' desire that the one Arab nation should have one state. This national tendency does not imply restoration of the past. . . . Arab nationalism is born of modern history, of need and necessity, it is constant straining after the future. . . .

Even if the Arab had (specific) characteristics and tendencies molded throughout history . . . socialism is an all-human trend that does not rest on such characteristics and tendencies. Socialism aims at man himself, meaning that man upholds his value as a man. . . .

1. Socialist thought is born of modern times, of a secular mind, emanating from belief in man's ability to legislate his system and arrange his affairs himself . . .

2. The socialist method of social and economic analysis is a dialectical one, that is, a method stemming from affirmation of the existence of a conflict in society and struggle between men. . . .

3. . . . Socialist revolution is not an historical inevitability, but necessity, and the efforts of men wanting socialism must be enlisted on its behalf. . . .

4. To replace an old order, inevitably one must destroy the state of this order and change the economic, social and legal structure on which this state rests. . . . The ways of the revolutionary forces to seize power may be violent or peaceful, according to circumstances and objective necessities. But an active element in these circumstances, that is, the force of change, is an organized revolutionary vehicle in the form of a party. . . .

5. . . . To become a revolutionary socialist party, this revolutionary movement must have a guide of action and struggle, a clear constitution for a revolutionary rule and a long-range plan for militant policy in government. . . .

Principles and premises on which a revolutionary movement and a socialist system rest are not peculiar to a nation or a people. Their first goal is to destroy delusions and myths spread by forces inimical to socialism in order to divert the people from uncovering the reality of needs and struggle. . . .

From the principle of unity of Arab destiny, on the basis of unity of struggle of the revolutionary forces in the Arab homeland . . . we proceed to chart guideposts of our Arab road to socialism. These are conditions determined by present reality and do not derive from "peculiarities" distinguishing the Arabs, nor from principles "flowing from substance," or from the world of fantasy, but from the needs and necessities of our liberation as humans.[3]


In *About the Ba'th Experiment*, Yasin al-Hafiz presents a Marxist, or rather Marxist-Leninist, critique.[4] It was a decade of many options: communism seemingly stripped of Stalinism, Communist dissidence of People's China, workers' management as an instrument of "withering away" of state in Yugoslavia, people's democracy of "a mere democracy for the people's masses." Al-Hafiz knows that "guided democracy" or "revolutionary democracy" could turn to bureaucratic or personal dictatorship, the remedy being a revolutionary pattern of democracy as the "widest and deepest pattern of democracy of the people's masses." An effective vanguard rôle of the working class is to prevent this kind of democracy from becoming dictatorship of bureaucracy or of a person.

With the merger of the two parties, in 1954, the characteristics of Hawrani's Arab Socialist Party — "populist scent and opportunism" — are said to have prevailed; its "petty feudalist leadership was after quick and cheap gains, so that the revolutionary zeal of the old Ba'th waned." Ba'th is charged with "ideological poverty," which made it hand over the reins — completely and exclusively — to 'Abd al-Nasir, whose rôle was great and important, and yet should not be considered a "revolutionary model of a revolutionary masses' movement."

Hafiz's study refers merely to the Syrian Ba'th, the "mother" of the party. Ba'th of 'Iraq is said to have given a "theoretical, revolutionary and scientific content to the party slogans." A few months later the author would have been spared this assertion.

Despite its firm ties with the masses, Ba'th was unable to play the rôle of an actual vanguard of the masses. . . . Not being intellectually and politically mature, Ba'th was floating with the spontaneity of the masses . . ., though it had a basic part in bringing about the first historic revolutionary Arab victory in modern times. . . .
The party's revolutionism was shrouded in romantic and metaphysical mist. The party seized upon general goals, large and distant, of the Arab struggle, but was unable to grasp the tangible Arab reality in all its aspects and contradictions. This disability has not allowed it to forge objective tools for struggle. . . . Objectivity is not safeguarded by a dictum like "in our movement belief precedes action."
Having shut itself off completely from reality, the party (or at least an important part of it) withdrew into itself and placed itself above the masses. . . . It fell prey to a state of mind recalling "narcissism" under various dicta: "the party is an historic necessity"; "the party is the destiny of the Arab nation," etc. . . .
. . . A section of the party crossed the "tabu" (of its slogans) and pierced the metaphysical fog, only to plunge into the mire of reality in a vulgar manner. Openness toward reality, if it is not stimulated by an original spirit and revolutionary methods, turns to cheap, vulgar opportunism leading to gradual surrender to rotten reality.
. . . They moved back to a kind of "new regionalism" enveloped in a disgraceful flimsy curtain of Arabdom. . . .
What afflicted the party was not the usual split wit-

nessed in socialist movements in Europe, that is, a split into right and left wings, revolutionism and opportunism. It was an explosion inside the party into grouplets and factions ... with no element of principle or class content to clearly delineate the aspects of every group. ... Ideological poverty blurred the image of the party as a whole.

*Slogans without theory.*

In a party publication, *On Arab Socialism* (1951), Ba'th is stated to be "an authentic inimitable movement. ..."

Throughout its history, Ba'th lived by spontaneity ... without trying to seek a road. ... Its road to the three goals — unity, freedom, socialism — was a dream with no signposts ... no theoretical program as a guide to action. ... The link between revolutionary slogans, method of work and the tool of action was neither clear nor defined, and this made the way easy for opportunist elements in the party.

In line with the logic of non-imitability, the party took a negative attitude to revolutionary and combative experiments in the world. ... In the name of "national peculiarities," Arab socialism was made contradictory to them, without trying to elucidate the national content, the characteristics of the Arab people and their impact on Arab socialism. ...

Every people rely on others experiments in building socialism, but it adds to them its own. ...

Owing to theoretical vagueness ... the party's organization and discipline were weak. With every crisis, ideological and organizational, convulsions shook the party. ... With this grew the danger of reformist opportunism. Lack of a theoretical base opened the way to cheap maneuvering and about-faces according to the circumstances. This reduced the inner struggle in the party and around it to a personal struggle, at least externally.


*Petty bourgeois socialism.*

... Though the party in many regions of Syria was able to filter into the masses of fellahin (including poor fellahin and agricultural workers), the general skeleton of the party in the countryside is middle-class. The bases of the party are elements of "non-owning — non-toiling" (village grocer, village *iman*, son of a prominent figure in the village, small farmer). As for the town, its petty bourgeois character is clearer (educated, clerks, professionals, craftsmen, etc.) ... so that the party was prompted to adopt attitudes that ensure the direct and immediate interests of these factions. ...

As for action, the party did not put complete trust in the ability and the revolutionism of the masses, and this is the deep explanation for its cooperation with military bureaucracy. ... Opportunism in political action stems from contempt for the masses. The claim that it is possible to save them from above is refuted by history. ... The problem of revolution is always the problem of organizing the toiling masses. ... Cooperation with this bureaucracy compromises the seriousness of the socialism Ba'th calls for.

... Game with bureaucracy is not a revolutionary game, it is always opportunist careerism. It was used as a scarecrow to reactionary forces, as a complementary element of "parliamentary game," as a way to gain a starting point on the bourgeois-reactionary political arena. ...

Parliamentarianism is a political jacket of capitalism.

... Is it possible to maintain that it will be a tool for basic social revolutionary transformation in our homeland? ... We don't try to renounce parliamentary struggle, we want to delimit it. ... There should be no confidence in parliamentary struggle as a road to democracy. It should be used only as one of the forms of revolutionary struggle.

... In a race to increase the number of votes in parliament ... the party joined groups of bourgeois and large landowners and notables ... and entered non-principled alliances to assure the success of its candidates.

... Democracy is not a gift of the bourgeoisie to the people, it is a fruit of long violent struggle by the people's masses. ... One should ensure the concept and frame of freedom — large profound freedom of the people's masses. ...

The vagueness of the party's concept of freedom and democracy and the failure of the experiment of personal power in the era of union induced a part of the party members to adopt an idea prevalent in the milieu of educated bourgeoisie that stresses the advantage of the classic form of Western democracy and freedom. Some opportunists and bourgeois intellectuals in the party dragged a part of the membership to positions commensurate with the interests of the bouregoisie and reaction. ... The experiment of union proved that personal rule is unable to bring about genuine revolutionary mobilization of the masses.

... The upheavals in the party, at times in cooperation with military dictatorship, at times playing the game of bourgeois democracy, are void of any doctrinal and revolutionary spirit.

... In the era of union there began serious Leftist revolutionary critique. ... Personal rule, even if it seeks progressive revolutionary horizons ... inhibits the masses in their drive to ultimate goals. It turns the operation of revolution from populist lofty organized thrust to an adventurous raid always threatened with encirclement and annihilation.

Muta' Safadi pursues the evolution of Ba'th ideology in terms of a generation's struggle intensely stimulated by intellectual currents in France. Endowed with flowery Arabic hardly warranted by the austerity of Marxist reasoning, he communicates the atmosphere of the early period of Ba'th.

Most Ba'th members kept their attachment to the traditional ideas of their society, without gaining from the party any basic change in their beliefs. The petty bourgeois concept was the official concept, tacitly agreed upon among men of the party's first ranks.

Leaning to personalism in organization, to collusion in exclusive circles battling each other, to popularization of the idea of middle-of-the-road solutions and avoidance of violence — in the past, of course — and clinging to traditional democratic means of action, such as criticism, leaflets and student demonstrations, all this left the main questions facing every socialist party in the world, such as: what is revolution, who implements a revolution, etc., ignored ... so that they became a monopoly of the 'Aflaqi élite.

This ban on Marxism and revolutionary thought has not deterred some of the educated in Ba'th from trying to open a window to the evolution of Marxist thought, starting with the twentieth congress of the Communist parties. This was sometimes reflected in the journal al-Ba'th, in translations, summaries and studies concerning the declaration of this congress.

A Leftist trend, on the point of raising some Marxist topics in spite of the 'Aflaqi ban, tried to form itself during the political conflicts, the organization crisis and the inner splits in the crowded years preceding the union with Egypt).

This trend, represented by intellectuals such as 'Abd al-Karim Zuhur, Jamel Atas and others, reflected a great rebellion against the shabbiness of the party due to frictions between its special commands.

This trend was growing within the party and enveloping many groups eager to get rid of the 'Aflaqi and al-Hawrani phase. It paved the way to a basic split within the party during the phase of reactionary secession (1961-1963). Two mutually exclusive fractions emerged from it: Hawrani's school of political opportunism and the wing of socialist unionists.

Ba'th socialism was a slogan with no theoretical content and no combative attitude: a kind of liberal socially, utopian socialistically, bourgeois in the nature of political action.

These rightist, mystical and utopian outgrowths in socialism have a direct bearing on the molding of the party in a fascist pattern carrying the banner of counter-revolution, when the 'Aflaq wing came into power after March 8 (1963).

'Aflaq's thought derives from various sources, but all go back to traditional metaphysics and neo-Romanticism, as represented by André Gide in the second quarter of this century, and to poetic mysticism whose source is the philosophy of Henry Bergson, whom 'Aflaq held in high esteem. . . .

'Aflaq imparted to his first party disciples the tradition of admiration for Western culture. Reading of Gide's or Bergson's works became an article of faith among the educated of that founding phase. Bergson's and Gide's attitudes —whatever the difference between them —were emulated. Romanticism and literary thinking prevailed in the first cells of the party. . . . French language and letters were studied, French books translated. In the first half of the 'forties, the party was rather a literary association, its publications were, in general, far more influenced by the works of rightist novelists and philosophers than by social and Marxist studies. Discussion centered on literary and philosophical problems, remote from politics. A dreamy air, replete with enchanting intellectual slogans, an air of intimate personal relations – these were the objective conditions of the party's intellectual and organizational growth.

Poets and adolescents, dreamers and Western mystics could not form a core of a revolutionary party. And yet later on, when the Hawranis, considered nearly ignorant of culture by comparison with 'Aflaq's disciples, joined the party, it gradually became, at least in some of its intellectuals, alive to trends of European leftist thought. Following the Bergsonian generation, the second generation, especially the Ba'th university youth since the early 'fifties, became attached to existentialism. Students turned more and more to the humanities, notably to the department of philosophy, whose teachers and students fell under the party's spell. So much so that most of the philosophy teachers at high schools were Ba'thists.

To the existentialist generation the slogan of freedom in politics assumed an "ethical, educational, and metaphysical meaning." Instead of revolutionary standards, literary and philosophical criteria prevailed within the party, educationalists vying with politicians for prominence.

This existentialist trend yielded literary produce in poetry, short stories and essays that helped spread the Ba'th message among the educated in the Arab world. Since the mid-Fifties this trend became alive to revolutionary developments within the existentialist trends, both secular and Catholic, in France.

Western culture that "took a basic turn in the mid-century" impressed the imagination of a group of party intellectuals. They closely pursued the ideological and political changes resulting from the twentieth congress of Communist parties and their impact on schools of thought opposing Stalinism, as represented in existentialist persuasions (Sartre, Camus) and other independent

Leftist circles such as the Marxist Catholic circle around *Esprit*.

The third generation of Ba'th, following the 'Aflaqi mystics and national Marxists, became alert to the changes in existentialism leading to the adoption of many of the Marxist premises.[5]

Egypt's appraisal of Ba'th is attuned to the addressee, so that a range of gradations is inevitable. Still, ideological exclusiveness is always the rule. Accordingly, the distinctions between, the original Ba'th and its left trend is reduced to trifles. In fact, in point of social concept the new trend markedly moved toward Egypt's ideology. Added to this, due to a new political constellation, the differences are being attenuated. This is what *al-Katib* had to say, by way of sweeping generalization, before the coup of 1966.[6]

The contention of some Ba'thists, especially after the collapse of the Ba'th ruin in 'Iraq, that the party is split into a "revolutionary socialist wing" and a "reactionary wing" headed by 'Aflaq, a "Fascist opportunist," a "corpse swimming in the swamps of the right wing," is refuted. Ba'th had no theory, no "basis for long-range strategic plans," over which a party sometimes splits into Left and Right.

Said Yasin al-Hafiz, one of the former Ba'thists: "When the party exploded into groupuscules and factions – after the secession or its collapse in 'Iraq – the whole of it, including what is called the left, stood on the same level of superficiality and ideological poverty."

Before Ba'th, the Lea  ie of National Action (*'Usbat al-'amal al-qawmi*), formed in 1934, called for "freedom and unity." At that time the imperialist powers were in collusion with the feudalists and capitalists in the Arab countries. The rising middle class was then prepared to carry the banner of a new revolution. The treachery of feudalism and capitalism made it inevitable to raise the goal of socialism and link it to the demand for freedom and unity.

Ba'th emerged as a mouthpiece of this trend and welded groups of the middle class and of the educated. Along with the irresolution of the middle class, it was afflicted, since inception, with two maladies:

1. The party was the first political organization to combine unity, freedom and socialism or to lend freedom and unity a social content, but it was not the first to discover the truth of Arab nationalism, to call for freedom and socialism. Owing to this delusion, it felt superior to the masse and insulated from the "real forces of revolution" — workers and fellahin. It imagined that by merely raising these three slogans it brought about for the Arab nations what they had not been able to do throughout their history. To 'Aflaq, Ba'th has become "the destiny of the Arab nation in this age." He calls the party to "activity and work in order that we should be equal to the destiny that led us to respond to our nation's needs." The destiny that loaded Ba'th with this vocation also "empowered us to command and speak with force and act with force."

In all its behavior Ba'th has been possessed by a superiority complex and placed the command itself above the party.

Said 'Aflaq in *Fi sabil al-Ba'th*:

"Real leaders are those who know how to abide by the idea; and devoted members are those who obey the leader, they obey the idea through the leaders." In consequence, Ba'th is a personalist, not a doctrinal party.

2. Ba'th rejected scientific socialism, consequently, also its basic pillar — class struggle. To Ba'th, "socialism should not be a factor of division or inner strife." Ba'th

187

didn't try to distill its slogans down to a theory that defined its goals.

Hence the complete estrangement between Ba'th and the masses. It was unable "scientifically to analyze society, to recognize the real forces concerned for the revolution — the basic instrument in struggle against feudalism, capitalism and imperialism." Hence the "fascism and opportunism" of Ba'th, its "romantic way of understanding nationalism." To Ba'th, nationalism is "beloved destiny," "love before all," an "intuitive, self-evident motive that imposes itself with no need to argue about."

Rejection of scientifism and class analysis of society made Ba'th incapable of understanding the forces of socialist unionist revolution that should be given all freedom, and the forces opposing this revolution that should be eliminated politically after having been deprived of economic power.

Ba'th ignores the experience of many states of the Third World that decidedly rejected the road of liberal democracy. Experience shows that liberal democracy in the Arab world is a tool in the hands of exploiting classes. During the negotiations on tripartite union 'Aflaq said: "From a theoretical viewpoint of national socialism a multi-party system is to a degree a safeguard of political freedom."

With Ba'th socialism became reformist propaganda. Said 'Aflaq: "The socialism of Ba'th confines itself to the economic sphere and aims to redistribute wealth and establish the bases of an economy that would ensure equality and justice to fellow citizens."

Ba'th cannot rid itself of old notions, including the notion of liberal freedom resting on a multi-party system, and of making good use of imperialism and capitalism for its interests in the Arab world. Its socialism being reformist or petty bourgeois, Ba'th considers socialism an economic regulation, not an enemy of the exploiting classes striving to eliminate their influence.*

Another view on Ba'th was presented after the 1966 coup, in the same journal.[7]

No doubt, Ba'th was a mouthpiece of the Left in Syria during the rule of the traditional parties before 1958, but it rejected collaboration with the socialist experiment under the auspices of UAR. In 1963, when Ba'th seized power, there appeared Leftist forces opposing its rule, such as Arab Nationalists, Arab Socialists.

The party underwent a grave doctrinal crisis because it supported secession.

No doubt, the removal of 'Aflaq and al-Bitar expresses the spirit of the new generation in the party. If it is true that the new generation unreservedly circumscribed its progressive way, then the source of conflict is the argument between the rightist and leftist factions in the party. Judging by externals, there are many proofs showing a real change leftward. After the movement of February 1966, a larger measure of nationalization was implemented. The neo-Ba'thists accepted Marxism as one of the sources of socialist thought. A Syrian delegation visited the Soviet Union in January 1967, to discuss the concept of socialism and the methods of its implementation.

'Aflaq understood freedom in a larger sense — liberation of man from exploitation by man or society; in this sense it is nearer to the concept of moral or psychological freedom than to the economic or political.

To the Syrian branch of Arab Socialists, the Leftism of Ba'th is not genuine because it rejects union with Arab revolutionary forces. The Ba'th fervor for nationalization of oil concessions is merely showing off, intended to drag the Arabs into a battle they cannot take up yet. Besides, Leftism is not judged merely by theoretical principles but by tactics or methods of work.

* At the time of this writing even the Rightist Ba'th was shaking off the notions of political freedom. When in power Ba'th never exercised it.

Al-'Aqqad suggests that the "secular propaganda" of Ba'th might be non-principled. The former head of Ba'th was Orthodox (Christian). 'Alawis and Isma'ilis dominate it and their representation there exceeds their numerical strength in the country, so that secular propaganda is a kind of "hidden communalism." Many are the proofs of discrimination in favor of the 'Alawi community since Ba'th came into power, in 1963. Some maintain that the urge of 'Alawis and Isma'ilis to join Ba'th can be traced to the new generation's desire to evade the domination of men of religion, hence the secret of Ba'th secularism.

A pamphlet by Mahmud 'Abd al-Rahim employs cadenced rhetoric, studded with images from classical poetry, in denouncing the foe and extolling the non-Ba'th ideas.[8]

. . . Mr. 'Aflaq had built his social and political philosophy as if there were an awful spiritual vacuum in our Arab East, which there never was. This raises a suspicion that these thoughts are drawn from alien movements that do not fit the East. Our East needs a basic creative revolution to change death to life, poverty to comfort, steam to smoke of factories, hunger and illness to care, sufficiency and justice, feudalism and serfdom to social justice and equal opportunities, monopoly and domination of capital to constructive socialism. . . .
Never was the Arab East in need of metaphysics or imported thoughts. . . . We repeat from the depth of our pure heart. . . . May the waters of the Nile turn to fire eating our intestines, may the waters of the Tigris and Euphrates become hot water broiling our hearts, may the water of Barada (in Damascus) turn to deadly poison wearying our bodies. . . . if we do not purge our pure Arab land from tyrants, false plotting propagandists.

Philosophers and thinkers never need vagueness and obscurity to present their thoughts.

With Ba'th socialism is a forged, a superficial veil.

By directing the fire of terror toward the classes of workers, fellahin and revolutionary intellectuals, Ba'th sets up a final barrier between itself and actual socialist behaviour.

Under the Ba'th command socialism became an empty slogan, a tool of maneuvers used in an opportunistic effort to hide a damned reactionary policy.

On April 19, 1963, two days after the union agreement between Egypt, Syria and 'Iraq was signed, five persons were killed in Aleppo in a clash between police and people demanding union.

In the era of Ba'th hundreds of officers were pensioned, many of them were given jobs abroad.

The Ba'th command pursued a clear dictatorial, fascist policy, deprived the masses and their national ideological forces (formations?) and people's organizations of freedom, banished freedom of thought, press and assembly, used the most violent methods of suppression against the masses, killed tens of fellow citizens, set up courts like those of the inquisition in the Middle Ages, threw into prison scores of Syrian unionist youths, also reform-minded individuals and journalists.

Socialism as implemented by Ba'th in Syria is a socialism of blood, jails and detention camps.

Unity means unity of the Ba'th party; national front — elimination of everyone who is non-Ba'thist; populism — abuse and vilification of the masses; people — a herd; public opinion — pressure of the mob; socialism — socialism of bloodshed; freedom of press — closure of all papers except the paper al-Ba'th; doctrinarism — bloodshed; democracy — Ba'th domination; army unity — dismissal of all national elements; freedom — waiver of immunity and unwarranted dismissal of officials, curfew for eighteen hours a day, shooting and shelling from armored cars, opening of the mouths of guns and the gates into jails and detention camps; liberation — getting rid of every non-Ba'thist.

Muhammad Hasanayn Haykal, editor of *al-Ahram*, isolates, rather waywardly, Fascist slogans from Christopher Hibbert's *Benito Mussolini* and finds them similar to 'Aflaq's dicta.

Haykal compares:

Fascism is the destiny of the Italian nation.
Fascism cannot be grasped by reason.
Fascism is not to be discussed but experienced.
Destiny that loaded us with the message of Fascism gave us the right to command with force and operate with force.

With the following:

Ba'th is the destiny of the Arab nation.
Ba'th ideology can not be grasped by reason but by belief.
Destiny that loaded us with the message of Ba'th gave us the right to command with force and operate with force. Ba'th is the vanguard, masses have to march behind it.

To Haykal, in the 'thirties Fascist propaganda impressed Aflaq, when in Paris, and he reproduced it in the 'forties.
"More than anybody he knows the true value of ideological camouflage. ... Ba'th is a movement opposing revolution, by its nature siding with reactionary secession."[9]
A National Charter, "agreed upon by the Arab Socialist Union,[10] ANM, the Arab Democratic Socialist Party

(formerly Arab Socialists) and "representatives of national progressive independent trends," bears the imprint of the first two groups. It was to be shortlived, hardly allowing the ink to dry. Here revolutionary impetus seizing even the third Hawrani's group, is let loose, so that foe within and without is presented in utmost dimensions. The phraseology is indiscriminately borrowed from foreign sources. Its main target is the neo-Ba'th régime in Syria.

The June war ... was also a war of American imperialism against the Arab revolution by the agency of and with Israel, the utmost phase of economic, political, and psychological war against the Arabs, and one of its fronts of aggression against the revolutionary world liberation movement, since the Arab revolution is an indivisible part of it, one of its main arenas.

... Egypt took the military blow nearly alone, whereas Syria that instigated the war engaged in secondary and partial battles whereupon her forces retreated arbitrarily on order of the political and military commands, after the maneuver of announcing the fall of Qunaytra.

... The Zionist-American alliance knows well what harms and threatens its interests and clearly distinguishes between verbal provisions and slogans with no real content, revolutionary hubhub ... and real revolution that blasts its basic interests.

... Israel fears Arab unity, and the Syrian régime has been a barrier to it.

Israel fears an authority that mobilizes the efforts and energies of the Arab nation to do away with backwardness, whereas the Syrian régime, in its actual conduct, has been a part of this backward structure.

Israel fears national unity of the people's masses ... whereas the Syrian régime tore up this unity within the region, dissipated the people's effort and killed its energies.

... The two main factors of the debacle are backwardness and dismemberment. Direct causes: ineptitude, corruption, weakness in the structure of the Arab revolutionary or so-called revolutionary régimes ... and failure of the responsible commands, political and military, to meet the needs and exigencies of the battle.

.... The UAR is the most advanced Arab country; its régime effected serious economic, social and political changes ... and yet this régime was unable to bring about a decisive change in the traditional structure of society and eliminate backwardness completely. ... The other régimes — traditional, half-traditional or so-called revolutionary — were unable to advance one serious step towards elimination of backwardness.

1. The basic conflict is the conflict between the Arab nation and the imperialist-Zionist-American alliance.

2. The struggle between the Arab nation and the Zionist-American alliance has a clear international aspect.

3. An armed struggle is an inevitable necessity for the Arab nation.

4. The Arab régimes that intend to confront Israel and imperialism lack a political and military strategy for this confrontation.

5. The supremacy of bureaucracy over the régime, army and people stems from lack or vagueness of a comprehensive theoretical and strategic vision, from deficient understanding of revolution and revolutionary proceedings. There dominates a notion that certain operations such as nationalization and projects of industrialization, irrigation and electrification are the whole revolution and all revolutionary accomplishments. Man, the only goal of revolution, is neglected. Emphasis is placed on the material side of revolution; as to the human, intellectual and spiritual aspect, man's value, his freedom and dignity, these occupy but a small place on the agenda of revolutionary actions.

This deficient understanding made the revolutionary

régimes ... mainly rely on official machinery ... that is a mixture of old bureaucracy, raised on submission to authority, and a new class of bureaucracy — military men and hosts of opportunists craving money, pleasures, luxury and domination. As for the people, it is barred from real participation in building its life and future.

These bureaucracies — military and civilians — are a steel ring gripping the people and keeping it from revolutionary creative activity.

These bureaucracies, installed as they are on rule of tyranny that spreads like a plague in the Arab homeland, so much so that they nearly planted in the minds a notion that revolution is black tyranny, leading, on account of vagueness, ignorance or eccentricity as regards the idea of revolutionary coercion, to despotic tyranny.

Revolutionary coercion can be applied against a dominating or tyrannical minority that was expolitative and is barred from exploitation, when it is plotting and resists, by violence, the revolutionary authority. But when violence is used against the people as a whole, it is tyranny incompatible with revolution, because the people are the source of revolution, its instruments and goal. A revolution that upholds its values in theory and strategy, a revolutionary apparatus that grew in the crucible of revolution, departs from its road and goals when exercising tyranny, and when tyranny persists the revolution dies. In an atmosphere of tyranny the existence of a revolutionary man is purified, a believing man, a man with a cause for which to sacrifice himself and to die as a martyr.

Given this situation, how could we conduct a methodical war marked by inventiveness in planning and heroism in battle? Moreover, how can we conduct a people's war when the people are ruled by terror, prevented from participation in determining their destiny and barred from having their place in this war?

6. Negative role of the military bureaucracy. There was a time when the role of the army in a number of Arab countries was not negative, moreover, it was positive in revolutionary struggle. Numerous Arab armies took part in eliminating the political influence of reaction and resisted the designs of imperialism. But the material and moral privileges of the military bureaucracy swelled, and by a kind of custody or terror it stifled the revolutionary advancement of the masses. Transformation of the military bureaucracy into a politically ruling class, in circumstances of backwardness, prepares the ground for bureaucratic military decay. A new military class inevitably becomes alienated from the people, thus supplanting the privileged traditional classes. Furthermore, the political mastery of the military bureaucracy affects the fighting capacity of the army itself and brings it down to the lowest level, transforming it into what resembles a quelling police force. This fact is not to be covered up with big labels such as "army of the revolution," "doctrinal army". . .

On the internal level:

1. A national progressive front should be formed in Syria. . . . Only extreme reactionaries, agents of American and Israeli and imperialist intelligences and emissaries of defeat and submission should be barred.

2. Democratic people's rule. On this basis of a front will democratic people's rule come up, whose duty will be to eliminate dominion, exploitation and corruption, to dissolve the services of intelligence and suppression, ensure legal safeguards of citizen's freedom and dignity and provide for freedom of national progressive parties and organizations, of press, opinion and criticism.

People's and professional organizations, such as trade unions, federations and associations should be given freedom to form themselves, to elect their agencies and manage their activities. . . . People's councils, starting with villages, boroughs, and ending with a supreme people's council should be elected. Elections to the supreme council should be arranged on the basis of segments of the people and its patriotic classes, taking into account their place in production and political vanguard role.

3. Arming, training and organizing the people . . .

4. The people's army should be governed by the principle of democratic centrism and equipped with proletarian efficiency and fighting spirit. The army is merely an armed branch of the people, with no material privileges, a branch of a poor people facing a heavy burden of defence and struggling to develop its economy.
The army's morale should be raised by the abolition of hierarchical paternalistic feudal centrism that is exercised by the bureaucracy not to keep up discipline but to make the army a tool of its aspirations for political power . . .

5. As long as all privileges are not abolished and decency does not obtain, as long as there is no adjustment of the standards of life of the people's classes, and a kind of consumption democracy does not prevail, the people will not accept such a hard life or carry it gladly.

6. Palestinians are the vanguard of the liberation army.

7. Complete coordination (by way of union) with UAR on a basis of mutual help. The UAR is the centre of gravity in the economic, military, political and cultural fields. Shé is the main base in the fight against im-

perialism and Zionism. The people of UAR are enduring a crisis of catastrophic depth and painfulness. . . .

The policy of the Syrian régime *vis-à-vis* the UAR after the debacle has not changed. It could be summed up as embarrassment, vilification, threats, covert or overt . . .

On the international level:

10. Strengthening and coordinating relations with the Soviet Union and socialist countries, Asian and European.

11. Tightening relations with neutral states and paving the way to the Islamic countries and the states of the Third World.

12. Taking advantage of all contradictions between the capitalist countries and scientifically presenting our case to leftist organizations, the press, oppressed classes and groups among European and American peoples.

The national progressive front is a populist democratic outlet for Syria to avert disintegration . . . minority rule and power struggle within the military structure.[11]

The editor of *al-Hurriyya*, organ of ANM, reasons that this Charter "partly criticizes the Syrian régime and analyzes some of its external manifestations and deficiencies, but does not delve into its petty bourgeois class character." "This part critique makes the Charter stand, as regards class character and ideology, on common ground with the present Syrian régime, in spite of its different attitudes . . ., in consequence, it could not embark on a new struggle."[12]

After two months ANM left the Front. In the view of *al-Hurriyya*, the basic constituents of the Front, should they ever come into power in Syria, are "petty bourgeois groups" more backward than the present Syrian régime with its petty bourgeois program and "operations of police suppression against the movement of working and poor masses." The Arab Democratic Socialist Party is the group of al-Hawrani known for his "conspiratorial attitude" against the "petty bourgeois union between Syria and Egypt for the benefit of Syrian reaction." Al-Hawrani insisted on including the national Ba'th in the Front because it has a backing in the army, hence a potential coup. During its "petty bourgeois, rightist, backward" rule — (February 8, 1963-February 23, 1966) — national Ba'th "imposed police dictatorship on other groups of the Syrian national liberation movement and on the revolutionary classes in society." "The Hama slaughters under Amin al-Hafiz are not distant." ANM in Syria works for a "wide-range secession from the petty bourgeois ideology prevalent in all segments of the Syrian national liberation movement" that has to undergo a "decisive proletarian, critical scrutiny."[13]

ANM is implacable in its attitude to the "Fascist rule" of neo-Ba'th in Syria. *Al-Hurriyya* complains about a "wide range terror" and "campaign of jailing, widening day by day," of patriotic politicians, trade unionists, university professors and students, physicians, lawyers, members of the Popular Front for the Liberation of Palestine, etc.[14]


Ironically, Ba'th, extremely nationalistic in its simplicism, came into power in two ethnically complex minorities-countries. In Syria Ba'th has been weakest among the economically stronger and largely urban Sunni Arabs, whereas in 'Iraq it is relatively stronger among the Sunni Arabs. Here, to a lesser degree in Syria, Ba'th rule has to contend with the Kurds in the north.

Customarily, at the initial stage of every coup the Kurds

have been placated with promises of fair treatment (the authors of the last Ba'th coup in 'Iraq promised a "fair and wise solution of the North in accord with 'Iraq's interests, her stability and her national unity"). In fact, the fiercest campaigns against the Kurds were launched by Ba'th rulers (June-October 1963; April 1969-February 1970).

Apart from the now defunct National Democratic party in 'Iraq, it was ANM, namely, its Leftist wing that was outspoken in its critique of the treatment of the Kurds at the hands of Ba'th in Syria.

To ANM, the Kurdish problem is one of the problems of the "patriotic (*wataniyya*) revolution," and its solution is "dialectically" linked to them. The "chauvinistic reactionary" attitude of the successive governments of 'Iraq to the national rights of the Kurdish people is class-bound. ANM stands for a "democratic populist rule, for a Leftist Arab-Kurdish front, to conduct the struggle of workers, poor peasants and soldiers, both Arabs and Kurds, and to eliminate the bourgeois military chauvinistic and rightist state." The recent "demagogic" promises of the régime of July 30, 1968, issued from a military coup, the same Ba'th régime that waged a "military chauvinistic campaign in 1963 to subdue the Kurdish national movement," are no more than a "temporary truce" in order to tighten its "police grip" on the country. By its very "class and ideological (bourgeois, petty bourgeois, rightist) nature," this régime that "slaughtered the Left of the 'Iraqi national movement in 1963," is not capable of solving the Kurdish problem from a progressive outlook.

But ANM is also tough on the Kurdish leadership. The chief command of the Kurdish movement, namely the "feudal military" Barzani command, known for its policy of "maneuvering and truce-making" with 'Iraqi rightist governments, is again capable of committing an "historic error." After having eliminated the revolutionary progressive force in South 'Iraq, a "military chauvinistic campaign" will again be launched against the Kurdish move-

200

ment. A true democratic way to solve the Kurdish problem, is "an organic linking of the populist armed
struggle in North and South 'Iraq and stimulating the revolutionary class vigilance in the whole of 'Iraq, to remove the régime of the bourgeoisie, kulak and neo-
imperialism that grips the throat of the economy in 'Iraq
(oil), a régime whose political face since July 1, 1958 has
been military bureaucracy."

The Kurdish minority in 'Iraq should enjoy complete
national rights on a footing of complete equality with the
Arabs. As for Syria,

whereas the petty bourgeois military (neo-Ba'th) régime continues to subdue the movement of the toiling
Arab masses, throws hundreds of democratic militants
into jails and suppresses the workers — the vanguard of
the poor people's masses — it employs the most disgust-
ing methods of racial persecution against the Kurdish
minority in North Syria.

Recently, the régime devised a project of an "Arab
Belt," aiming at displacing tens of thousands of
Kurdish peasants from the Turkish-Syrian frontiers inside Syria and replacing them with Arab peasants. The
régime fears that the Kurds might demand secession
from the Syrian homeland. For this reason the implementation of the agrarian reform and distribution of
land to Kurdish peasants was halted. Arab peasants are
expected to get the land. Since the advent of the Ba'th
rule in 1963, a policy of racial discrimination is in-
tensified, so much so that Kurds are barred from
teachers' seminaries, from public offices, from the
military academy, and the Kurdish language and
culture are kept suppressed. The present régime continues to deprive tens of thousands of Kurds of their
citizenship rescinded in 1962 by the reactionary régime.

ANM declares:

1. By its actions the régime has created a problem not in existence before. No Kurdish source has ever made a demand or allegation calling in question the unity of Syrian soil. The Kurdish minority in Syria demands no more than cessation of oppression and complete equality of rights.

2. Operations of displacement in the "Arab Belt" carried out under the name of "state farms" and "agrarian reform" are despicable acts of repression and dispersal, whatever their excuse.

3. ANM with tens of Kurdish militants in its ranks knows that the Kurdish people have always sided with the Arab people in all national and patriotic trials that befell Syria. The acts of the régime cannot but lead to further disintegration of the national unity caused by Ba'th since 1963. In final analysis these measures are in the interest of imperialism and Zionism.

ANM states:

I. The Kurds in North Syria are a national minority. It should enjoy all the rights of a national minority:

1. Complete equality with other fellow citizens in rights and duties.

2. The right to revive their national heritage and language, to hold fast to their nationality, and open schools of their own.

II. Kurdish youths should not be reprimanded merely on account of displaying their feelings and support of the revolution of their brethren in Kurdistan.

A solution of this crisis and cessation of racial oppression in Syria is bound up with remedying the general crisis in Syria, by ridding it of the petty bourgeois class régime that pursues these chauvinistic policies and is unable to carry out the tasks of a national democratic revolution. . . . [15]

**Footnotes**

1. **Fi 'l-fikr al-siyasi, op. cit., I, II.**

2. **Watani** is sometimes used interchangeably with **qawmi**, meaning national, related to the whole Arab homeland, or pertains mostly to one Arab country, patriotic.

3. **Fi 'l-fikr al-siyasi, I,** pp. 140-144, 152-160.

4. **Ibid.,** pp. 176-178, 184-201.

5. **Hizb al-Ba'th, op. cit.**

6. Ahmad 'Abd al-Ghani, **Hizb al-Ba'th wa-tariq al-la 'awda** ("The Ba'th Party and the Way of No Return"), **al-Katib,** August 1965, pp. 172-181.

7. Salah al-'Aqqad, **al-Yasar fi Suriya** ("The Left in Syria"), **al-Katib,** April 1967, pp. 68, 69, 70.

8. **Qiyadat hizb al-Ba'th al-murtadda ("The Secessionist Leadership of the Ba'th Party"), series Kutub Qawmiyya,** No. 249, Cairo, pp. 11, 12, 119, 120, 114-115, 92, 121, 171, 139.

9. Weekly Supplement, December 6, 1963; summed up in 'Abd al-Majid Shawqi al-Bakri, **al-Ba'th ratl khamis li-'l-isti'mar** ("Ba'th Fifth Column of Imperialism"), **Mosul,** 1964, p. 4.

10. According to **al-Hurriyya,** August 29, 1966, the Arab Socialist Union, Syrian region, came into being in 1964. "Revolutionary elements in it wanted it to be equipped with scientific socialists thought." The unionist movement in Syria comprised "large masses of workers, fellahin and oppressed classes, but leading in it were the petty bourgeoisie and elements of the big bourgeoisie." Rightist and median trends rejected scientific socialism, arguing that union can be effected without it. Religion was used to serve "non-progressive" positions. As against this, 'Abd al-Nasir, "leader of the Arab revolution," espoused scientific socialism.

Rightist trends, fed and "philosophized" by elements of the big bourgeoisie, rejected it openly. Owing to their social composition and mentality, the median trends dreamed of political action allowing "oscillation and political acrobatics . . . with no doctrinal deterrent." They deemed themselves superior to the masses, while fearing that the Union would turn to an organization of "oppressed toiling classes." "Empty political idleness froze the activity of the masses."

At this stage revolutionary elements in the Union saw their task in renewal of the masses' struggle against reaction and imperialism as well as against "reckless trends of dictatorship detached from the masses and dominating the government." These trends militate against the claims of popular democracy.

Being opportunistic, the Rightist and the median trends tried, "hoping to get some chairs and bits of power," to come to terms with the government.

They became estranged from the Arab Socialist Union, so that the revolutionary elements deemed necessary to purge them, to enable the Union to become an organization that represents "an alliance of toiling people's forces proceeding toward resumption of a revolutionary course."

11. **Ibid.**, May 20, 1968.
12. **Ibid.**
13. **Ibid.**, July 22, 1968.
14. **Ibid.**, June 10, 1968.
15. See **al-Inqilab al-'askari al-akhir fi 'l-'Iraq** ("The Recent Military Coup in 'Iraq"), **ibid.**, August 12, 1968.

Chapter IX

# MARGINAL COMMENTS ON BA'TH

As far as ideology in action can be divorced from the workings of the practioners' mind or from the Syrians' mind, the evolution of Ba'th, its gains and failures, seem inherent in its initial ideological premises. Treatises on Ba'th in the earlier era tend to give precedence to the writings of 'Aflaq, the chief theorist, and a few others over party statements that, though often bearing 'Aflaq's stamp, may also represent a sum total of divergent views. The latter are less given to abstraction, in consequence truer to the hustle and bustle of the party's practice. From the start a streak of over-assertiveness and exclusiveness, hence intolerance, marked Ba'th ideology, in part stemming from the sense of vocation of the founding fathers—a streak that promises the Arab fatherland will never come to rest. Here is tne verbal boundlessness of the visionary, the unquestioning excitement of the pathfinder, a strange sounding neglect of facts, an over-glossing of the evident, be it deliberate or, at least, imagination-bound.

Researchers dwell on Ba'th primacy of birthright in socialism, but they tend to forget that 'Iraq's National Democratic Party was socialist, albeit implicitly, from its inception in 1946, as was its embryo—the Ahali group—in the 'thirties. True, it was only in 1950 that the party openly espoused democratic socialism without labelling it Arab. Unlike Ba'th, it stood for an Arab federation whose links are to be defined by democratic decisions. Intra-party dissensions and successive coups bringing sole saviours to the fore caused its extinction.

The ideological evolution of Ba'th seems to have come full circle. At the onset Ba'th vehemently challenged the premises of Marxism and communism, but in its 1966 metamorphosis a kind of Marxism peppered with Leninism, Maoism and all kinds of Third World maxims has openly been espoused. In between, notably since 1961, there were internal deliberations of "fathers and sons," betraying adaptation due to "national front" exigencies and closer rapprochement with the Soviets. On the other side, some doctrinal continuity has prevailed in this ideological process. From the start seized by the mystique of revolution, be it national or social, it ended with the glorification of the idea of permanent rebellion, to be applied to Arab non-"progressive" states and to Israel.* The "eternal Arab mission" is still upheld.

Ba'th, then, claims precedence in launching the idea of Arab socialism. Cherishing an idea of originality is not to be confused with the unqualified originality of an idea. Nowadays any idea, whatever its claims to be rooted in native soil, consists, in the main, of reactions to ideas from outside. This goes for a national and social, even a religious idea. In his *Islam in India*, W.C. Smith has admirably shown how Indian Islam argued out and absorbed philosophical and social ideas from the West. Political exigencies and fascinations have a part in it. A strenuous assertion of originality notwithstanding, Egypt's socialism, though Islam-bound, is a rather eclectic assemblage of foreign versions of socialist or communist provenance.

---

* All offshoots of Ba'th are relentless in their opposition to a peaceful solution of the Arab-Jewish problem.

Ba'th was founded in 194, when an apocalyptic National Socialism was thought to prevail in Europe. The preceding decade was an era of *ideendämmerung*: Arab nationalism indiscriminately tended to confound Western democratic socialism with colonialism and imperialism. Triumphant fascism and National Socialism, unchallenged in Ethiopia and Spain, promised and were believed to hasten national liberation. Sympathies, "nationalist in motivation," prompted Ba'th to launch a "Victory for 'Iraq" movement in support of the pro-Axis revolt in 1941.[1]

Any attempt to pursue the evolution of Ba'th ideology comes to grief with the startling gap between the party's theory and practice. It is due not only to Tuman frailties or pressures from outside. With all the generalization, the state of affairs as presented by Khaldun S. al-Husri seems compelling.

> The Ba'th, and here we exclude from it all the military, who at one time or another took its name . . . That never been the monolithic and popular party it has claimed to be. It owed its dominant position in pre-union Syrian politics to its alliance with some of the more militant officers in the Syrian army, and wanted to keep this position after union through its alliance with Nasser.
>
> . . . The Ba'th had been only one among many groups that plotted the March coup, but the accidental circumstances of the coup at first, then their manipulation of the rivalries of the individualistic Syrian officers, gave them power. But that power lacked substance and was in fact illusory. Real power lay in the hands of the officers, who, in turn, manipulated the Ba'th, making full use of the schisms and the quarrels of the individualistic civilian leaders of the Ba'th . . . Salah Jadid today, like Hafez earlier, and Luay al-Atasi still earlier, and Ziad al-Hariri earlier still, rules in the

name of the Ba'th and is supported by certain Ba'th factions.

Al-Husri regards them all as "military dictatorships."[2]
Jebran Majdalani points to the absurdity of revolutionary euphory.

> Terms like revolution and counter-revolution are reduced *ad absurdum*. The overthrow of Qasim régime, in some ways and intermittently supported by the Communists, is named the "Ramadan 14 Revolution" fighting counter-revolution. Again the coup of November, 1963, against the "Ramadan 14 Revolution," ideologically soon to establish a regime of the Arab Socialist Union, is again called counter-revolution.[3]

Once a "coup" or "revolution" is made a legitimate means of ideological or political warfare, floodgates of violence are wide open. In the case of the "Ramadan 14 Revolution," army units fought army units, "two hundred civilian members and sympathizers of the Ba'th were killed mainly by Communist commandos"; as against this, Communists were tortured and "some leading Communist Party members" executed without trial.[4] A preceding link in the chain of violence was the unsuccessful, Egypt-supported attempt of Shawwaf, in 1962, to overthrow Qasim, when "approximately 5000 persons including a great number of women were killed" in Mosul. The "tragic memories" of this attempt "accentuated the thirst for revenge."[5]

### Footnotes

1.  In a lett of 1961, 'Aflaq sees in it "an opportunity to bring home to our young generation the significance of our Party's doctrine of Arab unity.' See Seale, **The Struggle for Syria (London 1965), p. 10.**
2.  "The Checkerboard of Arab Politics," **Middle East Forum**, 1966, No. 3, p. 87.

3. "The Ba'ath Experience in Iraq," **Middle East Forum**, 1965, No. 2, pp. 44, 45.
4. **Ibid.**
5. **Ibid.** — According to Éric Rouleau, (**Le Monde**, October 11, 1968), the Ba'th government of 1963 was responsible for ths massacre of "some twelve thousand of sympathizers or militants of the extreme Left and the jailing of over a hundred thousand others."

Chapter X

# BA'TH VERSUS ARAB SOCIALIST UNION

The degree of originality, at least of innateness, of both Egyptian and Ba'th ideologies may be claimed to be a criterion of validity. Egypt's and Arab nationalisms have grown, in the main, from protest against foreign domination.[1] Still, they have drawn from various and varying theories of nationalism, European and non-European, and in this sense also mirror, in Arabicized form, the evolution of non-Arab thought. True, here subtler, discriminative aspects of nation and nationalism have remained *terra incognita*.

Since the mid-forties, socialism, at the start vaguely indicating the need of change, has been linked more and more to Arab nationalism, and finally proclaimed coextensive with, even flowing from it. Curiously, these two or, in view of the schisms within Ba'th, three or four brands of socialism, all authoritarian and vocation-minded, hence in theory mutually exclusive, all discard regionalism,[2] and, at least initially, had claimed validity for all Arab countries.

Ba'th came into "sole" power in 1963, so that since the 'forties its ideology evolved, and to a degree was argued out, its secretiveness notwithstanding, on a voluntary basis. For ten-fifteen years it bore the ideological imprint

211

of one man, a kind of visionary turned politician, at most two—three men. It was voluntarily seized upon by an élite—students, teachers, professionals—and engendered a *movement*. Once in power, the highly personalized argument over matters of ideology ended in bloodshed — - between or within the military and civil wings—and schism. Since the late 'fifties theorists have moved away from Ba'th drawing ideas pointing to Nasserism combined with Marxism-Leninism (Unionist Socialists).

By contrast, Egypt's ideology was, from the start, devised and constantly modified by men in power, that is, never freely argued out.[3] As a consequence, it seems far more a patchwork of political and social scientists with little grace of creativity. The amalgam of socialism and Islam—far from being an innovation—sounds rationalized. It is felt ulteriorily motivated and lacks the force of religious spontaneity.

Both ideologies claim history as a midwife (Egypt's trend is linked to Islam, Ba'th purports to be rooted in Arabdom, hence, in spite of not being committed to religion, in Islam as a legacy of Arabdom).[4] But both are militating against history in that they tried to ignore the individuality—geographical, ethnic, cultural and religious—of each Arab country, that is, its historic sum total. Egypt's new ideology nearly disregards the pre- and non-Islamic components of her personality; only at times of trial or disillusionment writers fall back on Egypt's singular identity. Both employ ideas, patterns of argument and terminology at best Arabicized.

In both cases we have detected a movement of ideas towards Marxism, inevitably if unavowedly, Leninist. This brand of Marxism, often argued for by theorists insufficiently versed in the evolution of Marxist thought, even disregarding its pre-communist phase or non-communist aspect, echoes or tries to vindicats tactics rather than conviction. We witness arbitrary use of Marxist terminology, violent exegesis of events by pressing them into Marxist formulae and intoxication with revolutionism, a kind of new utopianism couched in "scientifism."

Having no tangible opposition to contend with, Egypt's Arab Socialist Union purports to embody all "progressive" or "working" forces of the country. Ba'th could hardly raise such claim; it is unable genuinely to coalesce with other "progressive forces." Even a longer essay in unity than that of U.A.R., in 1958-1961, would probably have shown that in each country the régime has to assume regional, in fact near-national characteristics. Besides, Egypt's ideology traces its origin to Islam. Ba'th is "this worldly," ancient mythology and hagiography have no part in it. As said, both absorbed the main elements of Marxism-Leninism, while shunning identification with communism. No doubt, the military, political and financial aid from the Soviet Union prompts or exacts an ideological alignment, but both are keen to elaborate distinct features.*

This ideological shift has occurred while Communist theory fell in disarray. It could be gleaned from both Egyptian and Syrian writings that the twentieth congress of the Communist party in the Soviet Union as well as the self-assertion of Yugoslavia's communism have made communism more palatable to Arab socialism. This was preceded by the Bandung conference, in 1955, and coincided with the activities of the non-aligned "third force" of Tito's, Nehru's and 'Abd al-Nasir's provenance championing "positive neutralism." This "third force" concept has not prevented contending Arab socialist factions from toying with the explosive Third World formation, since 1966 transformed from the Afro-Asian Peoples Solidarity Organization into a Tricontinental People's Solidarity Organization, temporarily seated in Havana. Represent-

---

*One is tempted to see it also politically motivated: distinctness enhances bargaining power.

ing a "hungry" nation of some fifteen states, with immense oil wealth, they too are standard-bearers of a pan-proletarianism of the underprivileged nations, natural allies in generating a world revolution, which means oscillating between the various kinds of communism, Latin American guerrillism and Third World socialisms.

It is in the mid-fifties, with the arms deal with Syria and Egypt, that communism has become *salonfähig*. The leap towards Leninist Marxism took place in the 'sixties, and yet it is safe to record that, for all the immense aid, the Moscow brand of communism has never called up fascination. Continuous Soviet aid prompts ideological alertnes *vis-à-vis* th e Soviet Union, and yet the then unruly spirit of Maoism and the cult of guerrilleros are felt to appeal more than the seemingly more disciplined, staid Soviet doctrine. Maoism's stand is not affected by being branded, in Soviet idiom, along with Trotskyism and anarchism —petty bourgeois. The effect is probably cancelled out by labeling Soviet communism as revisionism or social-imperialism. One recalls the late 'twenties and early 'thirties in Germany, when Communists would brand social-democracy social-fascism. Space is also given in the one-voice Arab press to other communist dissenters, though of late Yugoslavia's dissent has been put to near-oblivion.

Mao Tse-tung's vocabulary has struck the imagination deepest. To mention the terms ceaselessly used like magic formulas, some of them being titles of his works: mobilization of all nation's forces; people's liberation army; pople's revolutionary army; partial resistance, total resistance; guerrilla warfare; establishment of base areas; týpes of base areas; strategic base; roving insurgents; position or mobile warfare; encirclement and annihilation of the enemy; strategic defensive and strategic offensive in guerrilla warfare; protracted war; regular warfare; war of annihilation; war of attrition; new democracy based on democratic centralism; Marxism-Leninism verified in the practice of revolutionary class struggle; revolutionary national struggle; anti-bureaucracy. Added to this, the appeal to join the workers', peasants', youths', women's and cultural organizations.

Mao Tse-tung still quotes the unmentionable Stalin, but it must be a relief to know of Marxism-Leninism "ceaselessly opening, through practice, the road to the knowledge of truth," furthermore, that "it has been-verified in the subsequent practice of revolutionary class struggle and revolutionary national struggle."

A semblance of a historical parallel, if formal, seems not out of place. In the early 1880's, when the multi-facet and multi-level movement of Russian populism for a while reached a dead-end — as a social movement not as a state of mind or a way of living — and utter despair had led to *bezvremenye* (in our idiom non-time) and décadence, Marxism came to rescue mind and heart. New vistas had been held: no more wishful, at best "utopian" thinking — instead a theory distilled from insights in the evolution of mankind, aligned with the march of history and well-founded on economic and social laws. There is an iron-cast means of combat — class struggle, there is a legitimate carrier of social emancipation, heir of all the creative and viable values of bourgeois civilization and human culture in general — the working class. Its vocation is near messianic — by feeing itself it frees humanity. Even non-Marxist writers point to the then salutary effect of Marxism on the intelligentsia. It cleared the way for a purposeful and organized activity. Socially and culturally it was then a solidifying force.It stemmed the tide of individualistic self-indulgence and anarcho-terrorism. At the turn of the century fascination with Marxism somewhat faded, one of the reasons being its verification in practice. It branched out in warring trends. But here the tentative parallel ceases. In the Arab context we are dealing with what Arab opponents termed *"razzia (ghazw) of Marxism."* Here Marxism is the great discovery of the last fifteen years. A romanticized "scientifism" may affect consistent thinking, too. It may lead to horrendous utopianism strewn with myths of infallibility, to belief in unquestioned prowess of a few.

The Marxization of socialism is accompanied by Arabization of Marxism, perhaps one should add regionalization of Marxism. To the neo-Marxist Abdallah Laroui, *"La conscience arabe utilise le système marxiste à ses fins idéologiques."* He speaks of *"Marxisme objectif ... c'est-à-dire qu'il s'impose comme la conséquence nécessaire d'idéologies déjà courantes dans la Société arabe."* [6] 'Just as the Arabs had their own reading of Aristotle," *leur situation leur impose une lecture de Marx, qui n'est certes pas systématisée, qi est encore une possibilité plus qu'une réalité effective, mais qui déjà peut être nettement disinguée d'autres lectures courantes en Occident et adoptées individuellement par les intellectuels arabes.* [7] It is, so to speak, an absolute relativization of Marxism.

A retrospective glance may point to some formal consistency. It is a cast of mind that asserts itself. Here decades beg comparison. In the 'twenties Arab or Egypt's nationalism was linked to western democratic thought, in Gibb's idiom, "easternising" it in practice. In the mid-'thirties up to the early 'forties, a national-revolutionary mood was fanned in the wake of rising National Socialism and in the teeth of western mandatories that brought about the dismemberment of the Ottoman empire and within 15 years prepared some Arab countries — administration, judiciary system, communication, an élite reared in the West — for independence.

The younger generation of the Thirties discarded, in the mouths of youth movements and parties (League of National Action in Syria; in Egypt Young Men of Muslim Association and Young Egypt; *Futuwwa* in 'Iraq). the "decadent" western concepts of democracy, namely "capitalist plutocracy." Although the Arab nation occupies a low rung in *Mein Kampf,* Hitler youth prompted emulation.Fascism, too, spoke for the hungry nations, and its exploits in Ethiopia and Libya — both later to be liberated by Great Britain — didn't deter the Emir Shaqib Arslan, an ideologist of Arab nationalism, from seeking common ground with Italy. Glory in the past, cult of the leader, approval of violence, and last but not least, delusions about the ultimate victory of the creed — all combined here.

In 'Iraq we witnessed — in 1936 and in 1941 — two military *coups d'état* named *thawra* (revolution, also *wathba* —leap), thus inaugurating the era of coups. The nationalist press of 1936-1941 in 'Iraq and Syria betrays fascination with fascism and National Socialism, both bound to remove imperialism and Zionism. The ardor in favor of the new tide seems resuscitated in the present ardor for the Third World revolution.

In 1943, when the outcome of the war was shaping up, the infatuation with fascism faded and the minds turned to democracy and socialism, so much so that nearly every party, even of fascist provenance or religious orthodoxy, espoused it.

Will the new ideological servant maid — Marxism-Leninism — be a proper means for annihilation of Israel?

### Footnotes

1. It is well worth mentioning that it is the West that destroyed the Ottoman empire and opened the way of independence by carving out 'Iraq, Great Lebanon, Syria, Transjordan, later Jordan, and after the Second World War was instrumental in establishing Libya.

2. Except for Syria and 'Iraq, recently Lebanon, Ba'th is proscribed in all Arab countries. The ruling Ba'th wings in Syria and 'Iraq pursue policies of eliminating each other. The perennial appeal for unity of all progressive forces' there has remained a smokescreen.
   The recent experiment of a "national front" in Syria has not proved yet its solidity.

3. In may 1962, the draft of the Charter of National Action was discussed by a National Congress and approved as submitted by 'Abd al-Nasir. — See P. J. Vatikiotis, **op. cit.,** p. 377.

4. Ba'th may have taken note of Syria's ethnic composition and of religious affinities there. Not so Egypt with her some six million strong Coptic minority.

5 *L'Idéologie arabe contemporaine* (Maspéro, Paris), 1967, p. 139.

6. **Ibid.**, p. 153.

7. **Ibid.**
By marxisme "objectif" he understands "une situation particulière et passagere; celle d'une societe qui, a un stade determine de son evolution, ... est obligée de recourir, pour se comprendre et pour agir, a un ensemble non systématisé d'idées, de notions, de théories dont chacune peut être rattachée par un biais ou par un autre au marxisme"(p. 10).

Chapter XI

ARAB NATIONALISTS MOVEMENT

The full cycle of the Arab Nationalists Movement
(*harakat al-qawmiyyin al-ʾarab*)¹ from fascism to Marxism-
Leninism is candidly traced by Muhsin Ibrahim, whose
ideological itinerary covers that of his movement.² To him,
there were three stages in the ideological evolution of
Lebanon's branch, the mainstay of this movement.

1. The 'fifties: the fascist practices of ANM.
2. The 'sixties up to June 5, 1967: predominance of petty
bourgeois views and practices under the influence of the
Nassertite experiment and the nationalizations of 1961.
3. After June 1967, "basic leanings" became apparent
within the Left of ANM. On the whole, the conference of
1968 in Lebanon approved the analysis of the Arab condition as presented by the Left and officially espoused Marxism-Leninism. The struggle between the Left, bent on discarding the history of ANM, and the "rightist bourgeois
group," resulted, in the first half of 1969, in secession of the
Marxist-Leninist wing. It reconstituted itself in an
Organization of Lebanese Socialists, "embarking on a new
road, free of the burden of 15 destructive years and the
rightist nationalist and petty bourgeois practices."

ANM was launched, in 1951, by a group of youths with a
view of avenging the outcome of the 1948 war. "Unity,

liberation, vengeance (*tha'r*) was its watchword. Objects of revenge were also to be Communists and the Soviet Union. It was a kind of extension of a former terrorist organization- — Phalanges of Arab Redemption (*kataّ'ib al-fida al-'arabi*).[3] It seemed then to some Arab youths that the Arab problem could be solved by removing some "traitors" among Arab rulers, political and military. Gangs in Syria, Egypt, also Lebanon and Jordan planned or made attempts to assassinate traditional leaders who purportedly took part, by negligence or ill-will, in the "betrayal of the Arab cause," and to attack "Zionist and Western interests." It was also the beginning of the era of *coups d'états*.

ANM soon spread in semi-secret circles in the larger cities of Lebanon, in Jordan (here it had a part to play in the events of 1957-58), in Kuwayt, on account of the friction between the emerging bourgeoisie and the "tribal régime."[4] From its inception it was Palestine-centered, namely the Arab problem was viewed from the vantage point of the Palestine disaster that "exemplifies the weakness and retardedness of the Arab society."[5] Arab unity should ensure redemption of Palestine.

Not unlike Ba'th, ANM began as a movement of a non-confessional élite. Having the organizational weakness of Ba'th in mind, it seems to have stressed the organizational rather than the ideological aspects in revolutionary activity. Its leaders may have reasoned that Zionism owes its prevalence to organizational prowess, just as it is argued that the outcome of the 1967 war was due to technological superiority. Likewise the Movement's Palestine-centredness seems to have made them assume that Zionism could be beaten without battling simultaneously "reaction and imperialism" and questioning their institutions and values. The goal of "unity, liberation and revenge" dictates that the conflagration with bourgeois forces should be deferred.

Up to 1954 ANM had neither program nor constitution. On account of ideological differences, a draft of constitution in 1956 was not given approval. In talks and pamphlets ANM called for a "political solution" to problems of union. This was to be achieved even by backing "imperialist union projects" such as Greater Syria and Fertile Crescent sponsored by Great Britain. It saw in communism a great danger to the national struggle. First comes "political liberation"; social liberation and forging a revolutionary doctrine for it are left aside. In consequence, any form of unity at any price is welcome. Once the greater state is formed, foreign influence should be easy to eliminate. In Ba'thist view, it was an attempt to enslave the socialist idea resulting in a society dominated by the bourgeoisie.[6]

In those years ANM line of argument against the Jews, all of them enemies of the Arabs, recalls that of the al-Azhar socialists, the difference being that ANM did not draw inspiration from the Koran. It is the line of argument of the Protocols of the Elders of Zion and of Alfred Rosenberg. Judaism and Zionism are synonymous. "All Jews, from the far left to the far right, have the same clear and definite aims."[7]

ANM is charged with having, at this stage, completely ignored the "objectivity of class struggle" and opposing "political class agitation" against feudalism and the big bourgeoisie, on the ground that this would "dissipate the nation's unity and ruin the national struggle."[8] Furthermore, even the petty bourgeois vision of Arab national liberation (agrarian reform, democratic and social changes for the benefit of the masses) would set off "side- and part-battles," thus weakening the struggle against division, colonialism and Jews.[9]

Subsequently, ANM moved toward the concept of a phased struggle and envisaged two stages in it:

The first is political — unification of the nation, liberation from colonialism and elimination of the Jewish entity (*kiyan*) in Israel. At this stage all the nation's classes, save "dangerous and traitors," unite in his effort.

The second stage is "social construction," building a

"national society," not by pursuing class interests ("nationalism denies existence of classes"), but "for the benefit of the nation as a whole."[10]

To Muhsin Ibrahim, the ANM slogan of "liberation of Palestine" was in keeping with the fascist usage that fed the movement's original theory. The policy of "verbal racist primitive underrating of the objectivity of class struggle" deterred from "analyzing the Zionist movement scientifically and uncovering the dialectical relationship between it and the capitalist interests of world imperialism with all its ramifications and class bases in the Arab homeland."[11]

ANM assumed, rather confusedly, that realization of "political liberation" would not set off a violent struggle between the revolutionary movement and "reaction-imperialism." To 'Allush, they failed to see that it is impossible to free a country politically and recover lost parts of it by traditional methods of struggle, namely relying on "emaciated institutions." "Reaction-imperialism" represent and defend standing interests and violently reject any attempt at a change. Consequently, political liberation is only one of the aspects of a revolutionary battle.[12]

Their first serious study (Maq' al-qawmiyya al-'arabiyya, 1957) reasons that "elimination of poverty and economic and social injustice presupposes elimination of economic partitition of the Arab homeland, with a view to Arab union, and elimaination of exploitation in the direction of socialism. But imperialism, Israel and the devious and selfish ruling Arab groups are bound to fight these trends violently. Consequently, before turning toward economic or social struggle, these three factors have to be done away with."[13] It was a move away from their original stand.

During the Suez crisis, Egypt's challenge brought ANM—in this instance Ba'th as well—nearer to 'Abd al-Nasir, in the 'fifties himself a sponsor of the *fida'iyyun* in the Gaza strip. In the years of union (1958-1961), Ba'th, ever since averse to the dogma of sole leadership, modified, even questioned the belief in 'Abd al-Nasir's inevitability. ANM gloried in it. They moved toward the idea that Palestine could be recovered only through unification of the Arab régimes.

'Abd al-Nasir's turn towards socialism in the late 'fifties, more so in 1961, challenged ANM to a clear response. At the beginning of the 'sixties they knew a sharp struggle of currents. Exclusive nationalists vied with groups courting "scientific socialism." In 1963, their line of reasoning, at least that of the stronger wing, seems to have outstripped Egypt's ideology. Elements of their reasoning could even be traced to Mao Tse-tung.

In a declaration of March 16, 1963, they call for a tripartite union — Syria, 'Iraq, Egypt — with "deep populist roots." A "serious socialist revolution enjoins a deep limitless belief in the people, in the role of the masses, their creative ability and their being the first and last source of revolution." They speak of the oppressed "people's masses" becoming a revolutionary community. What is called "traditional democracy" is rejected; a pattern of democracy is envisaged that is "based on national socialist guidance and linked to elimination of reactionary class factionalism and anti-national (shu'ubi) and non-national forces." "True freedom and actual democracy are not realizable outside the framework of socialist revolutionary guidance and outside the scope of the basic interests of the masses."[14]

In a sense their name belies their ideological evolution. More than any other group they exemplify a chain of reactions to non-Arab radicalism, stretching from Fascist tendencies to various versions of Marxism-Leninism. Furthermore, it is also a chain of ideological experiments to achieve the main goal — annihilation of Israel.

In about 1964-1965 ANM set out to form military commandos. In January 1967, Dr. Habash and his collaborators formed a Popular Front for the Liberation of Palestine by uniting three groups, the most important being ANM (Palestine branch) and its military wing, Youth of

Vengeance (*shabab al-thą'r*). In February 1969, a Marxist-Leninist minority wing, under Na'if Hawatmeh as well as Muhsin Ibrahim and Muhammad Kishli from *al-Hurriyya* seceded from the Front to form a Democratic Popular Front.[15]

Another offshoot of PFLP is PFLP General Command, under Ahmad Jibril, started in 1968. Its practice — murder with no scruples of ideology or morals.

Abstracts of the PFLP-ideology, as presented by Hisham Sharabi[16], betray some sources of inspiration (Ho Chi Minh and Mao Tse-tung are quoted, the latter variously). As late as December 20, 1969, Habash speaks of a "three-dimensional framework" of the struggle: a "revolutionary Marxist-Leninist party" mobilizing the workers and the peasants and basing the movement on scientific socialism; a "broad national front" that "mobilizes the various national classes and groups willing to join the battle of liberation"; and the "Principle of Armed Struggle" that transforms guerrilla warfare into a people's war of liberation. Clearly, before the confrontation with Jordan's army PFLP was far from attaining even the first dimension.

Interviewed for the West German News Agency, G. Habash said:

"The future state of Palestine after the liberation will be run according to Marxist-Leninist principles. There will be a Marxist-Leninist party, and the people's front will be the leader of the revolution. The fight for the liberation of Palestine will take another 20 to 30 years, and after the victory everything will be different; not only will Palestine be free from Zionism, but Lebanon and Jordan will be free from reaction and Syria and 'Iraq from the petite bourgeoisie. They will have been transformed in a truly socialist sense and united. Palestine will be part of a Marxist-Leninist Arabia.[17]

"We wage a national democratic war of liberation of a socialist nature; the objective is to put an end to Israel's existence as a hostile, racist, robber state which is connected with world imperialism.

"When our war is finished, every Jew in Palestine will enjoy full and equal rights."[18]

Despite the "Marxist-Leninist" line of argument of PLFP (having a "proletarian ideology and program," the real people, the proletarian masses follow its lead), it is safe to argue that it is an opportunist one, the deeper motivation being that of the first stage of ANM. The capitalist countries "conceived the Hebrew state and use it as a bastion to protect their interests." China's attitude to Israel is supposed to be the fiercest, hence her ideology might be the most useful. The friendly attitude of U.S.S.R. is marred by having adopted the peace resolution of the Security Council.

The megalomania of Dr. Habash is a case in point.

"We want a Vietnam war not just in Palestine but throughout the Arab world.

"Our best friend, in fact, is China. China wants Israel erased from the map ...

"We believe that to kill a Jew far from the battleground has more of an effect than killing 100 of them in battle; it attracts more attention.

"We don't want peace, we will never agree to any peaceful compromise. And China sees eye to eye with us on this issue.

"Every day a tank gets destroyed somewhere, a soldier is killed, a traitor executed."[19]

A testament of PFLP, the self-confessed "vanguard of the armed revolution of the masses," declares that in "today's world" no one is "innocent," no one is "neutral." A man is either with the oppressed or he is with the oppressors. He who takes no interest in politics gives his blessing to the prevailing order. "International law only serves to make the mentality of exploitation legitimate."

Hence the exposure of innocent people to danger by

bombing, by hijacking or blowing up planes is justified.[20]

One can't help placing the leader of PFLP alongside of Nechayev. To strike the imagination of the "Arab masses" it crowned its exploits with the Lod massacres by terrorists from Japan. The exploits of the medieval Assassins or *fida'is*, combining ideas with terror, also come to mind. Another dictum of PFLP:

"The road to Tel-Aviv should pass henceforth through Beirut, 'Amman, Riyad, Kuwayt, even Damascus and Cairo." PFLP charges the Arab Communist parties, to be sure the Moscow-oriented ones, with betraying Marxism.[21]

Meanwhile Habash's vainglory and apocalyptic vision of an inferno prepared by spasmodic fits against the world has resulted in an inferno for the visionaries. Violent infighting before and after the split between members of the two factions make one imagine the events to ensue the moment all the ideological factions make a bid for power, or will have to share in it. True, Habash's prognostications had been made before the confrontation in Jordan in September 1970.

The PDFLP, too, argues for the elimination of Israel, but it claims to have adopted a "proletarian and international attitude to the national problem," not a *"position conjonctorelle."* It considers itself a segment of the "revolutionary world." For this reason it "recognizes the right of the Kurdish people in Turkey, Iran, 'Iraq and Syria to self-determination in its territory." It stands for a "democratic and internationalist solution of the Palestinian and Israel problems." It envisages in Palestine a "truly democratic state forming a part of a great Arab federation in which power, the whole power, would be exercised by councils of workers, councils of poor peasants and soldiers."[22] Another version: "a democratic popular state comprising Arabs and Jews within the framework of a socialist system, each community having the right to preserve its culture and work for its flourishing." "One could envisage a Yugoslav model — autonomous governments all under one authority on the plane of economics, security and foreign policy. By putting an end to all racial, religious and class antagonisms, socialism will help the new state to liberate itself from American imperialism, Zionism and Arab chauvinism."[3]

"The struggle for a democratic popular solution of the Palestinian and Israeli problem must be based on liquidation of the Zionist entity which manifests itself in all institutions of the state: army, administration, police and all political, professional, chauvinistic and Zionist institutions.

"(Hence the need) to provide the (striven for) Palestinian democratic popular state with a national liberation movement, realized only through an armed struggle and a popular war of liberation against Zionism and imperialism, leading to the destruction of the State of Israel and deliverance of the Jews from the Zionist movement."[24]

DPLFP rejects military coups whatever their ideological guise.

"The new coup (in 'Iraq) is a kind of a new link in a chain of struggles within the ruling bourgeois military class. These struggles differ as to political directions, connections and party identity, but in fact have an unchanging pattern: they are not capable of fulfilling the historic tasks of a populist revolution — from a basic agrarian reform to the liberation of 'Iraq from the influence of neo-colonialism."[25]

Both Fronts profess class consciousness, but Hawatmeh lays more stress on the theory of class struggle. To him, Israel is an enemy because it is ruled by a big bourgeoisie and exploiters' class allied with America. An Arab people's democracy and an Israeli people's democracy would find a common language.[26]

PDFLP purports to be averse to opportunism of PFLP and prone to ideological consistency. Their literary output betrays also some affinity for the line of argument of the New Left; they are even charged with "salon intellectualism." Even Trotsky's *The Permanent Revolution* is quotable. No doubt, personal and fractional rivalries had a part to play in this ideological argument.

And yet both Fronts pin their hopes on "forces of world socialism," profess Marxist-Leninist revolutionary purism and both are far from being excited about Moscow-oriented communism. Both link the Palestinian to the Arab cause and nurse objectives embracing the whole Arab world. Both seek to establish "liberation beachheads" in a number of conservative Arab states. Both share, along with Fath, revolutionary fervor in the cause of Palestine, but, unlike Fath, chided for its "technocratic concept" of commandos, they expressly extend their enmity to the Arab "reactionary régimes" and disapprove of the countries of Arab "petty bourgeois socialism," and yet both are variously supported by these countries.

Both Fronts purport to act in the name of the masses. PFLP is chided for an air of superiority (it aims to "organize, educate, mobilize" the masses), whereas PDFLP speaks of "daily relations with the large masses," of "drawing strength from them, learning from and teaching them." PDFLP believes in a "solid bridge between theory and practice."

Conspiratorial and unrelenting, PFLP yet clings to the need for the missing link, namely a party as "class expression." PDFLP sounds more supple, not lacking some substance in its Marxist-Leninist sloganeering. One is inclined to say that PFLP, its alternate relations with Arab régimes of "petty bourgeois socialism" notwithstanding, has not transcended the early age of Maoism, or headlessly leapt into the realm of Japan's Red Army, whereas PDFLP has somehow benefited from neo-Marxist self-criticism. PDFLP denounces "demagoguery of praise" favished on *fida'ism* at its heyday as well as" demagoguery of hate — often by the same persons — at its demise in 1971.[27]

In our context, Fath, though not an offspring of ANM, is well worth mentioning. As for the military nomenclature of revolutionism, the sources are identical, but in point of commitment to a social ideology, Fath professes neutrality. Depending on the leanings of various elements in it, it may be a tactical or a long-term attitude. But getting aid and support from any source, native or foreign, necessarily results in ideological mimicry.

In Sa'udi Arabia Fath "rejects any attempt to use Marxism and Leninism as the political base for the Palestinian armed struggle."[28]

To Husayn Shinnawi, Fath is "real Leftist revolutionary ... a total revolution, solving all outstanding problems, from those of the petty bourgeois régimes to those of Arab reaction."[29]

In the heat of revolutionary ecstasy, the *fida'iyyun* saw in the liberated zone of Irbid "the first Arab Soviet."[30]

As for the aims of the Palestinian revolution, they are attuned to the addressee.

In an official statement, distributed in Washington, Fath or the Palestinian Revolution stands for a "progressive," "democratic, non-sectarian state" meaning "destruction of the political, economic and militarist foundations of a chauvinist racist settler state." "The process of the Revolution will inevitably increase the tempo of emigration" from Palestine, "especially of those beneficiaries of the racist state who will find it difficult to adapt to an open plural society." Return of Jewish emigrants to the Arab countries is considered. A distinction is made between Jewish Arabs as against non-Arab (Western) Jews. "Liberated Palestine will be part of the Arab nation" and will "join the ranks of progressive revolutionary countries."[31] No word is wasted on Jewish immigration.

Hisham Sharabi speaks of two "schools of thought"

that preoccupy both Fath and the Popular Front — an "Algerian solution" and a "One-man, One-vote solution."[32]

Abu Iyad, one of the theorists of Fath:

" ... The Palestinian revolution is a revolution against racialism, fascism and imperialism, in consequence, it is completely void of racialism, fascism and imperialism. Hence it does not work nor carries arms against the Jews as humans, as an indivisible part of mankind. But it is against the Zionist Fascist racialist movement that carries out colonialist occupation of the people's homeland, of Palestine. Consequently, it is a colonialist movement closely linked to imperialism."[33]

Another statement, more outspoken:

"La violence révolutionnaire est la seule voie pour libération de la patrie. Cette violence révolutionnaire a pour but de liquider identité sioniste sur tout le territoire occupé de la Palestine, sous ses formes politique, économique et militaire."[34]

At a symposium with the editors of al-Anwar,[35] on the issue of a "democratic Palestinian state," Shafiq al-Hut, for Fath, said:

"There is no merit in talking at length about the slogan of a "Democratic State." It is not possible for such a state, devoid of affiliation, to come into being. If this slogan is only intended as an answer to the charge that we aim at throwing the Jews into the sea, it is a successful slogan and and effective political and propaganda act. But if we regard it as a matter of ultimate strategy of the national Palestinian and Arab liberation movements, then I think it calls for thorough examination."

A struggle, in some respects corresponding to that

within ANM, later within PFLP, took place within NLF of South Yemen that issued, in the main, from the local section of ANM. In November 1967, it prevailed over the pro-Egyptian FLOSY (Front of Liberation of South Yemen), in a mutual bloodbath, and seized power. On March 28, 1968, the Rightist or "pragmatic" wing in NLF led by al-Sha'bi defeated, due to the army, the Leftist or "idealist" wing under 'Abdu'l-Fattah Isma'il and for some time removed it from positions of power.[36] Some time back, at a conference of NLF on March 2-8, 1968, 'Abdu'l-Fattah, then minister of information, demanded a clear choice between "proletarian ideology and scientific socialism and ideology of the petty bourgeoisie (Nasserism, Algerian NLF, Ba'th, the Iraqi experiment), more concretely: on the side of the proletariat and the poor peasants and partisans allied with it or on the side of the rightist classes (feudalism, kulakdom, petty bourgeoisie)." The conference acceded to some of the demands. The weekly *al-Hurriyya* branded the partisans of al-Sha'bi as "petty bourgeois revolutionaries running a risk to turn counter-revolutionaries the moment they face a genuine people's revolution." Isma'il attacked the "phraseological, pathetic socialism of NLF leadership and called for people's democracy through councils of workers, poor peasants and partisans."[37]

Apart from Kuwayt, ANM seems to have been reduced to small groupuscules in a few Arab countries. Its Marxist-Leninist offshoots regrouped themselves under names of their choice. PDFLP and Organization of Lebanese Socialists have been mentioned. In 'Iraq it is named Arab Socialist Movement, close to the revolutionary strain of the communist party there; in Sa'udi Arabia it is christened Popular Democratic Front of Liberation of the Arab Peninsula, closely associated with PDFLP;[38] in Yemen—the Revolutionary Democratic Party of Yemen; in South Yemen—the left wing of NLF that seized power from its right wing in June 1969.

The Front of Liberation of Dhofar in 'Uman, also issued or inspired from ANM, renamed itself Popular Front of Liberation of the Occupied Arab Gulf, envisaging a popular republic comprising Dhofar, 'Uman, Trucial 'Uman, Oatar, Bahrayn and Kuwayt.[39] Here it will have to confront Iran and the missionary zeal of 'Iraq.

Fred Halliday ventures to apply to the events in North Yemen a time-honored terminology such as "counter-revolution," "republican feudalism," "Thermidor."[40] Evidently proceeding from myopic manichaism, he fails to note the utter exhaustion of the feuding forces in the 1962-1969 civil war (The estimate of killed Egyptians—15,194—is mentioned, but not the multitudes of Yemenis killed and wounded in action or by indiscriminate bombing of villages and tribal encampments, even reaching into Sa'udi Arabia.* One estimate suggests a quarter of a million). The "civil war" within the republican army is a contributory factor. The ensuing famine should make the compromise arrived at palatable even to upholders of a purified ideology.

Even Halliday's presentation makes it evident, if implicitly, that the ideological war between the two factions in North Yemen was, to a great degree, a sublimation of tribal or urban-tribal rivalries, in part stemming from religious affiliation of the Shafi'i minority. The party allegiance of republican officers (Ba'th, ANM, later renamed Revolutionary Democratic Party) should also be traced to tribal or denominational motivations.

*To put his revolutionary anger to rest: there is much bloodshed caused by the messengers from South Yemen.

## Footnotes

1. Hereafter ANM.
2. One of the editors of **al-Hurriyya**. See his preface to **Limadha munazzamat ishtirakiyyin al-lubnaniyyin (harakat al-qawmiyyin al-'arab min al-fashiyya ila al-nasiriy ya)**. Why an organization of Lebanese Socialists (The movement

of Arab Nationalists from fascism to Nasserism), Beirut 1970, pp. 5, 6, 7. Cf. Hani al-Hindi, Muhsin Ibrahim, **Isra'il: fikra, haraka, dawla (Israel: Idea, Movement, State)**, Beirut 1958.

In "The Arab Nationalists Movement 1951-1971: from Pressure Group to Socialist Party" (unpublished Ph. D. thesis, The American University, Washington D.C., 1971), B. R. al-Kubaisi sees in the history of ANM three ideological phases: Arab nationalist, Arab socialist and Marxist. As for its relationship with Egypt's new régime that greatly impressed this evolution, al-Kubaisi discerns five phases:

Phase one, 1952-54. Ardent approval and yet critique, albeit reserved, of the military aspect (**'askariyya**) of the revolution and of Egypt's policies vis-à-vis U.S.A. and Great Britain.

Phase two, 1954-58. A "new era of understanding" resulting from a widening dimension of Egypt's revolution — stress on "Arabism and revolutionism for Arab countries." Landmarks: struggle against the Baghdad Pact; a policy of neutralism; the arms deal with U.S.S.R.; nationalization of the Suez canal.

Phase three, 1958-61. ANM regards the U.A.R. as a nucleus of the future Arab union, accepts her lead and supports her "internally and externally." ANM struggles against the local communists as "the reactionary force in the Arab world."

Phase four, 1961-1967. Internal struggle within ANM, on account of the July 1961 socialist decrees and the National Charter of 1962, between the "historical leadership" — Habash, al-Hindi, Wadi' Haddad — and the "younger generation" (Ibrahim's group) that questioned the possibility of carrying out drastic reforms in the absence of a socialist party and the role of "nationalist capitalists" as a unionist force.

At the 1965 congress the Ibrahim group carried the majority for a program of creating a "new Arab socialist movement based on a working class structure and a clear socialist ideology." According to Ibrahim (in **Limadha** . . .) the Executive Committee of ANM demanded, in 1966, that the progressive elements in the Arab Socialist Union (the "Nasser Left") should ascertain their political independence. "ANM believed that they could bypass Nasser's bureaucratic machinery without affecting their relation with Nasser."

Phase five, 1967-1971. Since Nasserism failed to liberate Palestine — the main **raison d'être** of ANM — the movement "lost its faith in Nasser and his system." In 1968, Nasserism is denounced by ANM as "a petty bourgeois movement doomed to failure." The Left, by now the "dominant force" in ANM, attempts "to integrate Marxism-Leninism to the concrete conditions of the Arab world." To them, Cuba and Vietnam are "working examples" of victory. PFLP and PDFLP — both offshoots of ANM — are "vigorously upholding the political formulas of the Communist parties without losing their organizational independence." The question is whether Marxism-Leninism "will serve them as a vehicle to liberate Palestine."

Of "the deeper, unconscious or semi-conscious, motivations of the young Arab revolutionaries," al-Kubaisi mentions only "an element of frustration."

There are some illuminating data and some daring questioning in Kubaisi's work. Unfortunately, we miss here a coherent presentation of the ideological issues argued out within ANM. A scholarly approach would have enlisted more testimonies of trends outside ANM. This work sometimes impresses one as an attempt to mitigate Ibrahim's appraisal of the rightist trend in ANM. We are hardly able to pronounce on whether or to what extent the struggle within ANM immediately preceded or prepared the ground for the argument within PFLP.

3. **Limadha** ... , p. 16. "It was, by its idea and terrorist activities, a specimen of Fascist reactions current within the Right wing of the middle and petty bourgeoisie, namely reacting with ideas of violence, void of revolutionary content, to a deep social crisis."

   Along with Muhsin Ibrahim, a former member of the Political Bureau of ANM, in his **Limadha** ... , al-Kubaisi finds "reasonable evidence," the claims of ANM to the contrary, "to establish the relationship between the two organizations;" he even terms the **Kata'ib** "forerunner" or precursor of ANM and speaks of "the impact of **Kata'ib** on the organizational structure and the ideology of ANM, especially during the formative years of the latter." Hani al-Hindi and G. Habash were among the founding fathers of both.

   By the end of 1948 three groups (a Beirut-based and two from Damascus, a local one and terrorist fugitives from Egypt) formed the **Kata'ib**. Its leaders have "copied" from Ahmad Husayn's Green Shirts, "a paramilitary organization which was modeled after the S.A. and the Fascist phalangues," "doctrine and fundamental principles," also its organizational framework. Their terrorist activities (**inter alia**, an attack on a synagogue in Damascus and an abortive attempt on al-Shishakli, the then strong man of Syria, in October 1950.) Having been exposed to the authorities, **Kata'ib** disintegrated.

   To al-Kubaisi, "**Kata'ib** was envisaged ... as a political weapon to bring pressure on Arab rulers, by terrorist intimidation if necessary, to prepare for another **jawla**" (round) against Israel.

   We further learn from al-Kubaisi that Habash contacted the students' society al-'Urwa al-Wuthqa (The Firm Bond) on the campus of the American University of Beirut and at the election of its executive committee outran other groups. This society was to become a "workshop" of ANM "during its transitional period."

4. Also some fifteen members, "sons of bourgeoisie and aristocracy" in Syria (in 1960) and some twenty members in 'Iraq (in 1958), **ibid.**, p. 23.

5. The above source (p. 10) candidly states that "the Fascist trends in the Arab area had fed, in theory and practice, not only on the Palestine tragedy." In the 'thirties and 'forties "national trends and organizations looked with admiration to the European Fascist pattern and drew inspiration from it for a program to recover the glory of the Arab nation and her place in history."

6. Naji 'Allush, **al-Thawra** ... **wa-'l-jamahir, marahil al-nidal al-'arabi 1948-1961 (Revolution ... and the Masses, Stages of Arab Struggle 1948-1961)**, Beirut, 2nd ed. 1963, pp. 54, 107-109. See also **Limadha** ..., **op. cit.**, p. 19.

7. Hani al-Hindi, Muhsin Ibrahim, **op. cit.**, pp. 27, 30. The authors believe that "complete crushing of the enemy is a condition of our people's existence." The

enemy "knows that this land will belong only to one of the struggling peoples: Arabs or Jews." "True realistic information" is presented here, since "reality is to be seen with our minds, as it is, not with our emotions, as we long it to be." To show Jewish characteristics a vast spectrum of sources is enlisted: Karl Marx's **The Jewish Question**"(Capital is the real Jewish god"); the announcement of the Soviet government, in 1953, about the Jewish doctors plot to kill Soviet leaders; the trial of Slanski and his "thirteen Jewish friends" for plotting against the security of Czechoslovakia in 1953; an interview withKhrushchevin **Le Figaro** (the Jews inquire everything and are given to deep intellectual deviation; they are individualistic, secessionist, dislike collective work), Moses' law, the Talmud ("the Jews were the first to call for chauvinistic racism"); Gibbon ("the corrupting influence of the Jews caused the downfall of the Roman empire"); Nehru's **Glimpses of World History**; lastly, Adolf Hitler's **Mein Kampf** (the Jews caused the defeat of Germany in World War One). The authors pin their hopes on the United Arab Republic whose existence is "the beginning of the road toward their end . . . their return to life if dispersion and humiliation."**(Ibid.,** 5, 220, 6, 17, 18, 23.)

8. **Limadha** . . . , **op. cit.,** p. 17.
9. **Ibid.,** p. 18. This source also maintains that the "Jewish danger" is inflated by insisting on "complete congruence between Judaism and Zionism" ("Every Jew is a Zionist not vice versa") and on "war of death or survival with every Jew in all the corners of the world."
10. **Ibid.** To al-Kubaisi, the "idealist ideology" and the simplistic program "of the first stage demonstrates the "immaturity and weakness" of the movement. He suggests that ANM gradually conceded an "interlocking relationship" between the two phases, especially since the formation of U.A.R. Outside of U.A.R. the emphasis was still on the two phases concept. It was scrapped after the secession of Syria.
11. **Ibid.,** p. 19.
12. **Op. cit.,** p. 108.
13. **Ibid.**
14. **Al-Hurriyya,** March 18, 1963.
15. Michael Hudson, "The Palestinian Arab Resistance Movement," **MEJ,** 1969, pp. 297-299. See also Gérard Chaliand, **"La résistance palestinienne,"** Le **Monde Diplomatique,** March 1969.

    To Fawwaz Trabulsi ("The Palestine Problem," **New Left Review,** Sept.-Oct. 1969, pp. 79, 80), "both the Baathi and the Nasserite régimes . . . are the **régimes of an embourgeoisified privileged minority of petit-bourgeois origin which has merged with the remnants of the old social order** (bureaucrats, ex-managers of nationalized enterprises, etc.) **and which appropriates the national surplus product through its control over the bureaucratic-military machinery of the state."** "**The limits of such régimes are their incapacity to give rise to anything but privileged minorities which will quickly transform themselves into new ruling classes")** (the author's emphasis). To Trabulsi, the defeat of June 1967 "has spurred the process of disintegration of the Arab CP's and petit bourgeois nationalism . . . the latter . . . highlighted by the splits inside the Arab Nationalist Movement." ANM, "the only organized detachment of Nasserism, is now dissolved, leaving only Marxist-Leninist groups committed to a systematic and consistent anti-imperialist struggle " (p. 88).

16. "Palestine Guerrillas: Their Credibility and Effectiveness," **Middle East Forum,** 1970, nos. 2 and 3, pp. 61-62.
17. Quoted from BBC Monitoring Service, 18.1.1970.
18. **Al-Hadaf** (Beirut), organ of PFLP, quoted in **al-Masa** ('Amman), December 22, 1969.
19. From an interview in **Life,** June 22, 1970. "By 1967 we had understood the undeniable truth, that to liberate Palestine we have to follow the Chinese and Vietnamese examples . . . Israel is a product of colonialism, colonialism is a product of imperialism, and imperialism is a product of capitalism."
20. **Times,** September 21, 1970. Prior to that Habash argued that when Mao Tse-tung cooperated in the 'Thirties with Chiang Kai-shek against the Japanese, he did not dwell on adherence to the principles of proletarian revolution. See **Neu Zürcher Zeitung,** February 21, 1969.
21. Eduard Saab, **Le Monde,** May 31-June 1, 1970.
22. Nayef Hawatmeh, **Le Monde,** January 27, 1970.
23. Eduard Saab, **ibid.**; also **Christian Science Monitor,** February 21, March 8-10, 1969.

    A version in Arabic in **Hawla azmat harakat al-muqawama al-Filastiniyya** ("On the Crisis of the Palestinian Resistance Movement," Beirut 1969, pp. 155-156) differs widely: "a democratic state on the earth of Palestine in which cultural and religious rights of non-Arab collectives, including the Jewish human collective, will be safeguarded."

    The Israeli public opinion should be addressed in a democratic and progressive spirit, not by demagoguery to which organizations of the small bourgeoisie resort.
24. **Al-Masa,** October 10, 1969.
25. **Al-Hurriyya,** July 22, 1968.
26. **A.H., Neue Zürcher Zeitung,** October 16, 1969.

    In March 1972, a group split off PFLP charging the leaders round Habash with keeping fast to their pre-Marxist views. Having seized key positions, they are said to impede the movement by "reflexes inherited from the petite-bourgeoisie." See Sadek El-Azem, **Le Monde Diplomatique,** April 1972.

    This group is to operate as Revolutionary Popular Front for the Liberation of Palestine. It states its opposition to use of violence abroad including the hijacking of airliners **(Jerusalem Post,** March 12, 1972).
27. See **Shu'un Filastiniyya,** Beirut, November, 1971.

    To Gérard Chaliand, PDFLP is "the only one . . . of these organizations which is Marxist-Leninist in word and deed"; it is "the only movement to put forward the notion of a Palestinian state in which Jews would enjoy full national rights." Habash speaks of liberated Palestine becoming Arab once more. "Palestine will not be a mosaic of different nationalities: every citizen, whatever his social or religious background, will enjoy full democratic rights."

    Habash's vague allusions make one assume that Hawatmeh's group saw in transformation of PFLP from a nationalist into a Marxist-Leninist organization an expedient, not change of heart. Habash cited Cuba as an example. They also differed on the role of the lower middle class in the struggle, on relations with the Arab national régimes, on interpretation of "democratic centralism" (See **The Palestinian Resistance,** (Penguin), 1972, pp. 8, 168, 167).

    PFLP keeps fast to its nationalistic past. It stresses the similarity "between its strategy and the operations of Black September, that is, to strike the imperialist interests in general and their advanced bases in the Near East."

By contrast, PDLF denounced the "adventurism" of the murder in Khartum, of "actions against the enemy on foreign territory that could not be inserted in the strategic pattern of the Palestinian revolution." PDLF prefers action on "the enemy's territory" (**Le Monde,** April 1-2, 3, 1973).

To PDLFP, the Arab national liberation movement is led by the petty bourgeoisie represented in Ba'th, Communists and Arab Nationalists. The Right of the petty bourgeoisie is represented in the Popular Front; these "forces of backwardness" in the petty bourgeoisie are closely allied with the "forces of the big bourgeoisie and political feudalism." In the shadow of its rightist command are the "forces of the people's masses" kept in ignorance (See **Hawla azmat** . . ., **op. cit.,** pp. 94, 128).

PDLFP chides the Palestinian resistance movement for lack of revolutionary attitude and revolutionary culture, for emotionalism and personalism in its life and operations. It "has drowned in a sea of privileges and comfort, material and moral . . . prosperity (a rich revolution) produced by Arab reaction and bourgeois classes." In the ranks of the basic resistance groups prevails bourgeois ideology. See **Hamlat Aylul wal-muqawama al-Filastiniyya** (The September Campaign and the Palestinian Resistance), Beirut 1971, pp. 24-29.

28. **Al-Balad** (Sa'udi Arabia), January 4, 1970.

29. **Al-Anwar** (Beirut), February 1, 1970.

30. David Hirst, **Guardian Weekly,** September 19, 1970.

According to PFLP, the "alliance" recently agreed upon between Fath and PFLP "signifies cooperation with the world Left and the socialist and workers' forces in all countries." See L_ Monde, April 1-2, 1973.

31. **Al-Fath,** Vol. 1, No. 6, Beirut, 1970.

32. **Op. cit.**

33. **Al-Tali'a,** June 1969.

34. From a résumé by Gérard Chaliand, **op. cit.**

35. See the issues of March 8, 15, 1970.

36. Arnold Hottinger, **Neue Zürcher Zeitung,** December 29, 1968. Also: **New York Times,** April 16, 1968; **Times,** April 11, 1968.

37. See Abdul F. Ismail, **"Der nicht – kapitalitische Entwicklung-sweg,"** in **Na'if Hawatmah's Azmat al-thawra fi'l-janub al'yamani (The Crisis of the Revolution in South Yemen),** Beirut 1968, in Bassam Tibi (ed.), **Die arabische Linke,** Frankfurt M., 1969, pp. 121, 122, 144. Also: **"Résolutions publiques adoptées par le IV$^e$ Congrés du Front National de Libération du Sud Yemen,"** Orient, Nos. 43-44, 3$^e$-4$^e$ trim., 1967. Also: Jean-Pierre Viennot, Aden . . ., **ibid.**; Nos. 51-52, 3-4 trim., 1969 (June 1971)

The concept of reunification of historic Yemen, once the main object of struggle with the British of both North Yemenis and South Yemenis, assumed a new dimension. We witness a fierce struggle between the Yemen Arab Republic and the People's Republic of Yemen. It is a struggle for prevalence, ideologically overcoated: who will rule whom. By supporting the rebels of Dhofar in 'Uman, the latter also aims at extending the "revolution" to the Gulf emirates, thus embracing Sa'udi Arabia. Still, the ideological frontiers are blurred. The super-structure of this struggle is a tangle of integral nationalism, integral Islam and integral socialism, not easily to untangle. Sa'udi Arabia and Libya support in North Yemen an Army of National Salvation composed of refugees of various factions from South Yemen and led by Flosy. On the frontiers of Sa'udi Arabia, North Yemen and South Yemen wells are being poisoned and tracks mined. Sixty-five tribal shaykhs of North Yemen invited to South Yemen to discuss differences found death in tents purposedly mined. Modern ideologists don't shun modernized means of tribal warfare (Paul Balta, **Le Monde,** September 1, 1972: Roger-X. Lanteri, **L'Express,** August 28-September 3, 1972).

38. **Al-Hadaf,** February 21, 1970.
39. See Fred Halliday's exalted essay "National Liberation in the Gulf," **New Left Review,** Nov.-Dec. 1969, p. 36. Also: Jean-Pierre Viennot, **Le Monde Diplomatique,** January 1970.

PFLOAG has recently renamed itself Popular Front for liberation of Oman, to stress the immediate national task.

R. B. Serjeant ("The Two Yemens: Historical Perspectives and Present Attitudes," **Asian Affairs,** February 1973) sheds some new light on the rise of Nasserism (to him, meaning "furthering the interests of Egyptian imperialism and the Nasser clique under the cloak of nationalism and socialism") and on the activities of the Habash group (in the fifties pro-Nasserite, later non-Nasserite) and the agents of Nasser and Ba'th **(Sa'iqa)** in Yemen. We also learn that the coup ("corrective step") of 1969 brought to power not Southern Yemenis but "Hugaris of the Shafi'i (Sunni) district of the Yemen Arab Republic. These Hugaris are said to supply the jailers and torturers under East German security agents . . . Faisal al-Sha'bi, founder of NFL, was murdered in his cell."

For some intimations I am indebted to William B. Quandt's **Palestinian Nationalism: Its Political and Military Dimensions,** Rand, Santa Monica, 1971.

Chapter XII


## THE "NEW WAVE"


In a way, "Arab socialism" of Ba'th and of Egypt's coinage paved the way, even before the June 1967 war, to a "new wave" (*mawja jadida*) of more radical theorists. For many years have Mao's epigrammatic dicta been rehearsed, his terminology employed, his argument aped. Figuratively, his sayings were carried on the tips of lances not unlike the leaves of the Koran displayed by the Umayyads when battling the Shi'is near Siffin in 657 A.D. Added to this, Ho Chi Minh and Giap, Castro and Che Guevara have been glorified, national liberation front exploits extolled, in brief, the feuding two wings of Ba'th as well as the Arab Socialist Union saw themselves an integral legion of the tri-continental army of liberation. At the same time they continuously expounded the distinct features of Arab socialism.*

A feature common to all radical groups and parties, "petty bourgeois" and "proletarian" alike, is that all ruled out government by consent, or postponed it until the class enemy is eliminated; inevitably, violence and coercion in various guises and degrees became the vehicle of rule. First, "reaction" is to be eliminated —-

---

* Strangely, Marcuse's philosophical casuistry on violence serves to support all strains of Arab "progressivism." He is widely translated and discussed.

economically and politically. Then the non-Arab-socialism-minded who profess Western type democracy and socialism are silenced. Finally, other strains of Arab and non-Arab socialism are to be made harmless. Thus progressivism that monopolized justice and its implementation is reduced adsurdum. One day, when all class enemies and West-minded foes are eliminated and the various strains of Arab socialism in the "progressive" Arab countries are silenced or reconciled, the need for violence will fade (witness the Soviet Union, People's China and the discord between Communist countries).

Here self-gratification is also nurtured by the imagined integration with a larger whole—the mythical Third World. How exhilarating must it be to envision, together with Fanon in *Les damnés de la terre*, "the Third World starting a new history of Man," "to set afoot a new man" trying to "resolve the problems to which Europe has not been able to find answers." On the public level violence brings about "the liquidation of regionalism and tribalism," "of qaids and chiefs, a prerequisite for unification of the people." On an individual level violence "disintoxicates, unburdens the colonized of his inferiority complex ... rehabilitates him in his own eyes ... raises the people to the leader's height. What is more ... masses participating in violence, in a national liberation, do not permit anyone to present himself as a liberator." "Illuminated by violence, the people's consciousness rebels against all pacification." Violence is a cleansing force.[1]

After the June 1967 war the focal point of "Arab revolution" shifts from Nasserism to Palestine guerrillism. *Fida'ism* is thought to represent the acutest, the noblest cause; unlike the military-technocratic bureaucracy of countries of Arab socialism, the *fida'iyyun* are said to pursue their aims through self-realization, self-sacrifice and self-denial. The Arab régimes and their regular armies—progressive as well as conservative—had failed in their contention with Israel. Who is to blame?

The new generation witnesses bloodletting between Ba'thists and Nasserites and between the two factions of Ba'th in Syria, between Ba'thists and Communists in 'Iraq, between Arabs and Kurds there, between Arabs and non-Arabs in the Sudan. The deadlock after the 1967 war had to be overcome. Why not espouse guerrilla socialism chapter and verse? Razzias are a venerable tradition in Arab warfare, in Arabic classical poetry; now they are sanctioned by the most advanced ideologies of liberation. The many-winged New Left critique lends also an aura of Western respectability. It puts to a severe scrutiny the performance of communism in the Soviet orbit. Violence for the sake of genuine socialism assumes an ideal dimension. The inadequacies of analogy notwithstanding, why not follow the path of Vietnam in Palestine?[2] Che Guevara himself proclaimed that the world needs several Vietnams.

For a while the magic of fida'ism seemed to outshine other isms, even encompass all of them. All over the Arab world writers sang fida'ism's praise.[3] Palestinians take their destiny in their hands. Their "battle of destiny" could be supported by progressives and conservatives alike. Their movement inserted itself in the "world liberation movement." A shining example are the movements in Algeria and South Yemen (the conflagration between the Egypt-sponsored Flosy and NLF, later the contention between the two wings within NLF in South Yemen are glossed over; likewise the coup against Ben Bella and the suppression of the militant wing of NLF in Algeria).* In fact, every progressive or conservative régime, by nature exclusive, restricted or banned the activities of the *fida'iyyin* or espoused a

---

*Other snags could be ignored too: Tibet *realpolitik* fomenting rebellions of ethnic entities in India and Burma or mildly abstaining from it.

group loyal to it or willing to play its game in inner-Arab politics. Only Jordan and Lebanon nearly fell prey to them.

Muta' Safadi's attitudes of 1969 are well worth re-capitulating. Verbiage aside, metaphysics of fida'ism seem to overshadow metaphysics of nationalism. In Safadi's view, Arab society — all its classes, individuals and groups — undergo a "critical revolution." Lest this revolution turns "futile and abstract," it is linked to the *fida'i* revolution growing on the soil of reality and daily life. "The war of liberation from invaders ought to be supported by a war of liberation from delusions and inner obstacles that dissipate the forces of resistance or carry them astray from their authentic goal."

Traditional revolutionism is "activism of backwardness."

The *fida'i* revolution carries the Arab revolution, for the first time, to the terrain of a real bloody struggle as an absolute means of reaction against external invasion as well as against backwardness inside. With the infusion of *fida'i* morality into the generation, the nation is carried into an important purified age not yet experienced since the advent of decisive internal revolutions. Instead of political plotting and factional practices of immaturity within traditional revolutions, gushes a *fida'i* flame to draw the real front on the basis of blood sacrifice. Instead of personal forms of futile rebellion, of mental and moral aberrations that enveloped the generation of the first debacle (1948), the historical constellation of the generation of the *fida'i* revolution offers objective conditions to discard history and forge the promised history.

At the same time contemporary *fida'ism* is linked to a comprehensive movement of mental purge of mysticism, moral purge of hypocrisy of subservience by monitoring false values, and practical purge of exercises in perversion, deviation and putchist intrigues. The greater the battle of *fida'i* on the borders, the more consolidated are the moral bases of a real sound people's war, beyond slogans and groupuscles.

From here flows the consciousness of the *fida'i* revolution as an existential necessity to persist and evolve to an organized people's war from the depths of the inside to the borders of the outside. What this nation needs is to give real birth to a real war, war of peoples behind armies, not armies without peoples.

Reorganization of the Arab society in line with a strategy of a people's war means involving the whole society in its destiny, that is, eliminating all forms of political feudalism, old and new, and delving into the depth of the great multitude of masses still inactive, captives of negative susceptibility to what is told them, what is done in their behalf, forcibly or out of ignorance.

The effort of revolutionaries today is making *fida'ism* nonparochial, national, human, to be understood and supported by all the fighters in all the corners of the world.'[4]

Safadi disputes the usual explanation of the debacle (retardedness, technological deficiency, medieval mentality, struggle of culture with backwardness) that urges delay of the inevitable battle. The Arab people is "one of the important vanguards of the retarded world." Its capability is its position "at the center of the political challenges of destiny." It is the "daily political revolutionism," its infighting over power with a mentality of political feudalism that distorts genuine revolutionism and causes Arab society to be backward.[5]

Safadi's assertions ardently reach for the core of Arab revolutionism, but to a detached observer, they reflect its exterior. They may fit well with his concept of *thawra* as effervescence. Ali Ahmad Saïd (Adonis) presents its background:

> *L'homme arabe révolutionnaire perd la réalité tout en s'aggrippant de plus en plus à la théorie. Il néglige l'homme et se cramponne à la doctrine. Il méprise le citoyen et glorifie le mercenaire ...*
>
> *Le révolutionnaire arabe critique, détruit, juge et gouverne au nom de la Révolution. Mais son pouvoir n'atteint que les mots, non la réalité. Il transforme les mots par la prononciation ou la syntaxe, et s'imagine avoir transformé la vie.*
>
> *Il adopte le progrès théoriquement, et il vit pratiquement dans un cadre ancestral et traditionnel. S'il célèbre la liberté, c'est au niveau de la parole. Il se montre de gauche dans ces idées et pour les circonstances ordinaires, mais dans les situations décisives, où son destin est en cause, et même parfois dans les circonstances ordinaires, il se révèle de droit ... Il copie le monde sans le transformer et l'assimiler en son être. La culture est pour lui un gain qu'il conserve dans sa mémoire, et non un savoir qui pénètre son être et son existence.* [6]

Even Jacques Berque betrays verbal fascination with *"palestinisation, radicalisation ... mondialisation"* of the *"résistance palestinienne,"* hence *"moralisation du problème."* To him, the chances of the Palestinians are in realization of *"la fin des hégémonies"* and *"décolonisation de la Terre,"* whereas Israel pins its chances on Western hegemony. Israel proceeds from a messianic vision, that of return to the Holy Land and from "imported nationalism." To this Berque opposes a universal chiliastic vision:

> *Si la résistance palestinienne s'avouait pour ce qu'elle est: un cas entre autres de la lutte contre l'oppression et l'humiliation des hommes, elle déborderait l'adversaire de cela même qui, a l'échelle d'histoire planétaire, assure,*

*croyons-nous, la victoire à terme, des opprimés et des humiliés sur tous les groupements d'intérêt, et sur toutes les collusions de la prépondérance, de la force industrielle et du capitalisme et du passéisme.* [7]

This concept of history, issued from a social philosopher's pen, seems to have caught fire from the Palestinian cause. The slogan of "Arab eternal mission (*risala khalida*)" raised by Ba'th is studded in the planetary vision of deliverance of all oppressed and humiliated.

Ideology upheld with religious fervor of — to put it somewhat unfairly — finality implies: light will extinguish darkness. In view of the Stalinist performances, the Indo-China war, South Sudan, Biafra, Indonesia, Pakistan, Uganda, it seems that oppression and humiliation are not a mere upshot of *"la force industrielle, capitalisme et passéisme."* Actually and potentially there are in the liberated Third World and within the communist orbit manifold sources of oppression — new *"groupements d'intérêt"* and new *"collusions de la prépondérance."* Furthermore, this phenomenon of absolute evil — Israel — could not have come about without a culture grown out of the soil of this country, a community whose continuity was safeguarded by influx from the Diaspora and whose modernization started in the 'seventies of the last century. Admittedly, standardized thinking does not apply to a unique case, but it should be within reach of even a social visionary's imagination to contrast it with a case of a people having eighteen states and occupying an area from the Persian Gulf to the Atlantic. It is in this tiny country that the thread of an ancient culture was picked up, a language revived, and immense energies of creativity released. Furthermore, here contemporary trends of social thought have been put to creative scrutiny, thus making some contribution on a plane of "planetary history." And ways are shown to rehabilitate oppressed and humiliated.

Revolutionary mood is wedded to word-drunkenness, even to word addiction. Traditional leaning to affluent use of words, to synonyms, to alliteration and rhyme, to cadence in speech is spurred by the influx of new terms and idioms—in the main borrowed from foreign vocabularies—to generate a revolutionary stance. Indiscriminately used, their meaning may be blurred or perverted. Spontaneity or swiftness of action may prompt verbal improvization, but here it seems a substitute for action. A wave of inflation in derivation, word association, or arbitrary transfer of meaning to Arabic words—has swayed the language. In times of evolution quantitative and qualitative growth of a language is markedly qualified by the regulatory function of thought. At times of upheaval words and phrases may prevail on thought.[8]

A fervently used word is 'aqida (pl. 'aqa'id ) and the recent derivation 'aqa'idi, meaning ideology, ideological, or doctrine, doctrinal. The Syrian army is necessarily a doctrinal one. Originally a religious term, it has been transferred to the realm of "scientific socialism," Marxism-Leninism, neo-Marxism, or that strange concoction of anarcho-Marxism in the New Left. Likewise the myth of revolution prompts, obsessively, again and again to repeat thawra and its derivatives, as if the very use of it suggests promise and fulfilment. Recently revolutionism has been consummated in fida'ism. One circles in this dream-world, and yet ceaselessly points to "scientifism," "objectivism," and "reality." One juggles words over a timetable, i.e., stages of implementation, over strategy and tactics, over one's mentality (petty bourgeois or proletarian), etc. The factions charge each other with sloganeering, mystical, metaphysical or non-dialectical approach, with non-scientifism and disregard of reality.

Strangely, in matters of language Prof. Berque is all reason. The implicit doctrine of linguistic nationalism saw in bilingualism as exercised by the native *élite* a corollary of imperialism, but to Berque, use-in-depth of a foreign language and a foreign culture becomes a securest means of self-recognition and self-assertion *vis-à-vis* others.[9]

Is the Arab linguistic personality being restored? The era of revolutionary ideology with its vehement assertiveness seems to militate against it. The intrusion of manichaic ideas, as applied both to nationalism and socialism, inflates the lexical volume of Arabic with foreign words, loan-words, lan-arguments, but solidifying elements of reason and skepsis are weakening and under authoritarian régimes near-absent. There is an unconvincing attempt to relate modern revolutionism to precedents in Arab history, that is, to prove its continuity, but, perhaps except for Egypt, where stress on religion, albeit ideological, somehow involves in religious literature, this hardly affects the language. Besides, the idiom of modern ideologies is only one component here. What Berque labels "americanism" as opposed to culture, is the whole gamut of sciences (economic, social, political, natural) evolved in "America" and deeply affecting our planet, even the authentic French culture.

## Footnotes

1. Apotheosis of violence is not Fanon's innovation. Sartre's assertion: **"Fanon est le premier depuis Engels à remettre en lumière l'accoucheuse de l'histoire"** is not foolproof evidence. What he calls **"les bavardages fascistes de Sorel"** had affected Rightist as well as Leftist radicalism.
2. Western wizards of the media, fascinated by the resuscitated theories and refined practices of violence, embarked on a presentation of **fida'ism** that could easily be termed "commercials" for the revolution. From walls of venerable universities in Europe lurked the call of the future intelligentsia: Long live the Vietnam revolution! Kill Nixon! Long live the Palestinian revolution!
3. Their emotional appeal may have been genuine, but, for all the verbal fervor, support was flawed with opportunism. Conservative régimes, while financing and appeasing, could not but recoil from their revolutionism.

"Progressive" régimes have intermittently banned or restricted their activities. They formed or adopted commando groups (**Sa'iqa** initially sponsored by the civilian wing of **Syrian Ba'th**, Arab Liberation Front attached to the 'Iraqi Ba'th). Besides, depending on calculation or change of guards, support was given to or withdrawn from a commando group (PFLP and PDLFP in Syria and 'Iraq). Egypt's more non-commital approach often clashed with the puritan concept of adventurous guerrillism. Even Arab Communists condescended to form a small commando of the Communist parties of 'Iraq, Syria and Lebanon (**Ansar**). At present Ahmad Jibrils group serves Qadhdhafi's aims.

Opportunism had also a part to play in the variegated response of some Arab states to the September 1970 confrontation in Jordan. The Sa'udis, while giving refuge to stranded guerrillas, supplied "emergency ammunition" to Jordan's army. The strong men of the civilian Ba'th wing tried to intervene, only to be ousted by Hafiz al-Asad. The 'Iraqi units stationed in Jordan extended no help, as repeatedly promised, to the guerrillas, probably on account of being inimical to the Syrian Ba'th. (See David Hirst, **Guardian Weekly,** January 2, 1971: also the exhaustive studies by James A. Michener ("What to Do About the Palestinian Refugees") and Edward R. F. Sheehan ("In the Flaming Streets of Amman") in **New York Times Magazine,** September 27,1970.

4. **al-Thawra al-fida'iyya wa-'l-thawra al-naqdiyya** ("Fida'i Revolution and Critical Revolution") **al-Adab,** March 1969.
5. **Mushkilat al-taqaddum wa-'l-takhalluf** ("The problem of Progress and Backwardness"), **ibid.,** February 1969.
6. **"Le Manifeste du 5 juin 1967," Esprit,** March 1968, p. 435.
7. **Politique Aujourd'hui,** April 1970, p. 117.
8. Unlike Hebrew, the process of desacralization in Arabic extends to fiction too, to a degree due to the mood of social populism. In Hebrew fiction the trend is, in part, reversed: intense use is made of ancient, notably the postbiblical layers of Hebrew. Is it from aversion to depersonalization of Hebrew? Or affectation of a style of two great writers? An urge of aristocratization by injecting the utopian characteristics of the Aggada? Here profanation of the sacred in speech, in official and applied language coincides with sacralization of the profane.
9. **"L'Interaction des langues au bénéfice de la culture," Le Monde,** June 8-9, 1969.

    Chedli Klibi, minister of culture in Tunisia, echoes J. Berque's view: grâce au dialogue avec la culture française, elle (notre culture arabo-islamique) s'ouvre à nouveau a elle-même et prend conscience de ses valeurs fondamentales." — See Jean Egen, **"La Tunisie en crise," Le Monde Diplomatique,** February, 1972.

# CONCLUSION

A deluge of verbal revolutionism does not make the element of ideology overriding in human action. True, in part it is a motive power to stir up passions, but it may also be a smokescreen to other stimuli (personal, clannish, ethnic, confessional). To quasi-educated it may have the effect of alcohol or drugs. The "masses" on whose behalf the call is sounded remain unconcerned. It is not ideological zeal that drives them to give the men in power, at any election in revolutionary Egypt or Syria, over 98 per cent of the votes. 'Iraq has dispensed with elections since 1958. It is argued that the masses, still beneath the level of revolutionary consciousness, are to be led by a conscious élite. Against this could be maintained that by their massive vote the masses show contempt for or make fun of the rulers. One can't help thinking that just as dictators keep deceiving the masses by silencing opponents, so are the masses deceiving the rulers by approving their wayward suggestions and deeds. Of course, allowance is to be made for the element of fear and for the uncontrolled vote count.

This seems to hold true for the élite as well. Years of ideologization notwithstanding, it displays no revolutionary zeal to uphold positions that seem *raison d'être* of a party. When Hafiz al-Asad overthrew the Ba'th government in 1971, the "party," except for top opponents, acquiesced in the "procession of events," and the masses voted al-Asad into the presidency of Syria.

249

Anwar Sadat's dealings with the Arab Socialist Union and the resulting vote to the People's Council and the Union bear resemblance. Viewed from this point, ideology seems a mere mirage, at best a vehicle of political wheeling and dealing. And yet men of letters exert themselves or outbid each other in ideological sophistication. The year 1970 was a pinnacle of frenzied revolutionism. Armed with Debray's pamphlet Revolution in the Revolution?, young men made forays right into death.

Other than ideological reasons are to be sought for Syria's about-face. Why has the neo-Ba'th government whose "leftism" was tempered by the al-Asad coup joined in a "federation" with Egypt and the ideologically even more distant Libya whereas neighboring 'Iraq that has moved, semantically and in matters of implementation, to the "left," seems to have supported the authors of the Communist coup in the Sudan who upheld the idea of "national front" implemented in Syria? Ideological compatibility is to be excluded here; it is the motivation that plies or equalizes or glosses over ideologies. Is it from rationalization about the welfare of one's country, hatred of the opponent or sheer self-seeking?

In retrospect, the mutual deprecations of Egyptian and Ba'th theorists over positions that, on closer inspection, could be narrowed to insignificance, seem senseless. Parties outbid each other in adherence to the idea of Arab union, and yet, in practice, regionalism (iqlimiyya) motivated their behavior. Is it fear of losing the identity, of being overpowered, or concern over prestige that prevailed here? The bent for fissiparousness, to activity by plot inflated by a one-party system lacking mutual control of parties?

On the face of it the fierce ideological argument could point to the contrary. In the 'sixties it revolved on doctrinal issues such as Arab socialism, revolutionary tactic and strategy, interrelationship of proletariat and small bourgeoisie, stages of socialist implementation—all threshed out themes in Marxist literature. Having no strings of actual power, the radical strain discarded the national characteristics of socialism altogether.

The panorama of Arab or arabized socialism unfolds in coup after coup, and the other shore of the sea of repression is not within sight. Will there be a shore? In his *Republican 'Iraq*, Majid Khadduri speaks of the "July Revolution" (1958), "Ramadan Revolution" (1963) and November Revolution (1968), in sum of the "unfinished revolution." Rendered in prose, it means cliques plotting and succeeding each other, unaccountably wielding power over mind and body, the country's resources and the media of information, with no checks on greed and ambition.

In those turbulent years the voice of Dr. al-Bazzaz seemed crying in the wilderness, but he speaks of a potential trend frightened into silence. His is a call for a "prudent," "rational" socialism, "socialism as a means and not an end," socialism that has no pretense of monopoly or sole identification with a people's destiny, socialism that is no breeding ground of intolerance and violence. Unlike Egypt's one-voice theorists, he does not make religion part of an ideology.

For eleven months (September 1965-August 1966) Dr. al-Bazzaz headed the only civilian government in 'Iraq since 1958, to be ousted "by intrigue, inside and outside the country." He was to announce that "the time has come for the country to come back to normal life and conditions in which there is no place for military tribunals, military rulers, states of emergency or tanks in the streets, for those things which would give the citizens a feeling of lack of stability." He pleaded for a "firm parliamentary system" and sincerely planned to come to terms with Kurdish nationalism.[1]

Of the vast volume of writing, here merely alluded to, what is to survive not only as a testimony to human passions and vanities? Or to a chain reaction of militancy against Israel? All the movements raised claims to "vanguard leadership." Only Lebanon has allowed these ideologies to coexist, at least in print, and vie for the Arab mind. And the disputes in practice often call to mind the medieval battles of dogmatised masses, adherents of opposing law schools (*madhahib*) in the streets of Baghdad.

At present these ideologies seem to be overtaken by events. They needn't be rescinded, human sophistication is apt to make them serve new men in power and new twists of mind. And yet this era is marked by a third essay in enlightenment. The first—at the turn of the century—didn't go far beyond a call for education and emulation. The second—in the 'twenties—ushered in a literary renaissance utterly impeded by an oppressive, formally multi-party parliamentary régime; in its disregard for social ills and needs it *eo ipso* stifled the rights of the individual. The present one—fierce in its social critique and overstretched in its social message (for all the pressure of Islamic revivalism it is, in part, even outspokenly secularist)—is more than ever ruthless in violation of the individual's rights, glorying in violence for the sake of social or national redemption.

In aspects of Near East Society hope was voiced that the new generation would turn to a constructive argument. Meanwhile the keenest revolutionary ideas converged on it, and, having tried out all the means of warfare prescribed in the name of these ideas, it ended where it started. Is not the moment propitious to let the "still small voice" be heard?

In his essay on the "affirmation of Palestinian consciousness," A. Desvignes arrives at a bold conclusion:

*A vrai dire l'unique chance de réussite arabe aurait été*

252

*l'impossible 'déclaration de paix' à Israel. En établissant des relations pacifiques ils auraient été capables de contrôler largement son expansion, de limiter son influence: à la longue peut-être de la submerger. L'idéologie arabe interdit ce rêve, la guerre continuera, elle va s'exaspérer lentement, elle s'installe.*[2]

## Footnotes

1. See E. -F. Penrose, **"Essai sur L'Irak,"** **Orient,** No. 35, 1965, pp. 62-63; also his **"Une tentative de gouvernement civil en Irak,"** **ibid.,** No. 39, 1966; Majid Khadduri, **Republican 'Iraq,** 1969, pp. 255-259.
2. **Le Monde Diplomatique,** August 12, 1968.

# ANNEX I

In his annual report for 1970, Kamal Jumblat, head of the Progressive Socialist Party (*al-hizb al-taqaddumi al-ishtiraki*), speaks of the weakening or eclipse of the slogan of people's war of liberation and its upholders, the main reason being the "Arab bewitched mentality" that mistakes words and resolutions for their content (a "great difference between . . . reality and action, between word and work"). This mentality was at the base of the June 1967 debacle. Jumblat records the "shrinking of some small groups and emotional groupuscules" pretending to be new left and carried away by "fantastics and romanticism" of talk about people's war of liberation ("a healthy slogan *per se* ") without effort on its behalf. A great number of them are quasi-educated, alien from "objective mentality." Still, these "infantile, emotional, anarchic Leftist groups sometimes stirred up some problems, popular groups and some dogmatic Leftists from complacency."

Jumblat points out the "spontaneous self-purification" that produced some kinds of "genuine new left, meaning activism, social, political and psychological activism that meets the clear principles of our Charter," militates against phenomena of the industrial civilization and aims at releasing man from ills converging on his life and soul.

Against this, Jumblat's party adopted the idea of "comprehensive revolution (*inqilab*)," of "honoring the freedoms of the individual limited by freedoms of others and by necessities of public welfare." The impact of the armed forces is "limited by our confidence in the democratic order, in general freedoms and rights and by evading the tragedy of military coups that afflicted some foreign and Arab countries." The idea of political democracy and civic democratic order should be strengthened.

A kind of *oeuvre de synthèse* is presented here, choice ingredients of trends, old and new, for the sake of "human true socialism." Elements of incompatibility are glossed over. From the New Left he adopts "resistance to violence and non-violence naturally followed by the idea of love and no wrong doing," as postulated by Mahatma Gandhi, "one of the prophets of the new generation in the advanced industrial societies." Witness the struggle against the war in Vietnam, Cambodia and "at every place." Secondly, comprehensive human brotherhood (elimination of excesses of racialism, color prejudice and nationalism to be replaced by human internationalism between the peoples). Thirdly, change in the "system of affluence in the industries of consumption" and "return to natural life and to Eastern moral cultures and philosophies, meaning liberation from every domineering tradition, every religious or intellectual doctrine and from every psychic complex, return to genuine simplicity, absolute spontaneity."

"Movement of thought and scientific inquiry are a basic condition of Arab renaissance." Socialism has to adopt (or return to) "real scientific dialectic" and its "objective implementation." "The movement of modern youth accords, ultimately, with the idea of socialism aiming, in its last stage of implementation, at abolition of party and state and replacing them with voluntary free cooperation in all its meaning."

Jumblat has some unpopular suggestions, too. "It is necessary to restore political democracy to the socialist régimes in this area, perhaps through a two-party system based on proportional representation; basic rights and freedoms of the citizen as postulated by the United Nations should be upheld." All "elements and groups of the resistance" should unite in a "regular army of liberation," to function in Israel and in the occupied areas against economic and industrial installations and "real military targets." Jumblat envisages "imposition of a political solution in accordance with the Security Council resolution."

Finally, Jumblat rejects the idea of collective leadership. The party's charter necessitates a "commanding creative responsible personality." "Inevitably, the Arabs need one commander . . . and Egypt is the popular, economic, scientific, doctrinal and political base for such a command." 'Abd al-Nasir "led the movement of Arab resurrection and human comprehensive liberation, founded Arab socialism and built its palaces, set up the first Arab union, founded a school of political thought consonant with the requirements of Arab renaissance and man's perception of his humanity and his spiritual, moral and national value."[1]

1.  **al-Anba'**, December 28, 1970.

# ANNEX II

The wheel of the National Social Party (*al-hizb al-qawmi al-ijtima'i*), now legalized in Lebanon, has spun a full circle—from fascism and National Socialism to populism and pan-revolutionism. And yet the teachings of Antun Sa'adeh, the founding father, are made to feed the party's ideological about-faces all along. The party is known for its essays in collusion with the fascist Axis, with the imperialist West, and with the Hashimis, finally with the vanguard of world revolution, almost without relinquishing its original articles of faith. As for Lebanon, allusive sophistication helps confuse or synthesize the concepts of "Syrian nation" (implicitly comprising also Lebanon, Palestine, Jordan, 'Iraq) and of Lebanon's uniqueness ("cultural vocation, intellectual and educational line that draws upon the history of our national milieu, and participation in building the great Arab renaissance"); Lebanon ought to be pioneering in two fields—national (meaning within the Syrian nation) and (all-Arab). The party sails in all directions and addresses itself to manifold trends of thought, without expressly offending the sensibilities of pan-Arabists or regionalists(*iqlimiyyun*).

The party stands for elimination of political communalism in all its manifestations and setting up a "secular scientific" state; nationalization of all basic means of production; elimination of the vestiges of agricultural feudalism; comprehensive social security; elimination of foreign schools that implant Western concepts and building a national school to ensure "spiritual cultural unity." In line with the "logic of history" and the evolution of social life, Lebanon should effect the "logic of national solidarity and regional cooperation," another version: "unionist natural federal regional integration." Lebanon ought to defend and strengthen the Palestinian revolution and raise it to a level of a war of national liberation in cooperation with the states of the "national milieu." Lebanon should align itself with the forces "opposing imperialism in all its forms and policies."[1]

Dr. 'Abdallah Sa'adeh,* head of the party, expounds its programme:

"The socialist West was able to breach the traditional fence built by imperialism around the area." In their inimical attitude to "our national problems" the states of imperialist West have nearly forfeited their influence in "our Arab world."

At its inception the party stood for élitism — party power emanating from wardens considered select élite expressing the nationalists' will. Now party power should emanate from the base.

Armed struggle and unity of the fighting forces are to assume dimensions of a national revolution (the party fights the propagandists of a peaceful solution). It stands for a "positive dialogue" with all revolutionary movements "in the nation and in the Arab world" and with all revolutionary movements of liberation in the world.

The founder's doctrine is valid. It is a "resurrectionist revolutionary total doctrine with a comprehensive insight into life, being and art in the sphere of human national social existence, but it does not transcend into metaphysical in-

* A Greek Orthodox from North Lebanon.

terests." This doctrine could not be termed dogma or final premises, it rejects any inevitability or power except for reason in its gradual growth and integration."

Social revolution emanates from a national premise. A basic condition is "organic link between revolutionism of thought and revolutionism of practice."

From its inception the party "proceeds from the belief that the Syrian nation is an Arab nation and from the call of the national social renaissance to set up a front of the nations of the Arab world to be a formidable dam against foreign imperialist designs."[2] Remarkably, no mention is made of socialism.

Footnotes

1. **al-Nahar**, August 14, 1970.
2. **Ibid.**, January 29, 1970.

# ANNEX III

Revolutionary consciousness, ceaselessly extolled as if endowed with mythical power, stretches between the urge for "absolute separation of state and religious establishment" (Nadim al-Bitar) and fantastic essays in ideology, derived from foreign sources and yet made vindicated in the past. It is said that, for all the differences in circumstances and aims, the Prophet Muhammad was the first to employ the method of revolutionary *bu'ra,* in our times the Cuban *foco,* that is a nucleus of armed violence. He moved from bourgeois Mecca to the midst of rural Yathrib, assembled partisans and launched ambushes, then turned to the method of liberated areas that resulted in the seizure of Mecca. In our days *foco* is said to provide the fighter with a large degree of security and the best education before he sets out to stage ambushes; it is also the closest way to direct indoctrination of the masses.[1]

Che Guevara, "a prophet of an age having no prophets," "an audacious *jinn* ," "whose craft is death in order that the Third World lives," "friend of children in my country and all ill-fated countries," is associated with ancient names and places ("legacy of some words ... boiling, may they drip drops of blood from generation to generation"): Abu Dharr (Muhammad's Companion, noted for learning, humility and ascetism, a favorite of Arab Marxists); Tariq (Ibn Ziyad, landed in Jabal Tariq. *i.e.,* Gibraltar in 711); Dhu Qar (a place near Kufa in 'Iraq. The Prophet is reported to have said that here for the first time the Arabs got the upper hand over the Persians[2]); Falcon of Quraysh ('Abd alrahman I, survivor of the Umayyad dynasty who had fled from the Abbasids and established himself as amir in Spain, 756-788); Hittin (here Salah al-din won his victory over the Crusaders in July 5, 1187), Spartacus, Horatius and Mirabeau.[3]

Translated in modern terms, here revolutionism and imperialism, if religiously propelled, are peacefully aligned.

The same source points to the overt or covert struggle — from Ibn Khaldun to Marx — of materialism and metaphysics in Arab intellectual culture. Ibn Khaldun is said to be very close to Hegel in point of "dialectical philosophy," to Marx in point of materialism and class strife, and to Darwin in point of surplus value(?)[4]

Nadim al-Bitar decries the constant talk about imperialist manoeuvres and treacheries of the rulers as the prime source of defeat. Its roots are set in "traditional existence," in the souls and minds of the Arabs. A revolutionary ideology is to liberate them, producing new classes and a new "vanguard command." Consciousness is to be freed of past and present. A fervently praised panacea — "revolutionary dialectic" — of the debacle should be grasped and acted upon.[5]

Al-Bitar fails to mention that a dialectical approach should not stop at the new trends aspiring to replace the "progressive" régimes. It is hardly compatible with an absolute belief in one's cause representing the sole "power of light."

After September 1970 Bitar's critical attitude to *fidā'ism* stiffened; not so his self-critical attitude. He is panegyrist of Arab revolutionism and yet severe critic of Arab revolutionary thought ("missionary, idealistic, mystical, metaphysical, moralistic," "upholding unrealizable aims, not related to the social, historical, objective reality"). As in "religious mentality," words (revolution, unity) have a magic impact. "Fascination with words, phrases, slogans, embellishments, poetic images instead of conscious, ripe concepts leaning on objective, analytical probing, exact, comprehensive view." "Language of revolutionary aims stifles the language of transformational revolutionary dialectic." Resistance is presented as a popular war of liberation resembling that of China, Vietnam, Algeria, whose function is liberation of Palestine "from the river to the sea." For demographic, topographic and other reasons Arab resistance could not shoulder this task. It is the Arab nation's task whose focal point is Egypt.

Strangely, al-Bitar whose vision stretches the Arab area "from ocean to ocean" does not apply mental brakes asked of the *fia'iyyun* to himself. Verbal flights of fancy are not a proper guide to self-restraint.

Ghassan Kanafani, an ideological purist of PFLP, charges al-Bitar with petty bourgeois revolutionism, even with emulation, by phrases like "Arab substance," "Arab man," "thinkers of German national socialism." He, too, argues for scientific, objective evaluation. His strongest argument for resistance is that it is a "protracted war."[6]

An ideology of overheated nationalism variously combined with inflationary socialism could not but result in fratricidal tension, even within the revolutionary camp. It is a millenarian ideology, in its ardor breeding violent intolerance. For a while it seemed an overwhelming gale. It ranged from the world of *Mein Kampf* to dicta of Mao Tsetung, Régis Debray and the sophistications of the New Left.

To Richard Pfaff:

Manichaistic interpretation of history identified with the ideology of Arab nationalism ... not only serves to explain to its proponents why the Arab is in a disadvantageous political, economic, and social position today *vis-à-vis* the West, but also guarantees that the messianic mission of the Arabs *will* be fulfilled, just as the power of light will ultimately defeat the power of darkness.[7]

As usual, power politics and regional rivalries, even within one ideological creed, prove more resilient than ideologies. Exigencies of middle-aged revolutions and the need for constructive achievements dictate détente. Sources of inspiration are being shut: the authenticity of Maoism, the Giap method of struggle in Vietnam, the guerrilla exploits in South America, in part overtaken by reformist endeavors of the military there, in a new idiom a kind of Nasserism. Arab ideology seems to veer to "pure" nationalism.[8] Will it turn to all-inclusive violence where violence saturated with ideology failed? Arms aside, there remain two ways, running parallel or even across: creativity in all fields of human thought and endeavor and constructive argument. Both ways presuppose freedom of argument within.

## Footnotes

1. Nazih al-Hakim, **al-Adab,** May 1968.
2. **Encyclopaedia of Islam.**
3. **al-Ba'th,** December 19, 1967.
4. **Ibid.,** February 9, 1968.
5. **Fa 'aliyya al-thawriyya fi 'l-nakba (The Revolutionary Impact of the Catastrophe),** Beirut 1965, pp. 128-154.
     In another place al-Bitar, armed with L. Althusser and Feuerbach's **The Essence of Christianity,** speaks also of "revolutionary secularism" **(Mawaqif,** January-February, 1969).
     Adonis, too, claims "total secession from the past." Our past is a world of perdition in various forms — religious, political, cultural and economic . . . for all its "revolutionism," mostly due to it, Arab society's stand to religion (inherited, civilizational) is political and its stand to politics is religious" **(ibid.,** November-December, 1969).
6. **Shu'un Filastiniyya,** op. cit.
7. "The Function of Arab Nationalism," **Comparative Politics,** January 1970, p. 165.
8. In 1972, Ghassan Kanafani, editor of **al-Hadaf,** and two other still active founders of ANM, tried to "extricate" PFLP "from its present" and lead it back to "authenticity" of the 1948 vow, namely nationalism not diluted with socialism **(al-Jadid,** July 14, 1972).
     Knowing that he might pay a "heavy price," the editor of **al-Hawadith**

(Beirut) dwells on an old-new dimension of the problem. Before 1967, he argues, the 'Abd al-Nasir experiment seemed a focal point of hope, the road to meet the challenge of imperialism and Zionism. With the 1967 disaster new military remedies have been sought: electronics war, people's war or both coupled with commandos' war. Others termed the disaster either civilizational, to be remedied by progress, be it cultural, scientific, economic, or ideological, hence the argument over ideology — religious or Marxist of Soviet, Chinese or Cuban provenance. But all these endeavors of judgement **(ijtihadat)** were irruptions, "tending to simplify or touch on a part aspect of the disaster." The editor wants to see the people's intellectual and scientific abilities released, the "superiority tutelage" over it removed, the right to opposition made true ("opposition is not treason"). People ask for a" chance of democratic dialogue . . . in an atmosphere far from intellectual terror." Should a colonel overthrow al-Sadat or al-Asad, it would mean replacing one man by another. "A new intellectual pattern of Arab action couldn't come up in the absence of a dialogue, of freedom of discussion, that is, rejection of opposition and monopolization of power."